LET THE GOOD TIMES ROLL!

A Guide to Cajun & Zydeco Music

Pat Nyhan, Brian Rollins, David Babb

Upbeat
Books

Portland, Maine

Published by
Upbeat Books
142 Pine St.
Portland, Maine 04102

Printed in the United States of America

Front cover: C. J. Chenier in performance at the Muddy Waters Club in New Orleans, 1995. Photograph by David Babb.

Book design: Marcia Bernstein, The OverLeaf Office, Portland Maine

Publisher's Cataloging-in-Publication
(Provided by Quality Books, Inc.)
Nyhan, Patricia.
      Let the good times roll ! : a guide to Cajun & Zydeco music /
Pat Nyhan, Brian Rollins and David Babb. -- 1st ed.
    p. cm.
    Includes bibliographical references and index.
    Preassigned LCCN: 97-90429
    ISBN: 0-9658232-0-2
    1. Cajun music--Louisiana--Biography. 2. Zydeco music--
Louisiana--Biography. 3. Popular music--Louisiana--Biography. 4.
Cajun music--Louisiana--History and criticism. 5. Zydeco music--
Louisiana--History and criticism. 6. Popular music—Louisiana—
History and criticism. I. Rollins, Brian. II. Babb, David W.
III. Title

ML3560.C25N94 1997   781.62'410763
                          QBI97-40519

CONTENTS

FOREWORD

Everything you ever wanted to know about Louisiana Cajun and zydeco musicians and their recordings is included here, and more. From Nathan Abshire to Zydeco Force, this exhaustive collection includes splendid album reviews, historical perspectives and descriptions of all recordings available today. I believe that the authors actually listened to each and every one of them and had fun doing it! This collection is a monumental work, and the authors' love for our music and culture shines through.

A major factor to consider was the surprising amount of national commercial attention our Cajun/zydeco cultures were receiving in the mid-1980s. I see the film *The Big Easy* as detonating the "Cajun Craze," allowing non-Louisianans a safe and free ticket to join in the fun. In the zydeco realm, it was Rockin' Sidney's song "My Toot Toot" that opened the doors to English lyrics and catchy rhythms. Anyone who chooses to judge Louisiana French music should take into consideration the post-1985 "born-again-to-please" syndrome and its effects on traditional music.

An interesting tidbit I found was the circle of dates. Is it just a coincidence that a majority of artists were born or died with years ending in zero or one, and that major changes and outstanding music occurred during those years ending in five or six? I'd never really thought about it before I read this invaluable compilation of facts and related material.

Thank you, Pat, Brian and David for catching the Cajun/zydeco fever and putting so much love into your well-organized and insightful perspective of the French music made in Louisiana.

–Michael Doucet dit BeauSoleil • March 1997

PREFACE

Cajun and zydeco music have danced their way across America and abroad in recent years, turning up in music clubs, at concerts and festivals, on college campuses, in Hollywood films, on the radio and even in TV commercials. This explosion of interest has spawned a renaissance in recording these infectious musical styles. With so many new CDs and reissues of old albums coming on the market, we felt the need for a guide to sort out what to buy and listen to.

This book covers 132 musicians—virtually every Cajun and zydeco musician who ever recorded an album, from the 1920s to our cut-off date of January 1, 1997. That leaves out some influential artists who either never recorded, or recorded only singles. Because zydeco is a more recent genre with a shorter recording history than Cajun music, the zydeco chapter is shorter than its Cajun counterpart. Genre crossover exists, for instance among early black Creole musicians who played in a style more like their white Cajun contemporaries than like today's zydeco artists. That's why some Creole artists appear in the predominantly Cajun chapter.

We have listed all the artists' albums on which we could find information, even hard-to-find recordings. With the industry reissuing old Cajun and zydeco recordings at a fast clip, an LP that is unavailable today may become available as a CD quite soon.

A word about CD/LP/cassette formats: Although CDs have taken center stage nationwide, we chose to review LPs, too, because so much great music would be overlooked if we didn't; many are worth searching out wherever records can be found. We also indicated if an album is available on cassette because many listeners still prefer to buy cassettes. However, we did not review cassette-only releases because of their limited availability and their short life span. Although we tried to track down complete format information for every recording, it is difficult to find; always ask what format is offered when ordering.

Our reviews are based on listening to all the available albums of an artist from beginning to end, even if we've heard them dozens of times before. Our criteria are fairly simple: Does the album have a good overall sound? (A CD that has two great songs won't win out over another with more good songs.) Is it good music, well-performed? Does it have magic? Is the album well-recorded?

We admit to some prejudices.

Author Brian Rollins, who reviewed the Cajun albums: "I prefer traditional musicians such as the Balfa Brothers, Amedee Ardoin and Steve Riley. I have to work at accepting Cajun-country, but I try to be open to it."

Author David Babb, who reviewed the zydeco recordings: "I prefer the bluesy and the new funk zydeco. I look for that elusive groove factor."

Besides trying to be as comprehensive and open-minded as possible, we sought as much accuracy as the vagaries of the recording business allows, with its notorious information gaps about recording and issue dates and biographical data. One small problem was the variable spelling in the French language of southwest Louisiana. Also, as in any folk music, the same Cajun and zydeco song can crop up in various artists' albums under many different names. Although we took the vast majority of our discographical information from our own album jackets and cross-checked with several sources, some mistakes may have crept in. Please let us know if you find any.

It wasn't always possible to pin down facts. In some cases, musicians' own stories about themselves–birth dates even–differed from telling to telling. Like Cajun and zydeco music itself, the words and facts in this book matter less in the end than listening and dancing to the music!

Although we have enjoyed the music of southwest Louisiana for decades, we learned many things about it as a result of writing this book. For example, the depth and complexity of Cajun and zydeco music become more apparent the more you listen to it. We suspect that in future years, musicologists will refer to Amedee Ardoin, Dennis McGee and Clifton Chenier as geniuses. When you listen to zydeco music closely, new rhythms emerge all the time. With Cajun music, the intricacy of the harmonies stands out.

Both styles show healthy growth and expansion these days. Zydeco particularly is seizing on contemporary influences, like funk and Caribbean rhythms, although the traditional roots sound of musicians like Nathan Williams and Geno Delafose is alive and well. Likewise, Cajun musicians are experimenting. Some, like Michael Doucet and Steve Riley, are digging into old tunes and revamping them, as well as writing new songs in the traditional manner. Others, like Wayne Toups & Zydecajun, are blending Cajun and zydeco.

We'd like to see the recording industry do Cajun and zydeco artists justice by paying more attention to authenticity on recordings. Too many albums are overproduced–the kiss of death to the raw intensity of this music–and too many (although fewer lately) suffer from poor sound quality. The best way to hear Cajun and zydeco music is live; we're mystified why more live recordings aren't out there. Like other regional musicians before them, today's struggling Cajun and zydeco artists need good managers and supportive record companies to keep them focused on what they do best, rather than force them into the latest musical fad.

Finally, we've learned that no matter how much poor advice, poverty and bad luck these musicians are up against, their music will endure if it's the real thing. No one can challenge Dewey Balfa's greatness or take away Clifton Chenier's crown.

Acknowledgments

We wish to thank the Cajun and zydeco artists in this book who have given us thousands of hours of musical pleasure over the last quarter-century. Thanks, too, to the writers on whose source material we relied and to the record companies and photographers who generously allowed us to use photographs. Others who helped immeasurably include Michael Doucet, Marcia Bernstein, Charles Glasser, Jim Pinfold, Robley Dupleix, Scott Billington, Chris Strachwitz. and Cindy Laudati. Special gratitude goes to our families, who warmly supported us throughout this project.

About the Authors

Working on this book allowed Pat Nyhan to indulge her love of music and writing simultaneously, with Cajun and zydeco CDs playing on the computer as she typed. A former journalist who has written most often about social issues and the arts, she has worked at the Boston Globe, Portland Press Herald, Maine Sunday Telegram and Maine Times. Having followed her cross-cultural interests to faraway places such as Afghanistan and Africa, she has found no place richer musically than Louisiana.

Brian Rollins first got turned on to Cajun music 25 years ago when he lived in Nova Scotia, original home of the Cajuns. A former professional drummer who currently operates a home inspection service, his musical flame burns brightly once a week in the "Rubboard Review" show he hosts on WMPG-FM in Portland, Maine. He has made a lifelong study of Cajun music, of which he is an addictive collector.

David Babb is "the Blues Doctor" to fans of his longtime "Bon Ton Roulet" show on WMPG-FM, where he spreads the zydeco gospel. A former professional musician who plays accordion, piano and guitar, he became an early zydeco fan in the 1960s when he bought his first Clifton Chenier album. In his other life, he is assistant vice-president for St. Joseph's Federal Credit Union in Biddeford, Maine.

The three Cajun/zydeco fans from Portland, Maine, make musical pilgrimages to Louisiana as often as possible.

HOW TO USE THIS BOOK

Sample Listing

NATHAN & THE ZYDECO CHA-CHAS

Vocals, accordion

Nathan Williams is a gifted songwriter with a strong, distinctive voice. He is one of the few to play the piano accordion–a more versatile instrument than the button accordion favored by most contemporary artists. Stylistically, he follows in **Clifton Chenier**'s footsteps as a tradition-based ...

Name: Entries are alphabetized by artist's last name, or first word of stage name or band name.

Major instruments of the artist.

Biography: Length varies according to the importance of the musician. Places named are in Louisiana unless noted otherwise. Sources for quotes are listed at the back of this book.
***Boldfaced** names refer you to other artists' entries.*

THE BEST

Steady Rock

r. 1988; i. 1989/Rounder 2092 CD, CS, LP
A TOP 10 ZYDECO ALBUM

Williams burst upon the scene with this spectacular debut ...

The Best: The artist's single best recording, best buy and/or best first purchase. Many should be considered essential to a collection. However, not all artists' "best" albums are equally great, since we chose to single out the top album from every artist who recorded more than one.

EXCELLENT

Your Mama Don't Know

r. 1990; i. 1991/Rounder 2107 CD, CS

Just an iota below "Steady Rock" in excitement, Williams' ...

Excellent: The next best albums, listed in order of quality, best first.

GOOD

Follow Me Chicken

r. & i. 1993/Rounder 2122 CD, CS

Williams continues expanding zydeco's harmonic boundaries. ...

Good: Albums not up to "Excellent" standard, listed in order of quality, best first.

OTHER RECORDINGS

Zydeco Live!

(with Boozoo Chavis) r. 1988; i. 1989 / Rounder 2069 CD, CS

Other Recordings: Alphabetical discography of the artist's lesser recordings.

HOW TO USE THIS BOOK

How the Guide Works

The bulk of this guide is arranged in two chapters: **"Cajun & Creole" and "Zydeco."** The **"Top 10"** recordings that open each chapter are those we consider essential buys, because of their high quality and/or because they capture the essence of a major Cajun or zydeco performer. These recordings are highlighted in the text with the following symbol: 🪗

The third chapter, **"Collections,"** offers compilations of Cajun, zydeco and Cajun/zydeco recordings, If you're new to Cajun and zydeco music, these samplers are a good place to start.

Recording Information

Recording information mostly comes from albums in our collection; a few titles under "Other Recordings" have been taken from other sources such as the Schwann catalog.

THE BEST

Steady Rock 🪗

r. 1988; i. 1989/Rounder 2092 CD, CS, LP

A TOP 10 ZYDECO ALBUM

Williams burst upon the scene with this spectacular debut ...

Album title

Recording date (abbreviated as "r."): *Date the album was recorded, taken from the album. If we don't list it, the date is unavailable.*

Issue date (abbreviated as "i."): *Date the album was issued (released). Taken from the album; sometimes unavailable.*

Record label: *Taken from the album in our collection and usually the most recent release. The same album material may appear on another label, too.*

Album number: *Refers to the CD or LP we reviewed; cassette versions of the same album may have a different number.*

Format: *CD (compact disc), CS (cassette) or LP (long-playing record). Whatever format appears first is the format of the album we reviewed.*

INTRODUCTION TO CAJUN & ZYDECO MUSIC

A lot of people who are crazy about Cajun and zydeco music can't tell you what the words "Cajun" and "zydeco" really mean. They just know they love these infectious sounds from south Louisiana, where the motto is *"Laissez les bons temps rouler!"* (Let the good times roll!) But to enjoy this music to the fullest, it's helpful to know what it is and where it comes from.

First, it doesn't come from New Orleans, where in fact few Cajuns live. Only a fraction of it is made along bayous–to blow another stereotype. Nor is it simply folk music. Cajun and zydeco music have absorbed many influences over their long history and continue to evolve and gain vitality, making them two of the most unique and dynamic roots musical styles in America today.

What are Cajun and Zydeco Music?

Cajun music comes from the French-speaking white families who settled in southwest Louisiana's prairies after the British exiled them in the 18th century from what was then known as Acadie, Nova Scotia. The name "Cajun" is believed to be a shortening of *Acadiens*, and the area where Cajuns live today is called "Acadiana." Waltzes and two-steps are typically played by a fiddle and/or accordion, guitar and triangle (*tit-fer*); often a steel guitar, bass and drums are added. The melody line is important, with vocalists singing hauntingly in a forceful tenor over acoustic arrangements.

Zydeco comes from the French-speaking African-Americans of the same region and appeared in its present form much later than Cajun music. The term "zydeco" may come from an African word, but it is more widely believed to derive from the phrase "les haricots" (pronounced *layzarico*) from an early song, "L'Haricots Sont Pas Sales" (The Snap Beans Aren't Salted), an allusion to hard times. In the French Creole patois, *les haricots* sounds like "zydeco"; variations include "zodico" and "zarico." In the old days, a "zydeco" also meant a country party, as in, "Let's go to the zydeco!" Locals sometimes call it "French music," to differentiate it from other African-American music.

Faster and more syncopated than Cajun music, it is heavily influenced by Afro-Caribbean sounds and draws on blues, rhythm & blues, soul, funk and other urban styles. Zydeco's grittier sound adds to the traditional Cajun lineup a rubboard or *frottoir* (a corrugated steel washboard-style vest "scrubbed" with spoons or bottle openers), electric guitars, drums and sometimes horns and keyboards. Rhythm dominates over melody in zydeco bands, which usually play fewer waltzes than Cajun groups and only occasionally feature fiddles.

The accordions so characteristic of both styles hark back to a German model appearing in Louisiana in the 1870s. Most Cajun and rural zydeco musicians use a small push-pull type with one row of buttons, rather than keys; urban musicians often favor models with two or three rows of buttons. Bluesier zydeco artists like C. J. Chenier favor the large piano accordion for its greater harmonic range. Despite these differences, Cajun and zydeco music have much in common, springing as they do from a shared life in the region stretching roughly from Lafayette, La., to Houston, Tx. Both are homegrown forms of dance music sung in French or English or both languages. With a long history of cross-fertilization, they share a repertoire of songs whose lyrics often take a back seat to danceable rhythms. The exuberant sounds of both mask a painful history of hardship and loss.

Origins

Cajun music's origins go back to northwest France. In the 17th century, many families left there for Nova Scotia, bringing with them Celtic and other Old World musical influences. When the British deported the colony en masse in 1755 for refusing to swear allegiance to the Crown, most wound up in French-speaking Louisiana, along with other settlers from France. There they lived an isolated life, referring to non-Cajuns as *Americains*. They brought old European songs with them and created new ones reflecting their tragic exile, hardships of farming the prairies, and joys and sorrows of love. Some acquired fiddles and simple percussion instruments such as the triangle.

Also arriving in the 18th century were Creoles–French-speaking people of African descent including *gens libres de couleur* (free-persons-of-color) and slaves from the South and the Caribbean. Like Cajuns, they intermarried with French, Spanish, Germans, Anglo-Americans and native Americans. Many Creoles came to southwest Louisiana to farm or became sharecroppers after the Civil War, as did the poor whites. They brought with them Afro-Caribbean polyrhythms, syncopation, improvisational singing and African-style percussion instruments, of which the rubboard is a descendant.

The Creoles' early music featured field hollers, *jure* (call-and-response chants) and other singing accompanied by hand-clapping and foot-stomping. They acquired fiddles and began adding Cajun tunes to their blues and Creole folk songs, and began playing accordions as soon as they were introduced to the area. Into this mix of Cajun and Creole music also went influences from the native American singing style, along with Anglo-American reels and other dances.

Early 20th Century

The modern history of Cajun and zydeco music tells the story of two cultural neighbors that were assimilated into the American mainstream twice–in the 1930s and 1950s–and later re-emerged with a new sense of pride. Cajun and Creole cultures have always shared links such as language, Catholicism, cuisine and festivals. Music and dancing were central to both cultures, with the Saturday night dance the high point of the week for the hard-working farmers and sharecroppers. In the early days, Cajuns held house parties called *bals de maison* or *fais do-dos* (go to sleep), a term referring to bedding down the children so the grown-ups could dance in the next room. The Creole party counterpart was *la-la*–whence the term "la-la music" (*or la musique Creole*) for old-time music.

Drinking and pots of gumbo were natural accompaniments to the live music provided by a few local musicians at these gatherings, where mazurkas, polkas and many other Old World dances were popular up until the early 1900s. The fun reached a high pitch at Mardi Gras, when costumed troupes of horseback-riders joined by musicians rode from door to door across the countryside.

Eventually, dance halls took the place of house parties. Local performers filled the prairies with music loud enough to be heard above the noise–one reason for the intense, high singing style heard today and prominence of the accordion, whose volume is greater than the fiddle.

Due to the accordion's musical limitations and outside influences creeping into the region, the variety of dance styles shrank to primarily the two that currently dominate: the two-step and the waltz. Today, the dance hall tradition thrives in southwest Louisiana and east Texas, where Cajun and zydeco clubs tend to be frequented by their respective white or African-American communities but are increasingly visited by tourists from all over.

Cajun & Creole Recording History

The arrival of recording in the 1920s set Cajun and zydeco music's core repertoire by disseminating standard versions of songs that had formerly been improvised. Companies such as RCA Victor and Columbia cut field recordings of Cajun, Creole and other ethnic music to stimulate sales of phonographs. Louisiana's first Cajun recording, Joseph and Cleoma Breaux Falcon's "Allons a Lafayette" (Let's Go to Lafayette), created a sensation when it appeared in 1928. By then the accordion had overtaken the fiddle in popularity.

The Falcons made a dynamic accordion/guitar duo. However, very few female musicians ever followed Cleoma's lead, given the traditional strictures against women performing in public; to this day, only a handful can be found in Cajun and zydeco music. With her brothers, who included the influential Amedee Breaux, Cleoma also recorded and probably composed the most famous Cajun song, "Ma Blonde Est Partie" ("Jolie Blonde," or Pretty Blonde).

Black Creole musicians had a great influence on Cajun music and developed followings themselves. Accordionist Amedee Ardoin was a star performer in his day, recording from 1929 to the early 1930s both alone and with his partner, white fiddler Dennis McGee. Their collaboration laid the foundation for the style and repertoire of today's Cajun music. Ardoin created many of those songs, and his percussive accordion style can be heard today in zydeco music.

Despite racial separation in the community, black Creole and white musicians like Ardoin and McGee sometimes played together in the first quarter of this century, symbolizing the cross-fertilization that characterizes the region's music. Cajuns borrowed blues sounds from the Creoles, and Creoles adapted Cajun songs to their rhythmic sensibilities. In Ardoin's and McGee's music could also be heard influences from Nova Scotia, France, Ireland, Africa, the Caribbean, Spain, England, Germany, Anglo-Americans and native Americans.

During the 1930s, McGee made many recordings, while the sounds of prominent bandleaders like Leo Soileau and Lawrence Walker found their way onto recordings as well as the radio. The fiddle made a comeback as amplification arrived, boosting its sound, and German accordions became scarce. The pedal steel guitar, bass and drums were added to the lineup.

It was the era of Americanization. School boards had banned the French language from schools in 1916, and being "French" carried a sharp stigma by the '30s. The new oil industry and expansion of the highway system cut into the region's isolation, as did the popularity of radio music, with its influences from all over the U.S. Cajun musicians adapted these influences, particularly from country music.

This Americanization led to the popular western-style music of string bands such as the Hackberry Ramblers, one of the first groups to use electrical amplifaction. In the smoother, bigger sound filling dance halls and radio airwaves, French lyrics were often the only thing

Cajun about the tunes. English crept in; the Hackberry Ramblers even recorded in English as the Riverside Ramblers.

One immensely popular musician who blended tradition with modern trends was Harry Choates, "the fiddle king of Cajun swing." He played a wildly inventive fiddle and sang Texas-style songs whose "my lover left me to go to Texas" theme appears in so much Cajun music today. His 1946 western swing version of "Jole Blon" became a regional hit, turning it into the Cajun anthem.

The accordion reappeared during the 1940s, when returning World War II vets craved their distinctive Cajun music. Older accordionists such as Lawrence Walker and Aldus Roger were suddenly in demand again, and Nathan Abshire's "Pine Grove Blues" hit big regionally.

During the early 1950s, Iry LeJeune played a key role in reviving the accordion and traditional Cajun music. He struck a chord with his evocative crying-style singing and adept accordion playing. Soulful recordings like "La Valse du Pont d'Amour" (Love Bridge Waltz) had a huge impact on later musicians, including his son, Eddie LeJeune, who sings in the same style today.

Mainstream music won out again by the mid-1950s, when record companies abandoned traditional Cajun music to put rock 'n' roll and its south Louisiana cousin, swamp pop, on vinyl. Americanized Cajun-country music took off, with practitioners like Doug Kershaw of "Louisiana Man" fame and Nashville's Jimmy C. Newman making highly successful recording careers singing in English. Others like composer/guitarist D. L. Menard (who wrote "The Back Door") and popular crooners Vin Bruce and Belton Richard borrowed from country music but kept to a traditional Cajun base.

With the French language and Cajun culture suppressed, Cajun music was derided as "chanky-chank." This low period ended with fiddler Dewey Balfa's smash appearance at the 1964 Newport Folk Festival and his conversion to the cause of reviving Cajun music. Thereafter, the Balfa Brothers became the first internationally known Cajun band. Other festivals followed, exposing great artists like the bluesy Nathan Abshire, the brilliant, much-loved Creole fiddler Canray Fontenot and Creole accordionist Alphonse "Bois Sec" Ardoin to a national audience.

Behind these revival efforts was a group of folk music researchers like the Newport Folk Foundation's Alan Lomax (who had recorded Cajun and Creole music in the 1930s for the Library of Congress), Newport field workers Ralph Rinzler and Mike Seeger, Harry Oster of Louisiana State University (who also made field recordings), and local activists Paul Tate and Revon Reed. In 1968, the Council for the Development of French in Louisiana (CODOFIL) was founded, leading to the annual Festivals Acadiens in Lafayette and restoration of the French language in schools.

Dewey Balfa convinced Floyd Soileau of the local Swallow Records to make a traditional Cajun music record in 1965, and *The Balfa Brothers Play Traditional Cajun Music* led to other recordings. Other seminal musicians like fiddler Michael Doucet and accordionist/accordion builder Marc Savoy threw themselves into a Cajun music renaissance that continues today.

The hallmark of these world-class musicians and their younger counterparts such as Steve Riley is faithfulness to their Cajun music roots while constantly revitalizing them with experimentation.

Doucet's Beausoleil, the most famous Cajun band, brilliantly weaves rock, jazz and other styles into its authentic Cajun sounds. Some other important artists like Jo-El Sonnier and the mercurial Zachary Richard reach out to popular music without abandoning their musical heritage. And some, like Wayne Toups & Zydecajun, reach across the aisle to contemporary zydeco.

Zydeco Recording History

Zydeco arose from old-time Creole music, which had a lot in common with Cajun music during the early days of recording. *La musique Creole* combined accordion, fiddle and rubboard and played in a graceful style more rhythmic than Cajun music. Among the important artists who played in this style up until the present time were the Carriere Brothers, Bois Sec Ardoin and Canray Fontenot.

By the 1940s, Creoles were listening to R&B and jazz on the radio and juke boxes, as well as in clubs in Texas cities like Houston and Port Arthur, where they found work during World War II. Musicians added those urban influences to their rural *la-la* music. During the 1950s the King of Zydeco, Clifton Chenier, appeared on the scene. A legendary accordionist and creative stylist, he virtually invented the genre by blending Creole folk music with the blues and R&B and adding electric guitar, drums, bass and horns to the traditional accordion and rubboard. He was the first to play piano accordion, whose wide range could express his bluesy style.

Boozoo Chavis actually made the first modern zydeco recording, the popular "Paper in My Shoe," in 1954. However, he soon departed the music industry, leaving the field to Chenier, whose first national hit came in the mid-1950s with "Ay Tete Fee" (Hey Little Girl). Chenier also popularized the old Creole song "Les Haricots Sont Pas Sale" as "Zydeco Sont Pas Sale," making his name synonymous with the term "zydeco." His fame and recording output were monumental over his 30-year career and triggered the current zydeco explosion. Since his death in 1987, his son, C. J. Chenier, has continued his legacy with the Red Hot Louisiana Band.

As zydeco caught on outside Louisiana in the 1980s–boosted by the success of the California-based Queen Ida and a surprise hit called "My Toot Toot" by Rockin' Sidney–other heavyhitters from the Clifton Chenier school began to emerge to a national audience. Several have won major record label contracts.

Chenier protege Buckwheat Zydeco's multi-faceted talents propelled him to the top of zydeco's recording industry and broke new musical ground in the 1970s. His highly professional R&B and soul-tinged zydeco is the sound much of the world associates with the catchy style. Rockin' Dopsie pumped his earthy, down-home accordion to international recognition, with the help of a talented R&B-oriented band called the Zydeco Twisters. His son, Rockin' Dopsie Jr., took over the band in the early 1990s. Fernest Arceneaux, another Clifton Chenier stylist, also caught on in Europe.

Meanwhile, Terrance Simien charged ahead with a high-energy style. And Boozoo Chavis made a sensational comeback, becoming one of Louisiana's top draws among fans of down-home zydeco. Chavis has inspired still another generation of musicians pumping out a simpler, rural zydeco marked by Afro-Caribbean rhythms–newcomer Rosie Ledet is an example.

Old-style zydeco has kept a faithful following with traditionalists like the Ardoin Family Band and John Delafose, whose syncopated Afro-Caribbean sound found its way to regional fame with a hit record, "Joe Pitre a Deux Femmes" (Joe Pitre Has Two Women). In keeping with a pervasive "zydeco dynasty" tradition, both family bands had sons following in their fathers' footsteps. Geno Delafose carries on the Creole music legacy, but is also at home with a contemporary R&B sound. Lawrence "Black" Ardoin turned Bois Sec's *musique Creole* into zydeco and passed the torch to his own son, Chris Ardoin, who has modernized it further. Another father-son pair are accordionists Roy and "Chubby" Carrier. Still another example can be found in the up-and-coming Zydeco Force, a young band fronted by Jeffery Broussard, son of Delton Broussard, who led the old-style Lawtell Playboys.

Today zydeco thrives through important artists like Nathan Williams & the Zydeco Cha Chas, one of the most innovative bands around. Of this generation, two hugely popular musicians have emerged: Beau Jocque, with his funky urban zydeco with the deep grooves, and Keith Frank, a young favorite of the rural dance hall scene. Both mix rock and rap into their performances.

Record Companies

If national record companies began the story of Cajun and zydeco recorded music, local ones sustained it through the years—once they discovered the drawing power their Cajun and Creole neighbors had. Record producers George Khoury, Lee Lavergne, J. D. Miller, Eddie Shuler and Floyd Soileau all took chances on poor farmers who could play a fiddle or an accordion and had a certain musical magic.

Chapter 1•Cajun & Creole

TOP 10 CAJUN & CREOLE ALBUMS
(in alphabetical order)

We consider these albums essential buys, because of their high quality and/or because they capture the essence of a major performer. Please see artist entries in the book for reviews of the albums, which are highlighted in the text with this symbol:

CAJUN'S GREATEST-THE DEFINITIVE COLLECTION
Iry LeJeune/Ace (England) 428 CD

THE COMPLETE EARLY RECORDINGS OF DENNIS MCGEE
Shanachie/Yazoo 2012 CD

I'M NEVER COMIN' BACK-AMEDEE ARDOIN
Arhoolie/Folklyric 7007 CD

LA MUSIQUE CREOLE-ALPHONSE "BOIS SEC" ARDOIN
Arhoolie 445 CD

LA TOUSSAINT-STEVE RILEY & THE MAMOU PLAYBOYS
Rounder 6068 CD

LIVE! FROM THE LEFT COAST-BEAUSOLEIL
Rounder 6035 CD

LOUISIANA HOT SAUCE, CREOLE STYLE-CANRAY FONTENOT
Arhoolie 381 CD

PLAY TRADITIONAL CAJUN MUSIC-THE BALFA BROTHERS
Swallow 6011 CD

THE SWALLOW RECORDINGS-D. L. MENARD
Ace (England) 327 CD

WOMEN IN THE ROOM-ZACHARY RICHARD
A&M 5302 CD

CHAPTER 1: CAJUN & CREOLE

NATHAN ABSHIRE
Vocals, accordion

Arboolie CD 373

"A musician's life is hard, as hard as a man can have it," Nathan Abshire once told Louisiana author Barry Jean Ancelet. His lifelong poverty proved it. Yet his giant talent and exuberant personality won him thousands of fans, for whom he exemplified the Cajun musician.

Abshire helped revive accordion playing after it had fallen out of favor in the 1930s and went on to become one of the most popular Cajun recording artists. Of all the white Cajun performers, he was the most influenced by the bluesy, black Creole style. His accordion artistry, raw singing style and vast repertoire of traditional Cajun folk songs, hymns and blues made up a unique contribution to Cajun music.

Abshire was born into a humble, accordion-playing family of Cajun and native American heritage near Gueydan in 1915. He taught himself to play, making his accordion debut at age eight and soon playing at house dances and dance halls throughout the area. Abshire was heavily influenced by legendary Creole accordionist **Amedee Ardoin**, for whom he filled in during breaks at house parties as a teenager. Like Ardoin, the youthful Abshire would often walk up to 20 miles to a gig paying a couple of dollars.

In the mid-1930s he recorded briefly, backed by the Rayne-Bo Ramblers, for the Bluebird label. But when western swing caught on, he switched to fiddle for several years. During World War II, the French-speaking Abshire was drafted into the army, but was discharged early because of his limited English and illiteracy.

Once back in Louisiana, he joined the popular Pine Grove Boys, playing throughout southwest Louisiana and east Texas. During the oil boom years following the war, demand for Cajun music was high. The band's recordings on OT Records featured the spirited honky-tonk, barroom and dance hall music of those years.

In 1949, Abshire hit it big with "Pine Grove Blues" (also known as "Ma Negresse"), his signature tune that has become a Cajun classic. At the peak of his popularity in the 1950s he was heard every day over KPLC Radio in Lake Charles. In the early 1960s, Abshire recorded for the local Kajun label and played dances throughout the area. He continued with the Pine Grove Boys, who by then included renowned instrumentalists **Dewey** and Rodney **Balfa**.

Some of his finest recordings came in the late 1960s and early 1970s, with the **Balfa Brothers** on the Swallow label. As the Balfas became successful on their own, Abshire recorded with a new band for La Louisianne and Sonet Records and toured extensively. Festival and college audiences revered him, and he appeared in several films about Cajun music. However, alcoholism caught up with him by the late '70s, and his recordings for Folkways and La Louisianne weren't up to his former quality. The big-hearted, pot-bellied Abshire continued to please his many fans at local dances, smiling broadly and singing in an exuberant, sometimes off-key voice that expressed his emotional personality.

Like most Cajun musicians, throughout his successful career Abshire had to supplement his musical income with a string of odd jobs, finally winding up as longtime caretaker of the Basile town dump. Still, he was rich in visitors, who came from all over the world to see him. He said he gave up drinking in later years. However, after a period of failing health, he died in 1981, perhaps fulfilling the motto he displayed on his accordion case: "The Good Times Are Killing Me." Believing it wrong for a musician's music to be played after he was gone, he asked to have his music buried with him—a wish that went ungranted.

THE BEST

A Cajun Legend: The Best of Nathan Abshire

i. 1991/Swallow 6061 CD, CS, LP

For this CD, Swallow improved on its two earlier LPs–*Pine Grove Blues* (Swallow 6014) and *The Good Times Are Killing Me* (Swallow 6023), recorded late 1960s-early 1970s. Six of their weaker songs were dropped and two good ones added, "Belisaire Waltz" and "French Blues." The disc captures Abshire's spontaneous accordion playing and singing, whose strength is featured especially on the uptempo numbers. Blending well with his accordion are the plaintive vocals by Thomas Langley on "Tramp Sur la Rue" and Dewey Balfa on "Dying in Misery." Abshire's playing had a strong bluesy side, and even the waltzes have a pronounced beat. Outstanding songs include

his classic "Pine Grove Blues," "A Musician's Life," "Sur le Courtableu," "Choupique Two-Step" and "Tracks of My Buggy."

Nathan Abshire, Featuring the Balfa Brothers

i. 1991/Ace (England) 329 CD

This release contains the two Swallow LPs mentioned above in their entirety.

EXCELLENT

The Great Cajun Accordionist

r.1973, 1978; i. 1993/Ace (England) 401 CD (contains 12 cuts from Nathan Abshire: A Cajun Tradition, Vol. 1/r. 1973/La Louisianne 139 CS, LP & others from Vol. 2/r. 1978/La Louisianne 144 CS, LP)

Abshire sings best on "Cher Ti-Monde" and "La Valse de Choupique." "Hip et Taiau" features catchy lyrics, and this version of "Pine Grove Blues" shines. The combination of accordion and double fiddles lights up the latter tunes.

Nathan Abshire and the Pine Grove Boys: The Legendary Jay Miller Sessions, Vol. 13

i. 1978/Flyright (England) 535 LP (contains the best of the singles released by Jay Miller on his Kajun and Cajun Classics labels + 5 unissued songs)

This version of Abshire's classic "Pine Grove Blues" is required listening for fans of early Cajun music. It lacks Dewey Balfa's superb fiddle solo, but Abshire uses a slower tempo effectively and sings dramatically. The album offers strong vocals and terrific playing with a blues and swing flavor–Abshire's forte. There are a few weak songs and poor sound on two cuts, but the rest is great. The swinging "Popcorn Blues" and beautiful "Dreamer's Waltz" are other highlights.

Cajun Fais Do-Do

(collection) r. 1966;i. 1995/Arhoolie 416 CD (Selections from this CD also appear on Cajun Fais Do-Do/Arhoolie 5004 CS, LP)

The first part of this collection comprises *Nathan Abshire and the Balfa Brothers*–a gem recorded by Arhoolie producer Chris Strachwitz on portable equipment at the Frontier Bar in Basile. One of Abshire's most traditional recordings, the session captures two of the best vocals he ever recorded: "Ma Negresse" (also known as "Pine Grove Blues") and "Gabrielle Waltz." His accordion work is also good, especially on "Grandenuit Special." Playing with him are Dewey Balfa on fiddle and vocals, Rodney Balfa on guitar and Basile Marcentel on triangle.

The CD's second part features several traditional musicians who customarily gathered on Saturday mornings at the remote facilities of radio station KEUN in Eunice, and later Mamou. There a Mamou schoolteacher, Cajun music ambassador and self-styled DJ named Revon Reed emceed a two-hour live and recorded musicale called "Fais Do-Do"–hence the album's title. Musicians include the Breaux Brothers, Jerry Devillier, Cyp and Adam Landreneau, and Isom J. Fontenot.

OTHER RECORDINGS

The Cajuns, Vol. 1

(with the Balfa Brothers Orchestra) i. 1973/Sonet (England) 643 LP (unreviewed)

French Blues: The Khoury Recordings 1949-1956

i. 1993/Arhoolie 373 CD, CS (Selections from this CD also appear on Nathan Abshire and Other Cajun Gems/i. 1972/Arhoolie 5013 CS, LP)

ALPHONSE "BOIS SEC" ARDOIN
Accordion, vocals

Arhoolie CD 445

Bois Sec Ardoin is an important link to the *musique Creole* of southwest Louisiana–the Cajun-style "la-la" music that preceded zydeco in the African-American communities of southwest Louisiana. Through his Ardoin Family Band and recordings with longtime friend and Creole fiddler **Canray Fontenot**, Ardoin has kept old-style Creole music traditions alive.

Ardoin (b. 1914 or 1916) got the nickname "Bois Sec" (Dry Wood) in his youth, when he was the first one out of the fields and into the barn to keep dry during a rainstorm. He has lived all his life in a rural hamlet called Duralde, between Mamou and Basile. To make a living, he sharecropped and ran his own small farm, where he still lives.

At around the age of 12, Ardoin taught himself accordion by sneaking his older brother's instrument into the barn when his brother went to work. He drew inspiration from his famous older cousin, virtuoso singer/accordionist **Amedee Ardoin**. Bois Sec used to sit by Ardoin, watching how he played and learning his songs, which later became part of his own repertoire. In his teens, he backed up Amedee on triangle in a club in Basile and traveled with him to *bals de maison* (house parties) throughout the region. Unlike Amedee, however, Bois Sec did not become a professional musician–a career frowned upon by his mother.

In 1948, he and Fontenot teamed up to play house dances as the Duralde Ramblers. They performed regionally and at the Newport Folk Festival in 1966. They also cut some of the best la-la recordings ever made in a repertoire ranging from melancholy Creole tunes to old French dances.

By the 1970s, Ardoin was leading the popular Ardoin Brothers Band (which has also been known as the Ardoin Family Orchestra and Ardoin Family Band), made up of his sons and Fontenot. The group appeared at many folk festivals and has been recorded by several folk labels.

Three of his sons have played accordion at different times for the band. One, Gustave "Bud" Ardoin, was in line to take over from his father when he was killed in a car accident in 1974. The following year, Bois Sec retired from playing dances. Bois Sec's oldest son, Morris, also has played accordion and rhythm guitar, but left the band to run Club Morris, the family dance hall next to his home about a mile from Bois Sec's house. The family band often plays at the club, which is the center of Duralde's social life. The next oldest son, **Lawrence "Black" Ardoin**, played with the band and formed his own "French Zydeco Band" in the early 1980s.

A community leader and personable father of 14 successful children, Bois Sec hosts a family reunion with his wife Marceline every year where family members play music together. To honor his lifelong musical contributions, an "Hommage a Bois-Sec" concert was arranged at the Liberty Theatre in Eunice as part of the 1996 Festivals Acadiens. Continuing the Ardoin family tradition, one of Bois Sec's numerous grandchildren, **Chris Ardoin**, has also formed a zydeco band.

THE BEST

La Musique Creole

(with Canray Fontenot) i. 1996/Arhoolie 445 CD (contains all of Les Blues du Bayou/r. & i. 1966/Melodeon 7330 LP + 9 tracks from La Musique Creole/r. 1971, 1973; i. 1974/Arhoolie 1070 CS, LP)

A TOP 10 CAJUN ALBUM

This gem draws from classic recordings by two major artists. Ardoin and Fontenot's special interaction, brought about by years of playing together, is reminiscent of the classic duo of Amedee Ardoin and Dennis McGee. *Les Blues du Bayou*, one of the finest Cajun recordings ever made, was formerly available only on a rare Melodeon LP. Ardoin and Fontenot cut it at Wynwood Studios in Church Falls, Va., on their way home from a historic appearance at the 1966 Newport Folk Festival.

Ardoin and Fontenot swapped good lead vocals, backed up by Isom Fontenot and radio personality Revon Reed on triangle. Ardoin shines on "La Robe Barree" and "Fais Pas Ca." The strong swing beat in many of their songs lends a bluesy feel, as in the instrumental "Danse de la Misere." Even the waltzes have a strong beat, with only a tapping foot and a triangle supplying rhythm. Also on this CD are eight of the better songs from *La Musique Creole* (with Fontenot and the Ardoin Brothers) and one tune featuring the Ardoin Family Orchestra, "Ardoin Two-Step."

EXCELLENT

Cajun & Creole Masters

r. 1987; i. 1995/Music of the World CDT-138 CD (also available as Cajun & Creole Music 110 CS)

Recorded live at Washington Square Church in New York City, Ardoin and Fontenot were joined by Beausoleil's Michael Doucet and Billy Ware. Ardoin is featured on "Talles de Ronces" and "Blues du Voyageur." Not his best singing, but his accordion playing is superb.

GOOD

Louisiana Hot Sauce, Creole Style

(Canray Fontenot, with the Ardoin Family Orchestra)

r. 1971-1991; i. 1992/Arhoolie 381 CD, CS

A TOP 10 CAJUN ALBUM

Ardoin backs up his longtime partner, Canray Fontenot, on eight songs.

A Couple of Cajuns: The Ardoin Family Orchestra with Dewie (sic) Balfa

i. 1981/Sonet 873 LP

Ardoin and Cajun fiddler Dewey Balfa were longtime friends and neighbors and often played together, despite the fact that most Louisiana dance halls were segregated. Ardoin's vocals are excellent on "Two Step de Lans Prie Noir," "I Went to the Dance" and "Two Step a Mama's," weaker on other songs. Balfa's splendid fiddling swings more with this looser band than with his own Balfa Brothers. The full-sounding orchestra provides excellent back-up.

OTHER RECORDINGS

Louisiana Cajun French Music from the Southwest Prairies, Vol. 2

(collection) r. 1964-1967; i. 1989/Rounder 6002 CD, CS, LP

Zodico: Louisiana Creole Music

(collection) r. 1976; i. 1979/Rounder 6009 CS, LP

AMEDEE ARDOIN
Vocals, accordion

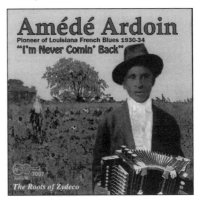

Arhoolie CD 7007

Creole virtuoso Amedee (also spelled Amede, Amade or Amadie) Ardoin probably had more influence on Cajun and zydeco music than any other musician, black or white. He was the star singer/accordionist for house parties and dance halls in the 1920s-1930s. Many nights, the tiny, energetic musician finished playing at a lucrative white dance for a couple of dollars, only to sing the blues until dawn at a Creole party where musicians took home only change.

"Then Amadie would really get hot. After playing for the white folks—you know, two-steps and waltzes—he would get down on some blues and just sing and sing," Creole fiddler **Canray Fontenot** recalled, according to **Michael Doucet** in John Broven's *South to Louisiana: The Music of the Cajun Bayous.* Similarly, Ardoin crossed the race barrier in the recording industry to become the most popular early black "French music" recording star (although not its first; Creole fiddler Douglas Bellard holds that distinction).

Renowned for his powerful voice, wide range and ability to perform for hours on end, Ardoin had a high-pitched, crying vocal style that became the model of a Cajun singer. He took care of his voice, soothing it with a lemon he carried in his pocket. Along with his emotional singing, he played the one-row diatonic accordion in a daringly freewheeling, syncopated style. Although he performed traditional French, Creole and African songs, this gifted musician wrote most of his own Cajun-style tunes, which are still played today.

Ardoin was born in 1896 to a sharecropping family in L'Anse Rougeau, near Basile. In his youth, he played parties and dances to earn his keep, walking to gigs throughout the area. He met another sharecropper, white Cajun fiddler **Dennis McGee**, on a farm near Chataigner, and the pair were encouraged by the farmer they worked for to play together for white house parties in the neighborhood. Another sharecropping stint on a farm near Eunice solidified their musical partnership; again they found a supportive boss, who drove them in his buggy to dances. Their fame spread as they traveled, performed and recorded together throughout the 1920s and 1930s in a collaboration symbolic of the common roots of Cajun and Creole music.

"Everybody went crazy when Amedee played. Oh, I loved that little guy's music…He had a song he'd cry out in—it would make me shake when he'd take to singing it," McGee told author/musician Ann Allen Savoy.

Despite Ardoin's widespread respect among people of both races, there were some who called him a bum because he shunned hard work in the fields to earn a living as a professional musician, hitchhiking around the countryside with his accordion in his flour sack. Others thought he went too far with cheeky improvisations commenting on people in the room during songs, a habit which forced him to flee dances more than once.

A racial attack in the mid-1930s is thought to have precipitated a tragic downhill slide. Two white men beat him savagely and left him for dead after a dance for accepting a white woman's loan of a handerkerchief to wipe his face on a hot night. Ardoin never recovered mentally from the severe beating and eventually was committed to the Louisiana State Institution for the Mentally Ill in Pineville, where he apparently died in 1941. His death is attributed variously to effects of the beating, alcoholism or poisoning by a jealous musician.

Ardoin does not fit neatly into either the Cajun or zydeco category; his recordings are generally more Cajun, but he heavily influenced zydeco music. He began recording in the late 1920s for Columbia, then recorded with Dennis McGee for Brunswick and Vocalion in the 1930s, as well as on his own for Bluebird, Melotone, and Decca—with all but the Decca recordings extremely rare today.

Ardoin's influence went beyond what his output of 34 recordings would indicate, because he played constantly in a great variety of places and tutored upcoming musicians such as his young cousin **Alphonse "Bois Sec" Ardoin** and **Canray Fontenot**. He created much of the core repertoire of later Cajun music and inspired the next generation of accordionists like **Iry LeJeune**, **Nathan Abshire** and **Clifton Chenier**.

THE BEST

I'm Never Comin' Back 📖

r. 1930, 1934; i. 1995/Arhoolie/Folklyric 7007 CD
A TOP 10 CAJUN ALBUM

Subtitled "The Roots of Zydeco," this CD does indeed show where zydeco began. It also offers the most comprehensive view of Ardoin's creative genius. Covering most of his recording history, the album features 26

Cajun dances and blues numbers from three recording sessions: New Orleans in 1930, with fiddler Dennis McGee; San Antonio in 1934, again with McGee; and New York in 1934, his last recording session, playing alone. The final session is particularly important for the chance to hear Ardoin perform without backing; he holds nothing back in piercing, emotional vocals giving us a glimpse into the very soul of Creole music. Luckily, superb sound quality allows us to enjoy his music to the fullest.

McGee's accompaniment at the two other sessions is nothing like the pair's earlier recordings, where he was close to an equal; here, McGee plays more of a timekeeper role except on "One Step des Chameaux" and a few other tunes. In a superb collection, these songs top the list: "La Valse a Thomas Ardoin," "One Step des Chameaux," "Les Blues de Crowley," "La Turtape de Saroied" and "Les Blues de la Prison."

EXCELLENT

Cajun Dance Party: Fais Do Do

i. 1994/Columbia Legacy CK 46784 CD

All of one side of the remarkable recordings with Dennis McGee from *The First Black Zydeco Recording Artist* are here except one, and the sound has been improved. An excellent introduction to one of the greats of Cajun music, along with some other good early music by the Breaux Brothers and Cleoma Breaux.

The First Black Zydeco Recording Artist—His Original Recordings 1928-1938 (Louisiana Cajun Music, Vol. 6)

i. 1981/Arhoolie/Old Timey 124 LP (also available as The First Black Cajun Recording Artist–His Original 1929-1934 Recordings/Arhoolie 9056 CS)

Note the terms "zydeco" and "Cajun" in the otherwise similar titles of this historic collection–an example of how difficult it is to classify Ardoin stylistically. The differing recording dates also illustrate the confusion that can creep in on album covers. In fact, one side of this disc features recordings Ardoin made with fiddler Dennis McGee in 1929 and 1930, while the other showcases Ardoin singing and playing accordion alone at a 1934 session in New York City.

All in all, it's a wonderful collection of 14 of Ardoin's 34 recordings. The pairing of Ardoin and McGee is a case of one plus one equalling far more than two. McGee's melodic back-up fits perfectly, with just the right note at the right time. Their duets are superb, as can be heard on "Madame Etienne" and "Quoi Faire." Ardoin was not only an accomplished accordion player; he had a voice that could chill your spine–high, nasal, dramatic and emotional. Listen to him on "La Valse a Austin Ardoin" and "Les Blues de la Prison."

Pioneers of Cajun Accordion 1926-1936: Historic Recordings of Louisiana Cajun Music, Vol. 9

i. 1989/Arhoolie/Old Timey 128 CS, LP

This LP has five cuts by Ardoin from a 1930 New Orleans session for the Brunswick label. Dennis McGee's back-up is more subtle than on *The First Black Zydeco Recording Artist* except on "Valse de Opelousas" and "La Valse de Oberlin." "Amede Two Step" is slightly scratchy, but it captures the emotional power of

Ardoin's vocals. "Blues de Basil" demonstrates that, like his successor, Clifton Chenier, Ardoin was a great bluesman.

THE BALFA BROTHERS
Group

The Balfa Brothers

Rounder LP 6007

The quintessential Cajun band, the Balfa Brothers formed the centerpiece of the Cajun music revival following the western-swing era. Led by the hugely influential fiddler **Dewey Balfa**, the band included his brothers Will on fiddle and Rodney on guitar, and occasionally Harry on guitar and Burke on triangle. Various fine accordionists such as **Nathan Abshire** and Hadley Fontenot also performed with the group over the years. Renowned instrumentalists, the band's trademarks were superior fiddle duets and Dewey's and Rodney's searing vocals.

The Balfa family lived in Bayou Grand Louis, a small farming community near Mamou. They were poor, French-speaking sharecroppers whose only entertainment was music. Charles Balfa played the fiddle and sang old Cajun songs for his six sons and three daughters, who in their isolated existence weren't exposed to any other type of music. Their grandmother, Marie Richard Balfa, also

passed down old French songs to them. Five of the boys–Will (b. 1917), Dewey (b. 1927), Harry (b. 1931), Rodney (b. 1934), and Burke (birthdate unavailable)–learned to play the fiddle and triangle using their great-grand-father's instruments, as well as guitar, harmonica, accordion and spoons. Life on the farm was hard; since they were needed for fieldwork, none of the five brothers finished high school.

During the 1940s, the brothers played for family gatherings and house parties until Dewey and Will formed a Cajun band called the Musical Brothers in 1948, with other musicians on bass, triangle, guitar and sometimes drums. The group became popular at local dances, often playing every night of the week, and had its own radio show in Opelousas.

Two events propelled the Balfas' band into the national orbit: Dewey's historic appearance at the 1964 Newport Folk Festival and another at the 1967 festival with brothers Rodney and Will, Dewey's daughter Nelda and accordionist Hadley Fontenot. Following the tumultuous receptions, the Balfa Brothers played with a new Cajun pride at music festivals the world over, clubs, colleges and two Presidential inaugurations. They relished their role as Cajun ambassadors, teaching as they performed.

However, it took longer to become recognized in their own region, where Americanization had all but eradicated Cajun music. Louisiana record producer Floyd Soileau's initial reluctance to record the Balfas' traditional, fiddle-based sound demonstrates how little interest there was in things Cajun in the early 1960s. After repeated trips to Soileau's Ville Platte studio, Dewey finally convinced him to put out a single of the Balfa Brothers, and the surprisingly good response led to their stunning first album in 1965. A decade later, the Balfas had stimulated widespread interest in Cajun music and become a symbol of renewed local pride. That didn't mean they could earn a living by music alone. None of the brothers could ever afford to give up their other jobs—in Will's case, operating a bulldozer, and in Dewey's, driving a schoolbus, among other things.

The band's brilliant career ended tragically in 1979, when Will and Rodney died in a car accident. A devastated Dewey carried on, playing with his daughter, Christine, on triangle and vocals, and Rodney's teen-age son Tony, who had joined the group on drums, guitar and other rhythm instruments as a youngster. In later years, Dewey recorded with other musicians and served as Cajun music's elder statesman until his death in 1992.

THE BEST

Play Traditional Cajun Music, Vol. 1 & 2 📖

r. 1965, 1974; i. 1990/Swallow 6011 CD (contains Play Traditional Cajun Music, Vol. 1/r. & i. 1965/Swallow 6011 CS, LP & Play More Traditional Cajun Music, Vol. 2/r. & i. 1974/Swallow 6019 CS, LP) (also available as Ace [England] 955 CD)

A TOP 10 CAJUN ALBUM

This CD combining two earlier LPs catches Dewey, Will and Rodney Balfa at their best—particularly the selections from their stellar 1965 debut album capturing Cajun's characteristic plaintiveness. On the 1974 session, the brothers are joined by accordionist Marc Savoy and Rodney's son, Tony, on triangle and drums, with a dubbed bass line for an experimental sound. Nearly all 24 songs are good, and the musicianship is superb. It's great to hear the interaction of the brothers, who played together for almost four decades.

EXCELLENT

Louisiana Cajun French Music from the Southwest Prairies, Vol. 1

r. 1955, 1956; i. 1976/Rounder 6001 CD, CS

Ralph Rinzler made these early field recordings under the sponsorship of the Newport Folk Foundation at the time when the Balfas were unknown outside southwest Louisiana. His recordings helped generate national interest in Cajun music and resulted in invitations for groups like the Balfas to play in the north. The album projects a raw honesty, partly due to Rinzler's crude equipment. Perhaps because recording was new to them at the time, the brothers generate an excitement worth more than sophisticated sound quality. You can picture the *freres* at your own Cajun house party on a Saturday night. Includes seven songs by the Balfas and others by Austin Pitre and Edius Nacquin that provide a glimpse at some other early Cajun music.

The New York Concerts Plus

i. 1991/Ace (England) 338 CD (contains The New York Concerts/r. 1974, 1978; i. 1980/Swallow 6037 CS, LP + 9 extra tracks)

This CD lets us listen in on two great concerts. The first was a 1974 performance at the New York Pinewoods folk music club, with Dewey, Rodney and Will, plus two non-Balfas on accordion and triangle. The second was a 1978 live appearance on a New York City "Cajun Jamboree" radio show with Dewey, Rodney, Ervin "Dick" Richard on second fiddle and Hadley Fontenot on accordion. The Balfas were obviously inspired by a full house of enthusiastic New Yorkers. The CD improves on the sound of the original LP without losing the spirit. It also adds nine songs, four of them previously available only on rare Swallow 45s. The other added tracks are from Balfa Brothers or Nathan Abshire LPs.

OTHER RECORDINGS

Arcadian Memories

Ace (England) 183 CS

Cajun Days

r. 1978, 1979; i. 1979/Sonet (England) 813 LP

Cajun Fais Do-Do

(Nathan Abshire & the Balfa Brothers) r. 1966; i. 1995/Arhoolie 416 CD; Arhoolie 5004 CS, LP

A Cajun Legend: The Best of Nathan Abshire

r. late 1960s-early1970s; i. 1991/Swallow 6061 CD, CS, LP

The Cajuns, Vol. 1

(Balfa Brothers with Nathan Abshire) i. 1973/Sonet (England) 643 LP (unreviewed)

The Good Times Are Killing Me

(Nathan Abshire with Dewey & Rodney Balfa) r. late 1960s-early 1970s/Swallow 6023 CS, LP

J'ai Vu le Loup, le Renard, et la Belette

r. 1975; i. 1988/Rounder 6007 CD, CS, LP (original release 1976 by Cezame [France] 1008)

Nathan Abshire, Featuring the Balfa Brothers

i. 1991/Ace (England) 329 CD

DEWEY BALFA
Fiddle, vocals

Swallow CD 6063

Today's Cajun music revival owes its greatest debt to Dewey Balfa. The gentle "king of Cajun fiddlers" became a passionate advocate for his culture, inspiring a generation of musicians to return to their roots. His recorded repertoire covers the best of Cajun music.

Balfa was born in 1927 in Bayou Grand Louis, near Mamou. Growing up in a large sharecropper family of nine children, he worked in the cotton and potato fields while in his free time playing the fiddle music of his father, grandfather and great-grandfather. He learned tunes from his father, as well as absorbing the popular sounds of J. B. Fusilier, **Leo Soileau, Harry Choates** and Bob Wills.

As a teen, Balfa played music with his father and older brother Will. He left home to work in a Texas shipyard during World War II and later joined the merchant marine. On the side, he played Texas swing music with various musicians. Eventually, he returned home, got married and started a family. Besides farming, he supported them over the years by variously selling insurance, working in an oil field, operating a discount furniture store and driving a schoolbus. From 1948, he and his brothers Will, Harry and Rodney played local parties and dance halls. Dewey developed into a virtuoso fiddler sought after by other musicians for gigs and recordings because of his flowing, precise style. He accompanied accordionist **Nathan Abshire** on popular records for several labels.

However, the Balfas' kind of music was endangered by commercial pop music during the 1950s and 1960s, when locals derided Cajun music as old-fashioned. In the mid-1950s, the Newport Folk Foundation sent Ralph Rinzler to southwest Louisiana to cut field recordings of the Balfas and other Cajun musicians, but it wasn't until a decade later that Cajun music broke through to a national audience. In 1964, Balfa substituted for a guitarist at the Newport Folk Festival, where his landmark performance with a group of Cajun musicians won a standing ovation from 17,000 fans. The experience transformed Balfa, whose hometown had predicted the countrified musicians would make fools of themselves. Three years later, he returned to Newport to another rapturous reception, this time with Rodney and Will, daughter Nelda and accordionist Hadley Fontenot.

Thus converted into a missionary for Cajun music and culture, Balfa began a tireless campaign to rehabilitate them. Rinzler and Balfa worked with the Council for the Development of French in Louisiana (CODOFIL) to teach French in schools and create a Cajun music festival. A Center for Acadian and Creole Folklore was established at the University of Southwestern Louisiana, where Balfa was appointed adjunct professor in 1987. He organized numerous events to stimulate young people's interest in Cajun music and introduced a Cajun music curriculum in public schools. His efforts—in conjunction with those of musicians **Michael Doucet**, **Marc Savoy** and others—paid off as a Cajun revival took hold at home and the **Balfa Brothers** band reached a growing audience at folk festivals throughout America, Canada and France.

On the recording front, Balfa repeatedly urged local record producer Floyd Soileau to release traditional Cajun records until Soileau relented in 1965, producing the Balfa Brothers' first album, *The Balfa Brothers Play Traditional Cajun Music*. Its success convinced Soileau to record many more Cajun traditionalists. Balfa also recorded with other fine musicians for Swallow, Arhoolie, Sonet and Folkways on albums greatly enhanced by his relaxed, masterful fiddling style and heartfelt singing.

Balfa's reputation as one of America's leading traditional musicians had gelled and the family band was at its peak in 1979 when a car crash took Will's and Rodney's lives; in the next few years, Dewey's wife and son died. Despite these shocks, he continued to perform—now with his nephew Tony and daughter Christine. In 1982, he won the National Endowment for the Arts' highest award for folk artists, the National Heritage Fellowship.

When Cajun music's best-loved ambassador died of cancer in 1992, he left an inspiring legacy that went beyond music. He used to tell audiences: "Don't be ashamed of your daddy and granddad. Don't be ashamed to eat your crawfish or gumbo. It's your way of life, your identity." **Balfa Toujours** (Balfa Forever), a Cajun group which includes two of Balfa's four daughters, Nelda and Christine, carries on the Balfa name.

THE BEST

Dewey Balfa and Friends

i. 1991/Ace (England) 328 CD (contains the Grammy-nominated Souvenirs/i. 1985/Swallow 6056 CS, LP & Fait a la Main! (Handmade)/i. 1986/Swallow 6063 CD, CS, LP) (Note: 13 tracks from Fait a la Main! and 8 tracks from Souvenirs can also be found on Cajun Legend/i. 1991/Swallow 6063 CD.)

Both LPs contained in this CD featured Balfa on fiddle, brother Rodney's son Tony on guitar, Robert Jardell on accordion, and Tracy and Peter Schwarz (father and son) on second and third fiddle. *Fait a la Main! (Handmade)* also featured Balfa's daughter Christine on triangle and Mark Miller on bass. The group has a good ensemble sound, with Dewey in top form. The best selections are the instrumentals "Valse de Balfa" and "Les Flumes d'Enfer," as well as "Quand J'etais Pauvre," which features excellent singing by Balfa. Great Cajun music from the master.

EXCELLENT

Cajun Fiddle Old & New with Dewey Balfa

r. 1975; i. 1977/Folkways FM 8362 LP

This instructional recording on how to play Cajun fiddle includes great live recordings of Balfa, five from radio broadcasts and three from dance hall performances. He is at ease with the other musicians, who include his brother Rodney. The sound is exceptional for recordings done in this way, but it is Balfa's spirit that gratifies. Waltzes such as "La Valse de Reno," "The 99 Year Waltz" and "J'aimerais te Pardonner" transport you back to a mid-1970s Cajun dance.

Under a Green Oak Tree

(with Marc Savoy & D. L. Menard) r. 1976; i. 1989/Arhoolie 312 CD, CS (contains Arhoolie 5019 LP + 6 previously unissued cuts)

Fiddler Balfa, accordionist Marc Savoy, guitarist D. L. Menard and string bassist Jerry Whiten join their considerable talents on some classics, with Balfa and Menard sharing vocals. Lifetimes devoted to playing Cajun music result in a good ensemble sound, even though the four musicians did not regularly play together. Savoy's wonderful accordion work makes you wish he recorded more, and Menard's singing is haunting. Balfa supplies good vocals and fiddle work. "Jolie Blonde du Bayou," "Ma Chere Maman Creole" and the title track are outstanding.

Les Quatre Vieux Garcons

r. 1984/Folkways FA 2626 LP

This session features Balfa with his nephew Tony on guitar, and Tracy and Peter Schwarz on accordion and fiddle, respectively. Balfa takes the lead vocal on three songs. The sound balance on "Dans la Coeur de la Ville" is a problem. Balfa's fiddle sparkles throughout, and Tony Balfa provides excellent rhythm with his guitar. Tracy Schwarz carries most of the lead vocals capably. His son Peter, a Balfa disciple later with Steve Riley and the Mamou Playboys, plays second fiddle and sings the lead on "Muddy Waters." Stand-out tunes include "Mardi Gras Song" and "Wedding March."

GOOD

A Couple of Cajuns

(Ardoin Family Orchestra with Dewie [sic] Balfa) i. 1981/Sonet (England) 873 LP

Outings like this are often just a famous name doing a few solos, but on this one Balfa gets into the groove as the band's fiddler. He joins the noted Bois Sec Ardoin and his family orchestra. Great music, with three top tunes: "Two Step de Lans Prie Noir," "Morris Special" and "La Cucaracha."

OTHER RECORDINGS

Cajun Honky Tonk

(Khoury recordings) r. 1950s; i. 1995/Arhoolie 427 CD

French Style

(Rocking Dopsie with Dewey Balfa) i. 1981/Sonet (England) 872 LP

Traditional Cajun Fiddle

(instructional) r. 1976/Folkways/8361 LP (unreviewed)

BALFA TOUJOURS
Group

Rounder CD 6071

This acoustic-based band stars Christine and Nelda Balfa, two of the great Cajun fiddler **Dewey Balfa**'s daughters. Along with Dirk Powell (accordion/fiddle), Kevin Wimmer (fiddle) and Mike "Chop" Chapman (drums), the Balfa sisters (Christine on vocals and guitar, Nelda on vocals and triangle) keep the traditional Cajun spirit. The group projects an open-hearted sound that has captured the hearts of club and festival-goers since they debuted at the Festival Acadiens in Lafayette in 1993, a year after Dewey Balfa's death.

Rare for daughters of Cajun musicians, both Balfa sisters played music with their father. Nelda, the oldest of Balfa's five children, performed with her father as long ago as the 1967 Newport Folk Festival. The group plays many of his classics, such as "La Valse des Balfa" and "La Valse de Vieux Vacher." This steadily improving band also writes many of its own tunes, adhering to Dewey's philosophy that Cajun music will thrive only if constantly revitalized.

Their first album, *Pop, Tu Me Parles Toujours* (Dad, You Speak to Me Still), is a tribute to Dewey that includes the touching original title cut as well as tunes in a lighter vein.

Their second CD, *A Vielle Terre Haute*, alludes to the band's hometown near Breaux Bridge in the heart of Acadiana.

In an affectionate swipe at traditional Cajun gender roles, the photo on the back cover of the album shows band members Powell and Wimmer cooking in the kitchen, in back of the two women, who are happily playing guitar and fiddle. The album's liner notes thank "Hilda Balfa (their mother) and all the wives and daughters of Cajun musicians who stayed in the shadows so others could shine."

THE BEST

Deux Voyages

r. & i. 1996/Rounder 6071 CD

Balfa Toujours has evolved into a powerful Cajun band showing immense improvement with each recording. The CD's best moments are five instrumentals featuring superb playing by Dirk Powell on accordion and Kevin Wimmer on fiddle. The rhythm section has always been strong, and Peter Schwartz adds some good fiddling on four numbers. Christine Balfa's vocals are satisfying; and although Wimmer is the best of the three male singers on the recording, he only does one tune, Canray Fontenot's "Bee de la Manche." Powell sings best on his own "La Musique de Ma Jeunesse." The tunes are a mix of original and traditional, with "73 Special" credited to Swallow Records owner Floyd Soileau. The title track and "Galop a Wade Fruge" are among the best songs.

EXCELLENT

A Vielle Terre Haute

i. 1995/Swallow 6121 CD, CS

This second CD picks up steam after their first release. Both the Balfa women have improved vocally in the two years since then and added a good drummer, Mike "Chop" Chapman. He provides a drive that was sometimes lacking earlier with just the triangle and guitar for rhythm. This time around, lead male vocals also offer variety. Kevin Wimmer on fiddle and Dirk Powell on accordion are strong instrumentalists, and Peter Schwarz (now with Steve Riley's band) adds good second fiddle on two songs. Christine or Nelda wrote five of the 15 tunes; three others are by their father. The three instrumentals, along with the title track and "Texas Two Step," stand out. One nice tune, "Les Fleurs du Printemps," was written by Christine Balfa and Dirk Powell, who are married. This is a strong band with a great beat for dancing, which is what Cajun music is all about.

Pop, Tu me Parles Toujours

i. 1993/Swallow 6110 CD, CS

The traditional Cajun songs chosen for this first CD are good, and both Nelda and Christine Balfa offer excellent new material. Kevin Wimmer's fiddle and Dirk Powell's accordion are fine throughout. Nelda's vocals are not as sure-footed as on the newer recording. Outstanding songs include "Tow Truck Blues," "Two-Step Des Vieux Hommes" and "Ayou Est L'amour," all written by Christine and accordionist Dirk Powell; and Octa Clark's instrumental, "Cajun Hot Shoes."

LE BAND PASSE PARTOUT
Group

This traditional Cajun band's goal of attracting old and young is reflected in its musicians' ages, which range from 21 to 59. Drummer/arranger/musical director Joe Lirette was born in 1937 in Houma and played guitar as a youth. Then he switched to drums and played Cajun dances at the Welcome Club,

which was owned by the late Joe Falcon. After serving 21 years in the military, Lirette resumed his musical career and formed his own band in 1990.

THE BEST

Cajun Heartland

r. & i. 1994/Swallow 6118 CD, CS

Although the plaintive voice of former band member Robert Elkins is missed, this release is slightly stronger than their first, *Cajun Sentiment*. Vocals are shared here by Percy Boudreaux Jr. and Larry Hoffpauir. The instrumental sound is fuller, and the fiddle work on "Les 'Blue Jeans' Serres" is just right. The Cajun waltzes, particularly "J'aimerais Te Pardonner" and "La Chanson de Mardi Gras," are pretty standards.

EXCELLENT

Cajun Sentiment

r. & i. 1993/Swallow 6105 CD, CS

This is a good first Swallow release by what was then a relatively new band. Robert Elkins' haunting voice is featured on five songs. The young Elkins (b. 1973) is a popular singer and rhythm guitar player who appeared on the 1985 Swallow recording *The Cajun Experience* with Paul Daigle and Michael Doucet, and more recently in the band Cajun Gold.

THE BASIN BROTHERS
Group

Known also as "Al Berard and the Basin Brothers," this much improved group of young traditionalists comes from the once-remote Atchafalaya River Basin, haunt of independent trappers and fishermen. The Basin—a marshy area between Lafayette and Breaux Bridge—provided Berard's family a livelihood; his father trapped and crawfished and taught his son the trade.

In 1982, Berard and some school friends including band members Keith Blanchard and Dwayne Brasseaux formed a group and named it after the Basin. But Berard, ridiculed in school for speaking French, didn't feel pride in coming from there until 1986, when on tour with fiddler **Hadley J. Castille**.

"We went to Canada, and the first few songs I played with my head down, I was so embarrassed. But when I saw the people respond to that French music, I couldn't believe it. It was a big turning point," he says in the liner notes for the 1996 album *Dans la Louisiane*.

Berard sings lead vocals and lends his considerable talents on fiddle and a variety of other stringed instruments in the band. Accordionist and accordion builder Errol Verret, who played with **Beausoleil** from the early to mid-1980s, has replaced Danny Collet, who left to follow his own career with the Louisiana Swamp Cats. Since then, the band's lineup has remained stable, with Keith Blanchard on drums, Dwayne Brasseaux on bass and Tommy Comeaux on mandola/guitar.

The Basin Brothers' *Let's Get Cajun* earned a Grammy nomination for best traditional folk recording in 1991. They have gathered steam ever since, touring the U.S. and abroad, playing a regular gig at Randol's restaurant in Lafayette and cutting steadily improving albums.

THE BEST

Dans la Louisiane (In Louisiana)

i. 1996/Rounder 6065 CD

The Basin Brothers' debut on Rounder holds their place as one of the best Cajun bands around. Al Berard has moved to the forefront as bandleader, and his singing/songwriting/ fiddling skills clearly warrant that change. He handles all the vocals with a clear, high-pitched voice and dramatic delivery. He also wrote six of the songs. The band has gone back to traditional material by Dennis McGee, Cleoma Falcon, Joe Bonsall and Nathan Abshire for inspiration. Tony Comeaux's mandola and guitar enrich the group's full instrumental voicing. Guest Hadley J. Castille lends his distinctive fiddle on one of the album's best tunes, Cleoma Falcon's "Baisse ta Tete et Pleurer" (Hang Your Head and Cry). Other great songs include "Petite ou la Grosse," "Mulberry Waltz," "La Valse du Pont d'Amour" and the title cut.

EXCELLENT

The Louisiana Music Commission & Mulate's Present The Basin Brothers

i. c. 1994/Bayou Teche Records CD

An excellent selection of mostly old Cajun favorites. The sound on their two previous CDs on Flying Fish Records was never right, but this one has a full, rich sound. The great accordionist Errol Verret has replaced Danny Collet. Al Berard was always an excellent fiddler and now does a fine job with lead vocals. The guitar, bass and drums, with the help of the accordion, lay down a beat that makes wallflowers dance. The group is cookin'.

GOOD

Stayin' Cajun

i. 1991/Flying Fish 70581 CD, CS

Danny Collet stars on accordion and vocals. The sound may be flat, but the spirited performances come through. Good Cajun material for dancing or listening.

Let's Get Cajun

r. 1989; i. c.1990/Flying Fish 70539 CD, CS, LP

Traditional Cajun music with a great dance beat and outstanding uptempo renditions of "Brune de la Compagne" and "Bosco Stomp."

BEAUSOLEIL
Group

Arhoolie CD 5040

If you know only one Cajun band, it is probably this one. World-famous Beausoleil outshines all others when it comes to excellence across a vast body of work. The band took its name, "Beautiful Sunshine," from the nom de guerre of Joseph Broussard, an 18th century Acadian resistance fighter–an indication of how seriously the group takes its heritage. But the eclectic, six-time Grammy-nominated ensemble is equally at home with a spicy blend of Cajun, zydeco and rock 'n' roll. Virtuoso fiddler/singer/composer **Michael Doucet** leads the group and enriches its repertoire with his own compositions and songs he's found through research.

The most sought-after Cajun band around, Beausoleil has performed everywhere from Garrison Keillor's National Public Radio show, *Prairie Home Companion*, to international festivals. They have recorded with Keith Richards, Mary Chapin Carpenter, Richard Thompson and the Grateful Dead.

The band had two incarnations when Doucet formed it in the mid-1970s. The original Beausoleil was a traditional folk trio with Doucet on fiddle, Bessyl Duhon (son of the great fiddler Hector Duhon) on accordion and Kenneth Richard on mandolin. In 1975 they also formed the electric rock group Coteau, the first band to fuse traditional Cajun with Gulf Coast rock. Called "the Cajun Grateful Dead" (a reference to their looseness and extended improvisations), Coteau drew younger crowds back into the dance halls and toured successfully, but produced no albums before disbanding in 1977.

Meanwhile, the acoustic, traditional Beausoleil sent young crowds wild at folk festivals and at small clubs with a blend of old and new Cajun music. With expanded personnel, they went on a cultural exchange to France, where they cut a record for Pathe Marconi EMI in 1976. Back home, their American debut album, *The Spirit of Cajun Music*, came out on Louisiana's Swallow label in 1977, which was a good year for Beausoleil: they also played at President Jimmy Carter's inauguration. Around this time, the band kicked off the Cajun restaurant-supper club phenomenon of performing live French music by playing weekly at Mulate's in Breaux Bridge.

In the mid-1980s, Beausoleil went from acoustic to electric and hit their stride, both propelling and benefitting from the Cajun craze. Their best-selling Swallow album, *Zydeco Gris-Gris*, won a Grammy nomination, as did their soundtrack for the Louisiana film *Belizaire the Cajun*. The band got a big boost when their music was featured in the popular film *The Big Easy*. They produced four albums in 1986, the year the band members left their day jobs to play music full time. Ever since, they have been in great demand at concerts and festivals throughout the U.S., Canada and Europe.

Beausoleil's core personnel have remained solid over the years, which is probably why the band has become one of the tightest and most exciting ensembles in any type of music. Michael Doucet's fiery fiddling adds rock and jazz improvisations to a traditional Cajun base. His younger brother **David Doucet's** acoustic guitar is one of Beausoleil's great strengths, as both rhythm and lead instrument.

Accordion players have included Bessyl Duhon; Errol Verret; Pat Breaux (grandson of accordion great **Amedee Breaux**), who also played tenor sax and triple-key, zydeco-style accordion; and Pat's brother, the gifted Jimmy Breaux. The rhythm section–fuller than in most Cajun bands–has remained steady with bassist Tommy Comeaux, who also plays mandolin; drummer Tommy Alesi; and percussionist Billy Ware, who plays the zydeco-type metal *frottoir* (rubboard) and congas as well as Cajun's *ti-fer* (triangle) and spoons. Producer and soundman Al Tharp completes the roster with fiddle, bass and banjo.

Beausoleil plays mostly traditional music, but their monumental repertoire extends to all types of popular music, while keeping Cajun rhythm and instrumentation. Doucet says, "You can take any song and cajunize it." Like the Chieftans of Ireland, Beausoleil revives and preserves its culture's music while constantly experimenting and updating. With integrity and grace, the band has recorded some of the best albums of Cajun music ever done.

THE BEST

Live! From the Left Coast 🪗

r. & i. 1989/Rounder 6035 CD, CS, LP

A TOP 10 CAJUN ALBUM

Even a great band is at its flat-out best only so often, so it was fortunate the tape machines were turning during these live concerts at the Great American Music Hall in San Francisco. Michael Doucet's superb fiddling, his brother David Doucet's strong acoustic guitar, and solid bass and drum work all add up to a memorable recording. From the rocking "Pine Grove Blues" to a hard-driving "Les Filles a Nonc Helaire" to a quietly beautiful waltz, the band was in top form.

EXCELLENT

Vintage Beausoleil

r. 1986, 1987; i. 1995/Music of the World 213 CD, CS

Recorded live in New York City at the Washington Square Church and Central Park Bandshell, this disc marks an extremely productive period for the band. In 1986, they released four albums and rode the crest of a growing acceptance of Cajun music nationwide. The CD captures the acoustic feel of the great old Cajun music. From the forceful, uptempo numbers to the pretty Cajun waltzes, *Vintage Beausoleil* has it all. Master Creole fiddler Canray Fontenot adds his vocal and fiddling magic to an old French drinking song, "Parlez Nous a Boire."

L'Echo

r. & i. 1994/Forward/Rhino 71808 CD, CS

As its name implies, this recent venture approaches old Cajun favorites from a new direction. Michael Doucet says in the liner notes that he wanted to spotlight songs by forgotten musical leaders such as Joe Falcon, Freeman Fontenot and the Alley Boys. The new treatment enhances thoughtfully chosen, sometimes obscure, Cajun and Creole material –a tribute to Doucet's sure judgment as a folklorist. Beausoleil's acoustic sounds represented here successfully conjure up those of 1930s Cajun bands such as the Hackberry

Ramblers, a Louisiana-Texas hybrid heavily influenced by Western swing string bands made up of fiddles and guitars. Doucet's vocals soar.

Parlez-Noux a Boire & More

r. 1981, 1984; i. 1990/Arhoolie 322 CD, CS (Tracks 1-13 originally issued as Arhoolie LP 5034, 16-18 on Arhoolie LP 5025)

Ten of the first 13 songs are an interesting mix of traditional and new, with fast two-steps and reels balanced by Cajun waltzes, all gracefully done. Beginning with "Pierrot Grouillette et Mamselle Josette," however, the band soars to new heights and stays there for the remaining seven songs. Doucet's vocal on "Your Mama Threw Me Out" shows him at his relaxed best, capping a brilliant arrangement. David Doucet drives the band along with strong guitar work and takes a great solo on "Le Bozo Two Step."

Bayou Deluxe

r. 1982-93; i.1993/Rhino 71169 CD, CS

Subtitled "the best of Michael Doucet and Beausoleil," *Bayou Deluxe* is close to it. This compilation is essential for those who love that unmistakable Beausoleil ensemble sound. Highlights include the under-appreciated David Doucet (Michael's brother) singing the classic "Les Bons Temps Rouler Waltz" by prolific songwriter/accordionist Lawrence Walker, and "La Chanson de Mardi Gras," said to be the oldest song in the Cajun repertoire. An excellent mix of traditional Cajun, zydeco, Creole and French material.

Hot Chili Mama

r. 1987; i. 1993/Arhoolie 5040 CD, CS, LP

This hard-driving recording with more than a touch of rock 'n' roll and blues is a favorite of many Beausoleil fans. David Doucet's classic "Les Bon Temps Rouler Waltz" tops the list of prime cuts. Michael Doucet's fiddle roars on the uptempo tunes like "Acadian Two-Step" and "Canray's Contredanse." The syncopated beat and Michael's good vocal also turn "Belle" into a winner.

La Danse de la Vie

r. & i. 1993/Forward/Rhino 71221 CD, CS

The popular country singer Mary Chapin Carpenter joins in on two songs to advantage in this consistently excellent performance. The instrumental "Menage a Trois Reels" by Dennis McGee, S.D. Courville and Michael Doucet alone is worth the price of the CD. Most of the other tunes are written by Doucet.

Cajun Conja

r. & i. 1991/Rhino New Artists 70525 CD, CS

A Grammy nominee, this hard-rocking CD earned Beausoleil wide national acclaim. It features strong ensemble work on material reflecting Michael Doucet's modern, experimental side. Noteworthy tunes include "Conja (New Orleans, 1786)," a song about voodoo, and the catchy "Le Chanky-Chank Francais," whose title refers to old-time music.

GOOD

The Mad Reel

r. 1981-1982; i. 1994/Arhoolie 397 CD, CS

An intriguing compilation of six numbers from a 1981 LP, *Dit Beausoleil*, the soundtrack by Michael Doucet and Beausoleil for the 1986 feature film *Belizaire the Cajun*, and hitherto unreleased tunes including three duets by the Doucet brothers. A great bonus are three songs recorded in the early 1980s with early Cajun fiddling luminary Dennis McGee.

Allons a Lafayette & More with Canray Fontenot

r. 1981, 1985; i. 1989/Arhoolie 308 CD, CS (includes all of Arhoolie LP 5036 + several cuts from LP 5025)

Strong performances with the extraordinary Creole fiddler Canray Fontenot, one of Michael Doucet's mentors. The disc covers a wide range of traditional-style material, old and new, some of it tunes from *Dit Beausoleil* not found on *The Mad Reel*.

OTHER RECORDINGS

Bayou Boogie

r. 1985; i. 1987/Rounder 6015 CD, CS, LP

Bayou Cadillac

r. 1988; i. 1989/Rounder 6025 CD, CS, LP

Belizaire the Cajun

(film soundtrack) i. 1986/Arhoolie 5038 CS

Deja Vu

r. 1976-90 ; i. 1990/Swallow 6080 CD, CS, LP

Dit Beausoleil

r. 1981; i. 1982/Arhoolie 5025 CS, LP

The Spirit of Cajun Music

i. 1977/Swallow 6031 CS, LP

The Swallow Recordings

Ace (England) 379 CD

Zydeco Gris-Gris

i. 1985/Swallow 6054 CS, LP (i. 1980 as Les Amis Cadjins/Modulation [Canada] 33000)

CEDRIC BENOIT
Accordion, vocals

Benoit (b. 1958, Abbeville) formed his first band in 1981 following his graduation from high school in Kaplan and a stint with the U.S. Marines. Involved in a 1986 near-fatal car crash that left both his hands paralyzed for a time, he recovered and formed his current band, Cajun Connection. The group played a long engagement at Silver Dollar City at Branson, Mo., before releasing their album.

Cajun! Cajun! Cajun!

i. 1988/Swallow 6074 CS, LP

Poor arrangements, weak songs and over production bury Benoit's talent on this LP. He could be an important songwriter and performer, but he needs some guidance. "The (Le) Blues" and "Another Lonely Night" show how good he can be, which makes the balance of this recording even more disappointing. "Gator Breakin' " is a prime example of a good vocal wasted on a terrible song. However, everything comes together well on "Le Blues," which is also available on the CD *Cajun Saturday Night* (Swallow 102).

SHIRLEY BERGERON
Vocals, guitar

Known for his songwriting and high, Cajun-style singing, Shirley Bergeron won a measure of local fame in the late 1940s when he played rhythm and steel guitar with the Veteran Playboys alongside his accordionist father, Alphee Bergeron. Made up of World War II veterans, the popular group played dances every night of the week and broadcast over local radio stations during the post-war revival of accordion-based Cajun music.

Shirley was born in 1933 in Point Noir near Church Point and grew up helping his father pick cotton on their small farm before and after school every day. Alphee encouraged Shirley to attend school so he didn't have to rely on farming for a living, and to play music on the side. He gave Shirley his first guitar when the boy was 11 with the words, "Son, beat on it." As a teenager, Shirley shared the Veteran Playboys' success, but gigs dwindled during the 1950s with the advent of rock 'n' roll.

Bergeron bounced back in 1960 with a hit recording of "J'ai Fait Mon Ede'e" (I Made Up My Mind), on which he sang and played steel guitar accompanied by his father and the Veteran Playboys. The record was the first for the local Lanor label. Several more Lanor singles led to a successful album, *The Sounds of Cajun Music*. A second album, *Cajun Style Music*, did not prove as successful. Bergeron retired from music and turned to selling insurance after stints as a bookkeeper and furniture salesman. In another comeback, he performed for a time with fiddling master **Dewey Balfa** before Balfa's death in 1992.

Besides his own contribution, Bergeron served as a link to the old-style Cajun music through his musical partnership with his father, Alphee (1912-1980). The elder Bergeron performed with many of the early greats such as **Amedee Ardoin**, **Joseph Falcon** and **Lawrence Walker**. Before World War II, he cut one single before recording the Lanor sessions with Shirley 1957-1969.

French Rocking Boogie

r. 1957-1969; i. 1992/Ace (England) 353 CD (contains 8 tracks from Sounds of Cajun Music/Lanor 1000 LP & all of Cajun Style Music/Lanor 1001 LP + 2 tracks formerly available on 45s)

This CD collects most of the Bergerons' Lanor recordings. Although the Cajun rock 'n' roll title cut is the song most often associated with them, the rest of the album features their more characteristic traditional tunes. Shirley's excellent singing, Alphee's outstanding accordion playing and a generous 22 songs make this release a must for traditional Cajun music lovers. The rough sound quality lends a dance hall flavor. An echo chamber treatment adds drama to Bergeron's powerful, high voice. Stand-out songs are his hit, "J'ai Fait Mon Ede'e," "New Country

Waltz," "La Valse a August Breaux," "Madam Sosthene" and "Chere Tou Toute."

JOE BONSALL
Vocals, accordion

Swallow LP 6049

Joe Bonsall is best known for his songwriting. Many of his tunes have become minor Cajun classics, among them "Hack a Moreau," "Chere Tout Tout" and the high-speed "Step It Fast." Born in 1921 in Lake Arthur, he started performing when he was nine, accompanying his accordionist mother on triangle. In 1948, he played guitar with "Moot" Harrington. Then he switched to the accordion in 1951 when he formed his own band, the Orange Playboys (several band members lived in Orange, Tx.). The Playboys filled Cajun nightclubs in east Texas and southwest Louisiana during their heyday.

Bonsall recorded for several Louisiana labels in the 1960s, starting with Goldband. He cut three singles and two LPs for Swallow Records that were popular regionally. Then he joined Cajun Jamboree Records, a label formed in 1965 by his producer, John Lloyd Broussard. "Tee Bruce" Broussard broadcast a "Cajun Jamboree" radio show in Orange at the time. In 1981, Bonsall was inducted into the Cajun Hall of Fame.

THE BEST

Joe Bonsall's Greatest Hits

i. 1983/Swallow 6049 CS, LP

This recording includes Bonsall's own hits like "Step It Fast," "Hack a Moreau" and "Chere Tout Tout," along with other traditional tunes. Bonsall assembled a good back-up band and shared vocals with Ivy Dugas and Clifton Newman. "Your Picture" has a great accordion opener and strong vocal, with Bonsall speaking French and English in the middle, then winds up with more good accordion. "Same Old Places" has a strong, slow beat with excellent singing by Bonsall, who has a deep, resonant voice.

GOOD

"Tee Bruce" Presents Cajun Jamboree

r. c. mid-1960s/Swallow 6008 LP

This was Bonsall's first album, probably recorded by John "Tee Bruce" Broussard. The recording suffers from weak back-up, but Bonsall plays accordion and sings well. Three traditional songs enhance it: "Chere Tout Tout," "You Can Blame Yourself" and "Step It Fast."

AMEDEE BREAUX
Accordion, vocals

One of the earliest recording figures, Amedee Breaux was also one of the last authentic Cajun musicians before sophistication set in around the 1960s. In 1929, he made the first recording of the most famous Cajun tune of all time, "Ma Blonde Est Partie," usually known as "Jolie Blonde." With him on that Columbia session in Atlanta were his brother Ophy on fiddle and sister **Cleoma Breaux Falcon** on guitar. (Cleoma is more famous as the popular singer/steel guitarist partner of her husband, accordionist **Joseph Falcon**. Although "Jolie Blonde" is often attributed to Amedee, she is thought to have written it, apparently about Amedee's first wife.)

Breaux was born in Rayne in 1900 into a farming family. His father, Auguste Breaux, was one of the best accordion players around during the pre-recording era, and his mother played harmonica. All five children played musical instruments. In the 1930s, Amedee recorded sessions on 78s for several labels with his brothers, fiddler Ophy and guitarist Clifford, as the Breaux Freres (brothers). Cleoma also played on many of their early recordings.

Typical of early Cajun singers, Amedee's vocals were high and charged with emotion. Known as a wild man at a dance party, he had a habit when drunk of pulling accordions apart in feats of showmanship. He also had a reputation for fighting at gigs, sometimes with his own brothers.

Pioneering Cajun record producer J. D. Miller recorded Breaux in 1948 on his Fais Do Do and Feature labels. But in Breaux's later years, he joined a church band and would only record sacred music, having promised God during an illness that he would never play Cajun music again. Luckily for posterity, he broke the promise by making several more Cajun recordings in the 1950s and 1960s before his death in 1972.

All the Breaux family recorded extensively, but Amedee's virtuoso accordion playing stands out. Most later Cajun accordionists, especially **Iry LeJeune** and **Nathan Abshire**, acknowledged his influence. He also composed many of the best-loved Cajun songs.

THE BEST

Cajun Vol. I: Abbeville Breakdown 1929-1939

(collection) r. 1990/Columbia CK 46220 CD

This CD features a variety of Breaux family combinations, from an instrumental with Amedee on accordion, Cleoma on guitar and Ophy on fiddle, to several Breaux Freres numbers. "Vas y Carrement," recorded in Atlanta in 1929, is a catchy instrumental with a great beat punctuated with Cajun-style shouts. Five songs recorded in San Antonio in 1934 show off Amedee's dramatic voice. His vocals and the entire group's talents stand out on "T'as Vole Mon Chapeau" and "La Valse du Bayou Plaquemine."

EXCELLENT

Cajun Dance Party: Fais Do Do

(collection) i. 1994/Columbia Legacy CK 46784 CD

These are among the first recordings made of Cajun music, mostly from the 1930s. Breaux and early Cajun recording stars Joe and Cleoma Breaux Falcon also appear here. Amedee Breaux's recording of "Ma Blonde Est Partie" was probably made in Atlanta in 1929. With good sound, this CD allows Amedee's singing to come through well. The other nine songs feature strong instrumental back-up from Clifford and Ophy Breaux for Amedee's accordion and vocals. Outstanding are "Fais Do Do Negre," "La Valse du Vieux Temps" and "La Valse d'Utah." The intensity of these early recordings stands unmatched.

Acadian Two-Step, Vol. 2

i. 1989/Flyright (England) 610 LP

Although this LP only has four songs by Amedee Breaux, they are different versions and different songs from those available on CD. Aside from a misplaced twangy steel guitar on one side, the instrumental sound is full and the vocals are excellent.

OTHER RECORDINGS

Cajun Fais Do-Do

(collection) r. 1966; i.1995/Arhoolie 416 CD

SIDNEY BROWN
Accordion

Brown (b. 1906, Church Point) is best known for his pioneer efforts in manufacturing accordions in Louisiana. Before World War II, German accordions were popular. After production ceased in wartime, Brown developed his own handmade design, ensuring the availability of Cajun accordion music. He was a good accordionist himself, having taught himself to play at age 13.

Starting off playing house dances in Church Point, Brown later moved to Lake Charles, where he formed his Traveler Playboys band in the early 1950s. The group recorded successfully for Eddie Shuler's local Goldband label. In fact, Brown's "Pestauche a Tane Nana" (The Peanut Song) was Goldband's third-best selling Cajun record ever. Goldband featured Brown's old-time sound in an album, *Sidney Brown: Collector's Item* (Goldband 7748 CS). He retired from playing in 1963 because of ill health and continued to make and repair accordions until his death in 1981.

The Best of Two Cajun Greats

(with Shorty LeBlanc) i. 1987/Swallow 6067 CS, LP

Brown was an accomplished accordion player and a good singer with a slightly rough edge. He stars on one side of this LP, sharing vocals with his fiddlers, Nelson Young and Venice LeJeune. Brown's strong accordion playing is evident on every cut. He was also a songwriter; his hit "Pestauche a Tante Nana" is included here. The best songs are "La Valse des Meche," "Sack Dress Waltz" and "Traveler's Playboy Special."

VIN BRUCE (Ervin Bruce)
Vocals, guitar

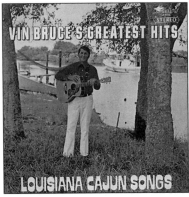

Swallow LP 6006

Sometimes called "the King of Cajun singers," Vin Bruce's popularity has held steady in south Louisiana since the 1950s due to a rich baritone that grows more velvety as the years go by. He has crooned in Cajun, country and swamp pop styles, in both French and English. And he is one of the few Cajun musicians to have recorded with a major recording company at an early age.

Born in 1932 in Cut Off, in southeast Louisiana's bayou region, Bruce listened as a child to his father, a fiddler who trapped and fished for a living. The boy started his career by playing guitar with two hillbilly groups, Dudley Bernard's Southern Serenaders and **Gene Rodrigue**'s Hillbilly Swing Kings. In 1951, a Columbia Records distributor discovered the teenager singing on a New Orleans radio show and promptly sent him to Nashville. There Bruce recorded hillbilly and Cajun songs, producing the hit Cajun ballad "Dans La Louisianne" and other tunes wildly popular in bayou country. This success led to appearances on "Louisiana Hayride" and "Grand Ole Opry." But before his career solidified, Columbia dropped his recording contract in the face of rock 'n' roll's popularity. Bruce returned home and raised cattle.

Rediscovered in 1961 by producer Leroy Martin, Bruce recorded for the Swallow label in Louisiana and again spun out a hit single—his version of the Cajun classic, "Jole Blon." During the 1970s, when country music swept away Cajun sounds, Martin produced three more Swallow albums featuring Bruce's country side. Martin also played bass guitar with Bruce's band, the Acadians, for which he assembled a group of talented musicians that included lead and steel guitarist Harry Anselmi and master fiddler **"Doc" Guidry**.

Like many Cajun musicians, Bruce prefers family life to the dubious rewards of the big time. He has reportedly resisted many offers to return to Nashville, including one from Chet Atkins to which Bruce replied: "Well, he can see me in Cut Off." Nevertheless, Nashville honored him in 1986 by adding his career memorabilia to the Country Music Hall of Fame. Bruce's low-key personal style runs to performing at house parties for free, although he does tour occasionally. At home, he is a respected carrier of the Cajun-country flame.

In yet another comeback, Bruce recorded his best release ever in 1993: *Chante: Les Cadjins du Bayou*. In it, he came full circle by returning to his Cajun roots.

THE BEST

Chante: Les Cadjins du Bayou

i. c. 1993/Lanor 1040 CD

Almost two decades after Bruce's previous album, Lee Lavergne, owner of Louisiana's Lanor Records, produced this excellent CD recapturing Bruce's original Cajun side, tinged with country. Lavergne assembled a quality band, and Bruce's voice is stronger and richer than it was in the mid-1970s. His full baritone can handle a wide range of songs. The waltzes stand out, among them

"Le Delaisse," "Ma Vie de Musicien" and "Si J'aurais des Ailes," with its country & western flavor. The fast-paced "C'est Malheureux" also features a great vocal, as well as excellent fiddle and steel guitar.

EXCELLENT

Cajun Country

i. c. mid-1970s/Swallow 6015 CS, LP (One Way S21-17609 CD also available)

"Doc" Guidry, one of the best Cajun fiddlers, adds greatly to every song on this recording. The LP offers solid Cajun standards and some C&W-influenced songs. Bruce's sumptuous voice stands out on "Made a Big Mistake" and "Maiden's Prayer." Good arrangements and talented back-up musicians round out this strong effort. Recorded at Cosimo's Studio in New Orleans, the album's sound quality is exceptional for an early LP.

GOOD

Greatest Hits

i. c. mid-1970s/Swallow 6006 CS, LP

An assemblage of talented musicians makes for a good LP, for which Bruce co-wrote nine of the 12 songs. The studio sound is a dramatic improvement over the first Swallow LP (*"Jole Blon" and Other Cajun Classics*, which was recorded at a radio station), although not as good as the two later Swallow LPs recorded at Cosimo's in New Orleans. Good music in the Cajun-country tradition so popular in the 1970s.

OTHER RECORDINGS

"Jole Blon" and Other Cajun Classics

i. 1961/Swallow 6002 CS, LP

Vin Bruce Sings Country

i. c. mid-1970s/Swallow 6016 LP

FIDDLIN' FRENCHIE BURKE
Fiddle, vocals

Burke comes from Kaplan, where he learned fiddling from his grandfather and started performing in his teens before his family moved to Port Arthur, Tx. He joined the Air Force as a medical technician and continued to play fiddle in his free time. After leaving the Air Force, he began playing with his band, the Soundmasters. They had a 1975 hit, "Big Mamou." In 1981, Cashbox magazine picked Burke as instrumentalist of the year. A Cajun/country fiddler, he has played with Willie Nelson and other country musicians.

Cajun Fiddle King

r. 1981; i. 1996/Collectables 5702 CD

Burke's zesty fiddling carries this recording. He sings and plays well on a nice mix of Cajun and country tunes, some of which don't work that well. A few that do are "Frenchie's Jole Blon," "Frenchie's Fire on the Mountain" and "Frenchie's Cotton-Eyed Joe," as well as the more Cajun "The Poor Hobo" and "Big Mamou."

CAJUN GOLD
Group

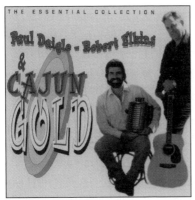

Swallow CD 6133

This traditional Cajun band records under the name "Paul Daigle-Robert Elkins & Cajun Gold," referring to the accordionist and rhythm guitarist, respectively, who co-lead the group. Daigle (b. 1958) comes from Point Noir, near Church Point, and runs a body shop between Branch and Church Point. Elkins (b. 1943) is a native of Church Point.

Cajun Gold is popular in Acadiana, where it has won a string of victories in band contests. It was voted the top Cajun band in 1986 by readers of *Times of Acadiana*, a Lafayette newspaper. From 1985 through 1990 it was an oft-requested group on Cajun radio programs, the club and restaurant circuit, and festivals. Unfortunately, burn-out set in at the height of its popularity, and the band has performed only occasionally in recent years. As of their 1996 *Essential Collection* CD, the band was playing selective engagements.

One of Cajun Gold's strengths is its unusually fine songs, many of which are written by the group's longtime producer, Pierre V. Daigle (no relation to Paul Daigle). Pierre is a prolific songwriter, as well as a novelist, playwright, teacher, and author of the book *Tears, Love and Laughter: The Story of the Cajuns and Their*

Music. In his book he describes discovering the 14-year-old accordionist Paul Daigle in 1972:

"I knew that, in my own judgement, I had found the one accordion player who has the things I consider necessary to be great: fingering and timing. Fidelity—no careless performance, and the gift for making whatever he plays sound exciting." Pierre eventually produced all of Paul's albums for Louisiana's Swallow label, starting in 1985. The accordionist's approach to Cajun music matches that of his mentor: preserving it by modernizing it, and avoiding a country or Nashville beat.

Daigle is an accomplished accordion player and a driving force in the band. Elkins has the requisite soulful voice, and his guitar provides a good rhythm bass line. Starting with **Michael Doucet** on Cajun Gold's 1985 debut album, the band has always had outstanding fiddlers in Tony Thibodeaux and, later, Ken Smith.

THE BEST

The Essential Collection

i. 1996/Swallow 6133 CD

The 18 songs on this CD capture the best of the five LPs released between 1985 and 1990—a tremendous output of high-quality music during a period when Cajun music was far less popular nationally than it is now. Most songs on the five LPs were written by producer Pierre V. Daigle; many are destined to join the standard Cajun repertoire. Highlights include "Je Suis Condamner a T'Aimer" and "La Lumiere Dans Ton Chassis."

EXCELLENT

La Lumiere Dans Ton Chassis (The Light in Your Window)

i. 1987/Swallow 6068 CS, LP

The consistently high quality of the songs (nine out of 10 written by producer Pierre V.

Daigle) and Tony Thibodeaux's top-form fiddling distinguish this LP from Cajun Gold's other outstanding releases. Elkins handles the vocals expertly on songs capturing the spirit of Cajun music, as best heard on "J'ai Conte des Menteries" and the fast instrumental "Le Two-Step a Paul Daig."

Est-ce Que Tu Pleur? (Do You Ever Cry?)

i. 1990/Swallow 6082 CS, LP

Another group of great songs, the two best being "Home Sick Waltz" and "Heritage Waltz." The title track and "Madelaine" are also good. Ken Smith replaced Tony Thibodeaux on fiddle, filling those large shoes well. Pierre V. Daigle wrote six of the album's songs.

GOOD

Cajun Gold

i. 1986/Swallow 6060 CS, LP

Excellent accordion playing by Daigle and fiddling by Tony Thibodeaux mark this LP, all of whose songs were written by Pierre V. Daigle. Among the best: "Ta Petite Robe Courte," "Je Suis Condonner a T'Aimer" and "La Valse du Coeur Casser."

The Cajun Experience

i. 1985/Swallow 6058 CS, LP

Michael Doucet's fiddling is featured on this debut album. Listen to "La Valse des Jeunes Maries," "Viens Me Chercher" and "Hackberry Hop."

Coeur Farouche (Wild Heart)

i. 1988/Swallow 6077 CS, LP

Becky Richard shares vocal duties with Elkins, with fine results. "L'Amitie d'une Femme" and "Pour Chaque Larme Que J'ai Pleurer" stand out, as do Elkins' "Un Vie a Vivre" and "Adele."

CALIFORNIA CAJUN ORCHESTRA
Group

Arhoolie CD 356

Since the early 1980s, this band has played dances in the San Francisco Bay Area, where Cajun music has a large following. Formed as an offshoot of the acoustic Blue Flame String Band, the California Cajun Orchestra plays a traditional Cajun style popular in southwest Louisiana dance halls. The band cites the **Balfa Brothers** as a major influence.

Accordionist Danny Poullard is a mainstay of the group. He comes from a musical family who farmed outside Eunice. In 1961, he moved to the Bay Area, where he played with the local Louisiana Playboys before hooking up with the CCO members. He draws on a repertoire handed down from his accordionist father. Early in his musical career, Poullard recorded with **Michael Doucet**, on *Cajun Jam Session* (Arhoolie 5035).

The other two mainstays are Suzy and Eric Thompson, on fiddle and guitar, respectively. They are versatile musicians who also have another Cajun band, "The Aux Cajunals." They recorded a 1989 blues CD, *Adam & Eve Had the Blues* (Arhoolie 5041), with several members of the later CCO, and Eric has cut guitar records on his own. Suzy grew up in Mt. Vernon, N.Y., in a musical family and studied classical violin before apprenticing with fiddler **Dewey Balfa**. Eric comes from Oakland and Palo Alto, Ca., and played bluegrass music for many years before switching to electric guitar for the CCO. He has traveled to Louisiana to visit and learn from musicians like **D. L. Menard** and **Marc Savoy**.

Fiddler Kevin Wimmer, from New York City, also plays in the traditional, Louisiana-based **Balfa Toujours**. Rounding out the lineup are rubboard player Charlie St. Mary, who comes from a rubboard-playing family in Louisiana; drummer Terry O'Dwyer; and bass player Sam Siggins.

THE BEST

Not Lonesome Anymore

i. 1991/Arhoolie 356 CD, CS

The CCO's Achilles' heel is its vocals. Suzy Thompson sings well, but none of the male singers except Charlie St. Mary do. However, the male vocals here are a slight improvement over those on the group's later album. The seven-piece band produces a rich instrumental sound behind solos by Poullard and the Thompsons. Song choice is excellent, as in the instrumentals "Hix Wagon Wheel Special," "Lake Charles Two-Step" and "Lake Arthur Stomp"; as well as "Valse du Mariage."

EXCELLENT

Nonc Adam Two Step

i. 1995/Arhoolie 436 CD

On this recent CD the CCO shows growth, and Poullard plays more inventively than ever. Eric Thompson doesn't solo often, but he is good when he does. The album offers a quality song collection, of which top tunes are "Chicot Two-Step," "Dog Hill," "Paper in My Shoe" and "Pleure Pas Mes Cheres Tee Yeux Bleus."

CANKTON EXPRESS
Group

The Cankton Express gets its name from its hard-driving sound. Founder Felix Richard (1918-1993) was from Cankton. He learned accordion as a child, then played guitar and sang at local house dances. As a young man, he did a stint with **Aldus Roger**. He dropped music for many years to support his family as a carpenter, then picked up the accordion again later in life.

In the early 1970s, Felix played with his sons Sterling and Kenneth Richard. They introduced him to **Zachary Richard**, whom Felix supplied with music, history and cultural background during this period of Cajun music renaissance. The better-known Zachary provided Felix with contacts. At the same time, Sterling and Kenneth joined **Michael Doucet** and Bessyl Duhon in the first incarnation of **Beausoleil**.

In 1978, Felix's family band represented Louisiana at the Festival d'Ete in Quebec, with Sterling and Kenneth in the group. In 1983, Felix and Sterling performed at the Smithsonian Institution's Festival of American Folklife, joined on fiddle by fellow Cankton native Gerald Cormier. Sterling died in 1996. At the time of their 1988 album, the band was playing a regular gig at Mulate's Restaurant in Breaux Bridge.

Live Chez Mulate's: Traditional Cajun Music

i. 1988/Swallow 6073 CS, LP

This aptly named band is exciting! Lead vocalist Sterling Richard has enough enthusiasm for several bands as he sings, shouts and exhorts his fellow players. His voice has the characteristic nasal quality of the early Cajun vocalists, as best heard on "Vien me Chercher." Felix Richard does a stellar job on accordion, as does Gerald Cormier on fiddle. Their zydeco selection, "C'est le Zydeco," is the only weak spot in a string of excellent songs such as "Valse de Bayou Chein," "Eunice Two Step" and "Bosco Stomp."

THE CARRIERE BROTHERS
(Eraste "Dolon" & Joseph "Bebe" Carriere)
Accordion, fiddle

As Creole performers of old-style "la-la" music, the Carriere Brothers provided a bridge from traditional Cajun to today's rural zydeco. Stylistically, they played a mixture of Cajun, blues and American music sung in French. The brothers used the term "la-la" interchangeably with "zydeco" to describe a fast dance as well as a party. Although zydeco music is generally believed to have appeared after World War II, the Carrieres said their father, an amateur accordion player, played it in the early 1900s.

They were a sharecropping family of six, raising cotton and yams near Lawtell. Eraste "Dolon" Carriere (1900-1983) couldn't attend school because Creoles were not admitted at the time; his brother Joseph "Bebe" Carriere (b. 1908) went as far as fifth grade. At 15, Eraste began playing single-row button accordion—the kind favored by most old-time accordionists. Because of its limited range, he often used it as a bass section for Bebe's fiddle tunes. From his father he learned a syncopated accordion sound and slightly more bluesy singing style than traditional Cajun. Often playing alone at white Cajun dances, he played the traditional Cajun tunes and the occasional zydeco in the old-time, Creole style.

When he was 12, Bebe made his first fiddle out of a cigar box strung with wires from a screen. Later, the brothers' father bought them proper instruments, and they began playing at parties. As a teenager, Bebe played with the legendary Creole accordionist **Amedee Ardoin** around Lawtell, Eunice and Basile. So good was he that a talent scout from a national record company invited him to make records in New Orleans, but, in Bebe's words in liner notes for *La La: Louisiana Black French Music*, "I was a young fella, near 18, and it just kinda slip my mind."

The Carrieres played house dances—both black and white—around Lawtell throughout the 1930s. Bebe traveled farther afield than Eraste, sometimes 60 miles away to Lake Charles, to play with other bands. He also performed with white musicians playing both "French" and hillbilly music, developing a fairly wide range of styles and writing some good blues-based songs. Until the mid-1960s, the brothers played often at Slim's Y-Ki-Ki in Opelousas with Eraste's son Calvin on violin and daughter Beatrice on rhythm guitar, calling themselves the Lawtell Playboys. The band turned zydeco when the brothers retired in 1966 and Calvin joined with Delton and Clinton Broussard to form a new Lawtell Playboys.

THE BEST
Cajun Fiddle Styles, Vol. 1: The Creole Tradition
(with Canray Fontenot) r. 1974, 1981; i. 1983/Arhoolie 5031 LP

It's hard to believe two musicians can produce such a full, rich sound. This is the original zydeco sound that Clifton Chenier probably heard growing up, and you can hear these roots sounds in his music no matter what changes he incorporated. Both Bebe and Eraste Carriere are excellent instrumentalists and good singers, with Bebe having the richer voice. Instrumentally they blend together beautifully to create an exceptionally robust sound. The sound quality is very good, considering the fact that one side, at least, is recorded in 1974 on portable equipment. Highlights include Bebe playing great fiddle and singing his own tune, "Madame Faielle," his outstanding vocal on "Barres de la Prison" and the brothers' unique rendition of "Home Sweet Home."

EXCELLENT

La La: Louisiana Black French Music

(with the Lawtell Playboys) r. 1976; i. 1977/Maison de Soul 1004 CS, LP

This LP is almost the equal of *Cajun Fiddle Styles*. Again, the sound is extraordinarily full with only an accordion and a fiddle. Eraste sings well on "Robe a Parasol," as does Bebe on his own composition, "Blue Runner." Together, they produce a spectacular instrumental duet on "Johnny Peut Pas Danser." If you want to know where zydeco came from, listen to this.

OTHER RECORDINGS

J'etais au Bal: Music from French Louisiana

(collection) Swallow 6020 CS, LP

Zodico: Louisiana Creole Music

(with the Lawtell Playboys, the Ardoin Family, Inez Catalon & others) r. 1976; i. 1979/Rounder 6009 CS, LP

HADLEY J. CASTILLE
Fiddle, vocals

Swallow LP 6057

Raised in the cotton fields along Bayou Teche, this son of a sharecropper sings stories from his youth and from visits with old friends and neighbors in the Opelousas-Port Barre area. An example is his best known song, "200 Lines: I Must Not Speak French," his account of being punished for speaking French on the Leonville schoolgrounds. The song won Castille the Cajun French Music Association's Heritage Award in 1992.

An accomplished fiddler, Castille learned Cajun music as a child from his uncle, Cyprien, a fiddler, and his father, Francois, who played the accordion. He listened to records by **Harry Choates**, **Leo Soileau** and Bob Wills to hone his own style. With his Louisiana Cajun Band, Castille plays Cajun and country-style tunes and has toured the U.S., Canada and Europe. He has appeared at the New Orleans Jazz & Heritage Festival and in a TV special for the Canadian Broadcasting Co. When not fiddling, he runs a plumbing business in Opelousas.

A heartfelt entertainer, Castille signals his Cajun pride by playing a custom-made fiddle in the shape of the state of Louisiana. His son, J. Blake Castille, plays guitar in the band and produces his albums. Castille has recorded seven albums since the mid-1980s.

Chapter 1 • Cajun & Creole

THE BEST

Cajun Swamp Fiddler

i. 1993/Swallow 6112 CD, CS (contains 7 tracks each from 200 Lines: I Must Not Speak French/i. 1991/Swallow 6088 CS, LP & Along the Bayou Teche/i. 1989/Swallow 6078 CS, LP + the title track from Going Back to Louisiana/i. 1985/Swallow 6057 CS, LP)

This CD makes some of Castille's best work over the period 1985-1993 available on one recording. The first three songs have been rerecorded or remixed with a stronger drum track, which drives them along better. The drum is slightly overdone, as on "Making Whiskey," but it creates a more exciting cut. "Nathan's Blues" and "Sugar Bee" don't measure up, but the balance of the songs are Castille at his best, displaying his considerable fiddle and vocal abilities. Castille wrote most of the songs. The best cuts are "200 Lines: I Must Not Speak French," "Hadley's Dream," "Chanson de Mardi Gras" and "Going Back to Louisiana," with a classic vocal by Castille.

EXCELLENT

200 Lines: I Must Not Speak French

i. 1991/Swallow 6088 CS, LP

Ten outstanding songs out of 10 makes this recording a rarity. Castille's fiddling is inspired, his singing excellent and the song selection perfect. The wide range of material includes beautiful Cajun waltzes, a rhumba beat, a bluesy swing tune, a strong instrumental and Castille as balladeer. The stars include "200 Lines: I Must Not Speak French," "Blue Acadian Sky" and "Fi Fi Poncheaux."

La Musique de les Castilles

i. 1995/Swallow 6123 CD, CS

This is all new material, with the exception of "Hadley's Dream." Castille's vocals and fiddling share the spotlight. Subtitled "The Third Generation," this disc features Castille's

son, J. Blake Castille, on guitar. He also wrote or co-wrote several of the tunes and co-produced the recording with his father. The cream of the crop are "Milk Cow Blues," done as a bluesy swing tune; "Sweet Suzannah," with a great vocal by Castille; and "Balfa's Waltz."

Cajun Fiddling and Singing Now and Tomorrow

i. 1983/Kajun 5020 LP

This early recording shows off more of Castille's fiddle expertise than do later albums, which emphasize his singing. "Prisoner's Waltz" and "Madame Sotan" feature singing; "Hometown Waltz," fiddling.

Going Back to Louisiana

i. 1985/Swallow 6057 CS, LP

Doug Kershaw adds his fiddle on three tracks, and Ann Savoy joins Castille on "Ma Negress" on this showcase for Castille's fiddling and balladeer-style singing. "Bayou Pon Pon" is one of Castille's best recordings; "La Dernier Waltz" and the title track also stand out.

GOOD

Along the Bayou Teche

i. 1989/Swallow 6078 CS, LP

A few weak songs can be overlooked, given the good ones: "Le Reve a Hadley," "Maudit Bayou Teche" and an outstanding version of "La Chanson du Mardi Gras."

OTHER RECORDINGS

Hadley Avec Sons Violons

Kajun 5010 (unreviewed)

HARRY CHOATES
Fiddle, vocals

Arhoolie CD 380

One of Cajun music's most infectious fiddlers, Harry Choates was also one of its more tragic figures. Born in Rayne in 1922, he grew up during the Depression with his mother in Port Arthur, Tx. On his own as a child wandering the streets, he learned to play guitar, steel guitar and fiddle. He got his education at local bars, where he would crawl under tables and listen to the jukebox. By the age of 12, the gifted musician was playing a borrowed fiddle for small change pitched to him in barber shops by customers. Unfortunately, he was also a heavy drinker by then.

In the 1930s, when Cajun string band music enjoyed wide popularity, Choates worked for awhile with **Leo Soileau**'s Aces, then Papa Cairo and Jimmy Foster, never staying long with one band. His tempestuous nature and alcoholism got him kicked out of the U.S. Army during the war, and he worked for a time in a Texas shipyard while playing dance halls with his own band. He first recorded as a fiddler with Happy Fats and the Rayne-Bo Ramblers in 1940 in Dallas for Bluebird. After World War II, when Cajun music moved into Texas and blended with western swing, Choates played a combination of both,

singing in English and French. A famous showman, he danced while fiddling with wild abandon, punctuating songs with his signature cry of "Eh... ha, ha!"

In 1945, Choates married, and he and his wife Helen had two children. Hoping to cut a record to promote his live shows, Choates persuaded an independent record producer in Houston named Bill Quinn to put a disc out on Quinn's new hillbilly label, Gold Star, and the result made musical history in 1946. "Jole Blon" (Pretty Blonde), sung in French, became the first Cajun hit outside Louisiana since **Joe Falcon**'s "Lafayette" in 1928. It swamped Quinn with orders for it from all over the country. Previously recorded by **Amedee Breaux** and others, the tune as recorded by Choates in western swing rhythm became the Cajun anthem, stimulating pride among Cajuns and spreading awareness of their music to the rest of the country.

Ever eager to please with his music, the tiny young musician with a zest for life traveled the Gulf Coast, where he was popular at clubs and dance halls. Like a Cajun Mozart, he played in a brilliant, idiosyncratic style given to note-bending flights of fancy, musical jokes and a remarkable sense of ease, considering the chaos of his life.

Choates sold the rights to "Jole Blon" for $50 and a fifth of whiskey and soon began a boozy descent that would lead to his death within a few years. Drinking steadily and unreliable in his work habits, he sometimes had to be dragged out of a stupor to gigs and supplied with a fiddle. Crowley record producer J. D. Miller, who booked him into his El Toro Club, once bought him a new fiddle to play at a gig, only to find it pawned by evening. On another occasion, Choates was playing a band member's fiddle at a Thanksgiving dance when the raffle prize, a live turkey, broke loose and flew towards the bandstand, whereupon Choates swung the fiddle and knocked the turkey out of the air, destroying the instrument. Because he always played on borrowed or inferior instruments (the good fiddles were in hock), the true sound Choates was capable of was never recorded.

Meanwhile, he carried on with abandon off stage, as well–sinking lower and lower into alcoholism and dissipation. In 1950, his wife divorced him, and the following year he was arrested in Austin for nonpayment of child support and thrown in jail. Three days later, he died mysteriously, apparently after an epileptic fit or head injury caused by banging his head on the cell bars in an attempt to overcome alcohol craving. Although the death raised suspicions of police brutality, the official cause was given as cirrhosis of the liver and complications due to alcoholism. Choates was 28.

Even though he was the most popular Cajun string bandleader of his day, Choates was never able to match the recording success of "Jole Blon." With Gold Star, he recorded more than two dozen sides, including his popular "Poor Hobo" and "Port Arthur Blues," often injecting English into the lyrics. Later, he made inferior recordings for De Luxe, D, O.T., Allied, Cajun Classics, Macy's and Humming Bird. By the later recordings, his voice had deteriorated and his fiddling had gone out of focus.

THE BEST

The Fiddle King of Cajun Swing

r. 1946-1950; i. 1993/Arhoolie 380 CD; 5027 CS, LP/i. 1982 (CS contains 14 tracks found on the CD + 2 others)

This CD collects the late-1940s Gold Star 78s that Choates made with his string band. The exuberance and abandon with which he lived

his short life can be heard in his fiddling and singing. His voice was good, but he took it above its limits; and his fiddle playing was extraordinary because he was not inhibited by any norms. Of the generous 26 songs, "Allons a Lafayette," the catchy "Port Arthur Waltz," "Poor Hobo" and especially "Grand Mamou" stand out.

GOOD

Five-Time Loser

r. 1946-1950; i. 1990/Krazy Kat (England) 7453 LP

Poor sound quality almost overwhelms Choates' incredible talent, but if you appreciate this truly one-of-a-kind performer, the aptly-named LP is worthwhile. His unhibited approach to music resulted in some spectacular performances, including "Louisiana Boogie" and "She's Sweet Sweet."

OTHER RECORDINGS

J'ai Ete au Bal, Vol. 1

(collection) Arhoolie 331 CD, CS (contains Choates' 1946 hit recording of "Jole Blon")

Jole Blon

i. 1979/D 7000

OCTA CLARK
Accordion, vocals

Rounder LP 6011

Octa Clark might have been the oldest Cajun musician to record when at the age of 89 he came out with the 1993 CD *You Can't Go Wrong ... If You Play It Right*. Just his third album in more than 75 years of performing, Clark preferred to stick close to home around Lafayette rather than tour or promote himself on recordings. Of the recording business, he said in liner notes for *Old Time Cajun Music*, "I always thought that my music was worth more than the little they offered me, and I never really liked what it did to most players who had recorded."

Born outside Lafayette in Judice in 1904, Clark grew up on a farm hearing the music of his accordionist father and other family members—waltzes, polkas and mazurkas. He learned to play accordion when he was nine. A farmer who had dropped out of school in third grade, Clark played house dances before teaming up in 1928 with Hector Duhon, a distant relative who played fiddle, in the Octa Clark Band. The two became lifelong partners. They played local dances for a few years until Clark, who drove a buggy and couldn't travel to far-off gigs, dropped

out of the string band that reformed as the Dixie Ramblers. But Duhon continued to second fiddle for Clark occasionally in local clubs from 1936 to 1948.

In the 1930s, recording legends **Joseph Falcon** and **Amedee Breaux** attended Clark's dances to learn from his accordion playing, and he was a major figure of the 1940s-1950s. In 1952, Clark reorganized the Dixie Ramblers with Duhon, and the band enjoyed another decade-long heyday in the Lafayette area. After another break, the Ramblers regrouped again and became part of the Cajun music revival of the 1970s.

Still active in the 1980s, Clark and Duhon played regularly at Mulate's in Breaux Bridge, with Beausoleil's **Michael Doucet**. The venerable "Mr. Octa" eventually quit the Dixie Ramblers but continued to hold court at Mulate's every Saturday night and occasionally sit in with the band. Clark, who refers to a gig outside the home as a "bal publique" (public dance), conveys the elegant, old-style music from France and Acadia rarely heard today. In addition to his recent CD, he and Duhon were recorded by the Louisiana Folklife Program in the early 1980s on two LPs illustrating the relaxed harmony that a half-century of musical partnership has wrought.

THE BEST

Ensemble Encore

r. 1981, 1982; i. 1983/Rounder 6011 CS, LP

There's variety in this consistently high-quality recording, with cuts from different musicians at three separate sessions. Five of the 14 songs were recorded at the Capitol Folks Concert Series in Baton Rouge in 1982. Clark plays accordion and sings, accompanied by Hector Duhon and Michael Doucet on fiddle and David Doucet on guitar. The addition of the Doucets results in some of the LP's best music. The three songs recorded with Michael Doucet on guitar in Lafayette in 1981 at the French American Music & Dance Tour are also excellent. The remaining six songs were recorded at Duhon's home in 1982 by folklorist Nicholas Spitzer, who also wrote the LP's informative booklet. Clark is clearly the leader, with his powerful accordion and full vocals, but Duhon's fiddle, when featured–as on "Acadian Two-Step" and "Cajun Twist"–is also good. Other outstanding cuts are "High Ball," "Allons a Lafayette," "Lafayette Breakdown" and "J'ai Ete-z-au Bal."

GOOD

You Can't Go Wrong If You Play It Right

i. 1993/Field Span Music FS2 0193 CD

At 89, Clark was no longer singing, but his accordion prowess was undiminished. With Steve Riley, David Greely and Christine Balfa, this should have been his best recording, but it is marred by a few flaws. Riley's guitar (played here instead of his usual accordion or fiddle) distracts from the other instruments due to poor mixing, and his singing doesn't come across as well as on his own recordings. Balfa's normally good voice sounds weak, and a hollow echo effect doesn't help. Clark wrote all 12 songs, several of them strong additions to the Cajun repertoire. Greely's fiddling is excellent, and Clark's accordion is a joy to hear. "La Valse du Grand Bois," with a good vocal by Riley, and "Cajun Hot Shoes," featuring Clark's strong accordion, are some of the CD's best music.

Old Time Cajun Music

r. 1981; i. 1982/Arhoolie 5026 CS, LP

Another of Arhoolie producer Chris Strachwitz's wonderful contributions to Cajun music, this LP recorded at Michael Doucet's home preserved the work of the two old masters, Clark and Duhon. The recording's only flaw is that Clark's accordion overwhelms the other instruments in the mix. These three talented musicians produce an outstanding version of "La Valse Criminelle," with an intense vocal by Clark.

DANNY COLLET
Vocals, accordion

Danny Collet is an up-and-coming musician who made a name for himself with the **Basin Brothers**. As a leading member of that quintet, the young Lafayette accordionist helped them win a 1991 Grammy nomination for their first album, *Let's Get Cajun*. Then he formed his own band, the Louisiana Swamp Cats, and has put out one CD so far.

He is a versatile artist, with a historically wide-ranging repertoire. His album contains traditional Cajun tunes by **Cleoma Falcon**, **Aldus Roger** and **Lawrence Walker**, as well as swamp pop's Tommy McLain. He also composes his own songs.

Collet was born in 1969 in Breaux Bridge.

Louisiana Swamp Cats

i. 1993/Flying Fish 70628 CD, CS

This CD has a good mix of old and not-so-old Cajun songs, as well as some zydeco, Texas swing, rock 'n' roll and even a polka. Collet is an accomplished accordion player with a self-assured style. He has a good, high-pitched voice reminiscent of early Cajun singers. The musicians he assembled are good, too, notably Jonno Frishberg on fiddle and Fabian Champagne on guitar. Jay Theriot on drums and Mike Meche on bass lay down a steady beat. The Cajun songs are the best; the rock, the worst. Outstanding tunes: "Quelle Etoille," "La Pistache a Tante Nana," "Year of '57" and "Chameux One-Step."

GLEN CORMIER & CAJUN COMPANY
Group

Formed in 1988, Cajun Company is a young band whose oldest member was 35 and all the others in their 20s or younger when they recorded their album.

La Bonne Compagnie

i. 1990/Swallow 6087 LP

The liner notes don't identify the vocalists, but bandleader and bass player Glen Cormier and accordionist Carl Hollier both have good voices. As a group, the musicians are strong, with accordion and percussion standing out. The sound mix is good on the LP, whose notable selections include the fast instrumental swing number "Who Diggie," the uptempo "Musique de la Louisianne" and "Family Waltz."

JOE WARREN CORMIER
Accordion, vocals

Joe Warren Cormier was born in 1945 in Church Point. After military service, he picked up his father's accordion and learned to play it, inspired by Cajun dances he attended. His "T Bec Do" was a Cajun hit recording in 1986 and has since been recorded by both Cajun and zydeco musicians.

Pure Cajun!

i. 1990/Swallow 6084 CS, LP

This recording shows that Cormier's "T Bec Do" was not a fluke. His accordion work is good and his band is very professional. But it is his singing that sets him apart from so many groups that are strong instrumentally but have little vocal talent; his voice is clear, powerful and bright. The songs he wrote here range from good to very good, the best being "Baton Rouge Waltz," "C'est Tout et C'est Bon," "T Bec Do" and the excellent instrumental "Cajun de la Capitale."

SHERYL CORMIER
Accordion, vocals

Swallow CD 6098

Billed as the "Queen of Cajun Music," Sheryl Cormier was the first female Cajun accordion recording artist, with 45s on various Louisiana labels before her two albums in the 1990s. Her band, Cajun Sounds, plays traditional music in the Acadiana region of Louisiana and east Texas, along with some touring. Cormier, outfitted in bright western garb, plays Cajun-style button accordion.

At the age of seven, Cormier taught herself to play an accordion belonging to her father, a sharecropper and part-time musician in Grand Coteau-Sunset, where Cormier was born in 1945. Bucking Cajun tradition regarding girls, her parents encouraged her to play music. Occasionally, she joined her father's band, Andrew Guilbeau and the Sunset Playboys, whose drummer was her mother. But she gave it up when she married–that is, except on her wedding day, when she was encouraged to strap on her accordion and play in her wedding gown, pinned all over with money, according to Cajun custom.

Later, after family duties, she returned to music, playing with various bands on weekends. Her own first band included her son, Russell Jr., on drums; then she fronted an all-female band for a brief period. Her current band once again includes Russell Jr., along with her husband, Russell Sr., who sings and manages the business.

THE BEST

La Reine de Musique Cadjine
(The Queen of Cajun Music)

i. 1990/Swallow 6081 CS, LP

Cormier is a strong accordion player but only a fair vocalist, although better in person than on recordings. She sings on only one of the 12 songs on this release, with other vocals split between her husband, Russell (who does a good job with those songs suited to his voice), Ivy Dugas (a gifted singer) and Russell Jr. (who does an excellent job on the Dewey Balfa tune, "When I Was Poor"). The band's strengths are Cormier's accordion, good fiddle and steel guitar work, and solid drumming by Russell Jr. Outstanding songs are the fast instrumental "Cajun Sounds Two-Step," the uptempo "Makes Me Feel Like Movin'" and the pretty waltz "Valse de Pont D'amour."

GOOD

Queen of Cajun Music

i. 1992/Swallow 6098 CD, CS

This CD has cleaner, more vibrant sound on four songs carried over from the above LP.

However, of the 17 tunes, seven are only fair and have weak vocals. Cormier handles the singing on "You Used to Call Me" well, and her duet with Isaac Miller on "Jolie Fille" is good.

SADY COURVILLE
Fiddle

Sady Courville (1905-1988) spent most of his many playing days as a second fiddler–one of the greatest. His best work was with **Dennis McGee**, with whom, over a 70-year partnership, he set a standard for twin fiddle playing. (See **McGee** for recordings made by the pair.) Courville came into his own late in life as the leader of the Mamou Cajun Band at the fabled Fred's Lounge in Mamou Saturday mornings.

This is Mamou Cajun Radio

i. 1979/Sonet (England) 802 LP

This album features the radio show's co-hosts, Courville and Revon Reed, along with the Mamou Cajun Band. The accordion dominates the sound, but Courville is heard on some solos.

BRUCE DAIGREPONT
Vocals, accordion, guitar

Rounder CD 6060

Bruce Daigrepont is one of the hottest Cajun musicians in New Orleans, where, contrary to popular belief, Cajun culture is hardly a fixture. His longstanding Sunday gigs at Tipitina's in the Crescent City are *the* event for Cajun fans, and it's easy to see why: Daigrepont and his spirited, five-piece band are a true modern Cajun dance band. Their songs are based firmly in traditional music, but have the energy and tunefulness of pop music. Daigrepont writes most of them.

Daigrepont credits musical influences from **Nathan Abshire**, **Belton Richard** and **Aldus Roger** to Creedence Clearwater's John Fogerty for his traditional accordion playing and clear, crooning singing style. An accomplished songwriter, he mines both the traditional Cajun experience as well as personal stories and contemporary issues. Many of his songs—"The Marksville Two Step" and "La Valse de la Riviere Rouge," for example—have made their way into other musicians' repertoires.

Although he was raised in New Orleans, Daigrepont (b. 1958) comes from a French-speaking Cajun family from Marksville. He soaked up the culture on week-end and summer trips to his grandparents' farm in the country. His father gave him a guitar when he was five, and he often played and sang at family gatherings and house parties. At 15 he learned banjo and toured with Luke Thompson and the Green Valley Cut-ups. In 1979 he got turned on to the accordion, after attending the Festivals Acadiens in Lafayette a year earlier. Seeing other young people playing Cajun music made him want to do the same.

In 1980, Daigrepont started his own group, the Bourre Cajun Band, which played to huge crowds at the Maple Leaf Club in New Orleans for five years and helped trigger the Cajun dance craze in the city. With his recent band he toured the U.S., Canada, Europe and Latin America before settling in close to home to spend time with his wife and two young

daughters. As a contributing member of the Cajun revival and linchpin of the Crescent City Cajun scene, he expresses no regrets about forsaking the career he trained for: accountant.

THE BEST

Petit Cadeau (Little Gift)

r. 1993; i. 1994/Rounder 6060 CD, CS

The songs on Daigrepont's most recent album are tradition-based but fresh, with a strong dance beat and full arrangements. Daigrepont wrote 10 of the 14 cuts. A wide range of contemporary music within the older Cajun style is represented by the uptempo waltz "Nonc Willie," the fast instrumental version of the classic "Perrodin Two Step" and the modern rhumba "Bebe," written for Daigrepont's young daughter. The talented Ken Smith replaces Waylon Thibodeaux on lead fiddle here, but Thibodeaux, who has gone out on his own, sings harmony vocals.

EXCELLENT

Coeur des Cajuns

i. 1989/Rounder 6026 CD, CS, LP

Just a notch below *Petit Cadeau*, this CD of almost all original songs is Daigrepont's most traditional. His knowledge of Cajun music's roots shows in his compositions "Acadie a la Louisiane" and "Les Main du Bon Dieu." Guest musicians David Doucet on guitar, Sue Daigrepont (Bruce's wife) on piano and others strengthen the already sharp band.

Stir Up the Roux

i. 1987/Rounder 6016 CD, CS, LP

Winner of the Cajun French Music Association's 1988 album of the year award, this first effort features Daigrepont's songwriting skills, rich arrangements and strong back-up from the band. "Laissez Faire," "Disco et Fais Do Do" and "Marksville Two Step" stand out in an album polished by Daigrepont's own mixing and production skills.

DEJA VU CAJUN DANCE BAND
Group

Formed in 1990, this Baton Rouge-area band has performed in several southern states and was chosen to represent Louisiana at the Kennedy Center for the Performing Arts in Washington, D.C., in 1996. Besides playing for dances and festivals, they have made several TV commercials and appeared on the *Today Show*.

The five-member band contains a mix of older and younger musicians: Fiddlin' Bill Grass (Louisiana's State Grand Champion Fiddler in 1994), rhythm guitarist/vocalist John Richard, accordionist Wes Thibodeaux, drummer David Monic and bass player Jerome Thomassie.

Juste Parce Que (Just Because)

i. 1996/Swallow 6132 CD, CS

Deja Vu has talent, but it is not realized on this outing. With the fifth song, "Une Heritage Perdu," they come alive and demonstrate how well they can play. "Lost in the Swamp" is enjoyable, too. Otherwise, the band is hindered by weak songs and arrangements. Several songs lack excitement, although John Richard is a good vocalist at ease with a tune.

ED AND BEE DESHOTELS
(Edward and Elby Deshotels)
Duo

The Deshotels brothers walk on the quiet side of Cajun music, with simple acoustic instrumentation and no "yipping" yells. The identical twins were born on a cotton farm near Mamou in 1920. They learned tradition-

al tunes from their father, who played the fiddle, accordion and harmonica. As young men, they served in the Navy in World War II and attended college–uncommon for musicians with similar backgrounds.

They often sing duets, while Ed plays fiddle and Bee plays guitar. Their style is low-key and dreamier than most of their counterparts, coming from a time when Cajun music was for private house parties, rather than raucous dance halls. Good musicians and fair songwriters, they adhered to the traditional sound of French and Canadian folksongs and were popular recording artists for Swallow Records in Louisiana in the early 1970s. Their recording quality varies, with each album having some gems as well as a few tunes marred by choppy-sounding vocals. These LPs may be hard to find today.

THE BEST

Cajun Troubadours

r. & i. early 1970s/Swallow 6025 LP

The highlights of this LP are two original tunes, "Sept Jours Sur L'eau" and "Cinq Frere et Deux Soeurs." The elements that create a captivating recording came together on these two songs–musicians, arrangement, singing, tempo, engineering and mood of everyone involved during the session.

GOOD

La Vie des Cajuns

r. & i. 1973/Swallow 6017 LP

Good singing and musicianship on uncluttered arrangements make this a pleasing album. "T'es 'Cajine' Et T'es Mignonne" and "Tolam Waltz" are excellent tunes, and Ed turns in a good fiddle performance on "La Vie des Cajuns."

GERARD DOLE
Accordion, other instruments, vocals

Dole is from France, where he recorded his two albums. Taken with Cajun music, he has visited Louisiana to learn songs from older Cajun musicians and made field recordings for Folkways Records. In 1975, he formed Bayou Sauvage, a Cajun-style group.

THE BEST

Hey Madeleine!

r. 1976-1984; i. 1985/Folkways 2627 LP

When Dole gets it right, he can play some fine Cajun music. This LP was recorded in studios in several different French cities over an eight-year period. At times, it has a French music hall feel. This album is more even than his earlier *Bayou Memories*. Dole plays Cajun accordion, fiddle, mouth organ, jaws harp, triangle and drums, as well as handling most vocals. Dominique Poncet sings on four songs, shining on "Jolie Catin," which also boasts some of the finest instrumental work on the recording. Other highlights include the vocal duet by Dole and Poncet on "La Valse du Pont d'Amour" and the instrumental "Vilaine Catherine."

GOOD

Escale en Louisiane/A Journey to Louisiana

i. 1995/Playsound 66511CD (contains 7 tracks from Louisiana Cajun Memories/PS 65049 LP, 9 tracks from Co Co Colinda/PS 65086 LP + 1 track from Musique Cajun/PS 65024 LP)

Dole plays accordion on all the tracks here and sings on nine–nicely on "Evangeline," but not so well on the others. Michael Doucet adds his fiddle prowess to "P'Tit Jean Domingue" and "Evangeline," as does Canray Fontenot on "Co Co Colinda." Another plus is Bobby Michot's vocals.

Bayou Memories

r. 1977-1978; i. 1982/Folkways 2625 LP

This home-recorded LP of "Louisiana French folk songs and dance tunes interpreted by Gerard Dole" features Dole on accordion and Marie-Paule Vadunthun on guitar. Although the album offers a wide range of good Cajun music, it is plagued by weak material.

CAMEY DOUCET
Vocals, drums

Doucet made a local splash in the mid-1970s with the double-sided hit "Hold My False Teeth (And I'll Show You How to Dance)" and "Mom I'm Still Your Little Boy" on Swallow Records, as well as a minor hit on Kajun called "Me and My Cousin." But after putting out three Swallow albums, he hasn't recorded since 1979.

Doucet writes his own songs, singing in French to a light rock/country beat. Accompanying his vocals and drum work on his last album was a six-piece band that included **Wayne Toups** on accordion, replacing Jimmy Thibodeaux, who shared billing with Doucet on his first two albums.

Born in 1939 in Crowley, Doucet has played professionally since he was 17, early on with Clint West and the Diamonds and a rock band, Sabu Gap. His father, Julian Doucet, played accordion for local dances. A popular disc jockey, Camey Doucet has spread the Cajun music gospel on several radio stations since 1972.

THE BEST

Cajun Good Time Music

i. 1979/Swallow 6034 CS, LP

On his third try, Doucet got a solid band behind him that allowed him to display his vocal abilities. The featured players are skilled musicians, and the rhythm section is solid. Wayne Toups' squeezebox contribution is mixed–notably quiet on one side, and strong on the other. Better material and stronger arrangements account most for this album's superiority over previous ones. The steel guitar is used to better effect, and Doucet's songs fit his voice better. The best are "I'm Lonesome," "Dans le Coeur de la Ville" and "La Langue des Cajuns."

GOOD

Et Musique

i. c. 1975/Swallow 6024 CS, LP

Doucet and accordionist/vocalist Jimmy Thibodeaux struggle against weak material, with the following exceptions: "La Valse Pour Tout le Monde," with a good vocal by Thibodeaux, "Quand Je T'ai Vu Pour la Premier Fois" and "La Valse de Broussard."

OTHER RECORDINGS

Cajun Gentlemen

Kajun 5011 CS (unreviewed)

Cajun Goodies

i. 1977/Swallow 6028 CS, LP

Pierre & the Squishy Squires

Kajun 5019 CS (unreviewed)

DAVID DOUCET

Guitar, vocals

David Doucet plays guitar as a lead as well as deep rhythm instrument in **Beausoleil**, where he has served as a linchpin since the famous band's early days. Like his older brother, bandleader **Michael Doucet**, David has a genius for blending traditional material with modern techniques. He is also a fine composer, arranger and singer.

One of the most underappreciated players in Cajun music, Doucet has his day on *Quand J'ai Parti*.

Quand J'ai Parti

r. 1990; i. 1991/Rounder 6040 CD, CS

Doucet's guitar solos and vocals appear on countless Beausoleil recordings, but are featured on this debut CD. Both his guitar playing and singing are top-notch. Doucet is at home with the Beausoleil band backing him up, and guests Josh Graves on bluegrass dobro and John Stewart on upright bass add to the session. With an imaginative selection of high-quality songs, the recording puts its best foot forward on "T'en as Eu," "Ton Papa," "French Blues" and "Les Bon Temps Rouler."

MICHAEL DOUCET

Fiddle, vocals

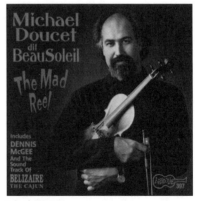

Arboolie CD 397

One of the founders of the Cajun renaissance, Michael Doucet is also one of its finest musicians. A virtuoso fiddler and appealing singer, he leads the world's most popular Cajun band, **Beausoleil**, with whom he has explored a vast repertoire of traditional Cajun and other styles since the mid-1970s. Doucet has done more to preserve and reinvent Cajun music than anyone, digging deep into folk archives to unearth forgotten songs, studying with older Cajun and Creole masters, arranging old tunes and composing new lyrics to old melodies. He also plays with the purist **Savoy-Doucet Cajun Band**, along with accordionist **Marc Savoy**, another key figure in the Cajun revival, and his wife Ann Savoy.

With his white halo of hair, Doucet looks the part of a middle-aged Cajun godfather. But he is at heart a youthful experimenter who has led Beausoleil through jazz, rock, blues and zydeco, always keeping to a Cajun base. On stage, his wildly inspired fiddling is likely to draw on many of these styles in a show propelled by his warm, engaging personality.

Born in 1951 in Scott, near Lafayette, Doucet grew up in a musical, middle-class family. His mother played clarinet, and several aunts sang traditional ballads. His father, an Air Force colonel, did not play music, but an uncle who played Cajun fiddle encouraged his nephew to play banjo and guitar. When Doucet was six, he played Elvis Presley songs on a banjo; later, he learned the guitar and trumpet, playing them both through high school. Early stylistic influences were classical, jazz and traditional Cajun music sung at family gatherings (where he picked up French, although his parents spoke English at home). Another influence was his sister Paulette, who was interested in folk music.

During the 1960s, when Cajun culture was at its low point, Doucet listened to folk music and rock 'n' roll. Off and on, he played Rolling Stones-style music with boyhood friend and distant relative **Zachary Richard**. Doucet was an English literature major at Louisiana State University, where he began his lifelong study of Cajun music in a folk music course. Upon graduation in 1973, he

and Richard accepted an invitation to play at a folk festival in France, where they were startled to hear French folk bands playing Cajun songs for enthusiastic young audiences.

Doucet began to appreciate his musical heritage. Returning to Louisiana, he and Richard formed the Bayou Drifter Band, which lasted less than a year in the face of a cool reception from everyone except an ardent group of French-Canadian Cajun music fans who were teaching French in Louisiana. Dropping plans for graduate school in English literature, Doucet split with Richard (who found fame in Canada as a Cajun rocker) and instead searched out and studied the fiddle with old Cajun masters like **Dennis McGee**, **Dewey Balfa** and **Canray Fontenot**.

"Before I could go and say that I knew Cajun music, I felt I had to know myself what Cajun music was," Doucet said in liner notes for *The Mad Reel*. Fortunately, he found a handful of others who shared his newfound passion. In 1975, he and the great fiddler **Dewey Balfa** started a folk-music-in-the-schools program and helped found what has become the annual Festivals Acadiens to showcase Cajun musicians.

By 1975, Doucet's broad musical reach appeared in two bands he founded: the acoustic folk trio Beausoleil (with Bessyl Duhon on accordion and Kenneth Richard on mandolin) and a "cosmic Cajun" rock band called Coteau. While the exciting, popular Coteau only lasted two years before collapsing from internal pressures and diverse musical tastes, Beausoleil caught fire with the college and folk festival crowd and expanded its personnel. On a cultural exchange trip to France in 1976, they cut their first record. *The Spirit of Cajun Music* followed the next year on Louisiana's Swallow label, kicking off what was to become a golden recording career and eventually fulfilling Doucet's dream of reviving Cajun music.

While researching Cajun music (with support from National Endowment grants), Doucet earned a living by working for the communications department of the Diocese of Lafayette producing radio and TV programs. By 1986, when Beausoleil had taken off nationally, Doucet dropped his day job and began to play music full time. Since then, he has turned up everywhere from Beausoleil's recordings to sessions with old-timers like Canray Fontenot and musicians in other genres—Keith Richards and **Nathan & the Zydeco Cha-Chas**, for example. All the recordings carry his stamp of impeccable musicianship.

THE BEST

Beau Solo

r. & i. 1989/Arhoolie 321 CD, CS

While Doucet's fiddling and singing fit Beausoleil like a glove, it's nice to hear him alone, backed up only by his brother, David Doucet, on a full-sounding rhythm guitar. Here Michael sings and plays accordion as well as his usual fiddle on traditional and original tunes. In a uniformly outstanding disc marked by his virtuosity and imagination, the following songs call for special praise: "One-Step d'Amedee" (written by Doucet), Dennis McGee's "Valse a Pop McGee" (listen to the fiddling!), Wade Fruge's "Wade's Waltz" and Ambrose Thibodeaux's "Two-Step d'Ambrose." An informative booklet written by Doucet, with transcriptions and translations by his wife, Sharon Arms Doucet, accompanies the CD. (Please note that songs #19 and #22 are transposed in the booklet and on the CD case.)

EXCELLENT

Michael Doucet & Cajun Brew

(with Richard Thompson & Sonny Landreth) i. 1988/Rounder 6017 CD, CS, LP

The fun that can come out of a high-level jam session comes through in this musical gumbo, the product of an unplanned recording session that just fell into place. Into the pot went a mixture of styles including rhythm & blues and rock, along with a dash of traditional Cajun and zydeco as Doucet used to play it with Cajun Brew at Mulate's, a Cajun restaurant in Breaux Bridge. Sonny Landreth produced the CD and plays lead electric guitar, with the brilliant British guitarist Richard Thompson sitting in on three cuts and contributing a quirky original composition, "Woman or a Man." In places, the ensemble lacks Beausoleil's characteristically rich sound, but the spirit of the session easily overcomes that drawback. Doucet does a great vocal treatment of "Louie Louie," "Woman or a Man" and the more Cajun "J'ai Passe Devant Ta Porte," with notable accordion playing by Pat Breaux.

Cajun Jam Session

(with Danny Poullard & Alan Senauke) r. 1983; i. 1989/Arhoolie 5035 CS, LP

Another jam session, this time a 1983 radio broadcast from the studios of KPFA-FM in Berkeley, Ca., on Arhoolie Records producer Chris Strachwitz's "Folk, Blues, & Jazz" show. Doucet's spirit and incredible musical abilities bring out the best in others, even relative beginners, as accordionist Danny Poullard and guitarist Alan Senauke of the California Cajun Orchestra were at the time. Sharon Arms Doucet also provides an excellent beat on triangle. The group is good, but Doucet's fiddling stars on "Grand Kaplan," "La Banane a Nonc Adam" and

"Eunice Two Step," on which Poullard sounds like anything but a novice. The talk between songs is entertaining, too, particularly Doucet's spontaneous radio ad for Louisiana boudin a la the Saturday morning radio broadcasts from Fred's Lounge in Mamou.

GOOD

Le Hoogie Boogie: Louisiana French Music for Children

(with family & friends) i. 1992/Rounder 8022 CD, CS

You only have to be a kid at heart to love this recording. Some selections are standard Beausoleil fare and the full band is on some tracks, while others are more specifically for children. Steve Riley joins the group with a good vocal on "Les Maringouins Ont Tous Mange Ma Belle." Sharon Arms Doucet, Melissa Maher, Jane Vidrine (now of the Magnolia Sisters) and a vocal chorus join in on some tracks. Musicologist Barry Ancelet narrates some nursery rhymes in French, and his family joins the group. An excellent booklet with translations and transcriptions by Sharon Arms Doucet comes with the CD, whose stand-outs include Steve Riley's vocal, "P'tit Galop Pour Mamou," "Paquet d'Epingles" and "Johnny Peut Pas Danser."

Christmas Bayou

i. 1986/Swallow 6064 CD, CS, LP

This recording captures the spirit of Christmas in Cajun country, where a lot of effort goes into making it special. The Beausoleil crew from the mid-1980s plus some guests create beautiful holiday music. Doucet's vocal duet with Annick Colbert on "Il Est Ne" is pretty, and flautist Richard Landry does a good vocal turn on "Trinquez, Trinquez." Another gift is the excellent instrumental version of "Little Drummer Boy."

JOHN DUBOIS
Vocals

Called the "Maurice Chevalier of the Bayous," Cajun balladeer John DuBois began his long career in summer stock. A trained vaudeville-style actor/singer, he performed in nightclubs and cabarets before appearing in TV's "Colgate Comedy Hour" with Eddie Cantor, Milton Berle, Jimmy Durante and others. Later he did a stint as marketing and sales promotion specialist in New York's hotel business.

After retirement, the Vermillion Parish native performed Cajun songs at festivals in Louisiana, New England and Canada, as well as in clubs and on public television stations. He has also recorded songs for the Folk Music Archives in the Library of Congress. DuBois, whose father and grandfather were fiddlers, learned unaccompanied Cajun ballads from his grandparents at his family's camp on Cow Island. While his first recording was an eclectic tribute to his Acadian heritage, his latest is for dancing.

THE BEST

Rendez-Vous Louisianais

i. c. 1995/Chaud Dog Jean CD

DuBois gathered an all-star group of musicians: Al Berard on fiddle and mandolin, Errol Verret on accordion, Kenny Allerman on drums and Cal Arnold on bass guitar. Guests include Sonny Landreth on slide guitar, Steve Riley on accordion, Christine and Nelda Balfa on triangle and producer Chris Foreman on percussion. DuBois's son, Andre John DuBois, is executive producer. In his 70s at the time, DuBois's voice is strong, and the mix brings it out. "Chanson de Mardi Gras" and "Tout les Soirs" are particularly fine.

GOOD

Dans le Creux du Bois (In the Deep of the Woods)

i. 1991/Chaud Dog Jean CD

Another stellar back-up featuring Dewey and Christine Balfa, Al Berard, Steve Riley and Vorance Barzas strengthens this disc, which finds DuBois in less robust voice than on his later release. In fact, his singing sometimes gets lost in the instrumental and vocal back-up. But several songs are good in the assortment, among them the Cajun classics "Les Veuves de la Coulee" and "Madame Sosthene."

EVANGELINE
Group

Primarily a Nashville-style pop-country band before it split up in 1995, Evangeline occasionally lived up to its name with a bayou ballad or *bon temps* rocker. Formed in 1988 in New Orleans, the all-female group's first recording, *Louisiana Aye Yi Yi*, had an identifiable Crescent City feel. They sound like a slightly updated and hipper Phister Sisters. However, by their second disc, under Jimmy Buffett's Margaritaville label, Evangeline became indistinguishable from the countless other Nashville female country & western groups.

The band went through several personnel changes. At their best, Evangeline's smooth harmonies, funky rhythms and original songs conjure up a pleasing Louisiana atmosphere.

THE BEST

Louisiana Aye Yi Yi

i. 1990/Renegade 004 CD

This debut recording, produced by David Doyle, shows a Cajun/zydeco influence. The songs by Clifton Chenier, D. L. Menard and Rockin' Sidney, plus some traditional Cajun

tunes, help create a Louisiana feeling. The title cut is excellent, as are Robbie Robertson's "Evangeline" and D. L. Menard's "Back Door."

GOOD

French Quarter Moon

i. 1993/MCA/Margaritaville 10879 CD, CS

Evangeline's final release contains stronger material than their second disc, *Evangeline*; but the sound is modern Nashville, with the exception of the title track. That tune, as well as "She's a Wild One" and Kelly Willis' "Let's Go Spend Your Money Honey," are the best.

Evangeline

i. 1992/MCA/Margaritaville 10582 CD, CS

Only the excellent Waylon Thibodeaux/Sharon Leger song "Bon Temps La Louisiane" has any sense of Louisiana, but the music is fine.

CLEOMA BREAUX FALCON
Vocals, guitar

Jadfel LP 101

Cleoma Breaux Falcon created the kind of sensation most musicians could only dream of in her day. In 1928, she made the first Cajun recording, "Lafayette" ("Allons a Lafayette") and "The Waltz That Carried Me to My Grave," accompanying her singer/accordionist husband, **Joe Falcon**, on rhythm guitar.

Soon after, she and her brothers Ophy and **Amedee Breaux** made the first recording of "Ma Blonde Est Partie" (later known as "Jolie Blonde" [Pretty Blonde]). Cleoma is believed to have composed the Cajun anthem, which was sung by Amedee.

She helped pioneer Cajun recording, cutting some two dozen singles from 1928 to 1937, including her hit "Mon Coeur T'Appelle" (My Heart Aches for You), a lament over the early death of a loved one.

Born in Crowley in 1905, Cleoma grew up singing and playing guitar in an unusually musical family, even by Cajun standards. With her brothers, she made a group of fine recordings. Joe Falcon often played triangle with the Breaux family band and married Cleoma after her divorce from a guitar player, Oliver Hanks. While the Falcons usually played as a duo, they sometimes joined Breaux Freres, the band three of the four Breaux brothers formed after Cleoma married Falcon and left home.

As a female performer, Falcon was a rarity in Cajun country. Dance hall crowds from Lafayette to east Texas were drawn to the petite, dark-haired beauty singing in an emotional voice of family loss and love gone wrong while strumming her National steel guitar with a basic, steady beat. Along with traditional songs, she also translated popular western numbers into French. The powerful Joe and Cleoma Falcon duo were mobbed wherever they went. During performances, their daughter, Lulu, slept on a quilt nearby.

Cleoma died in 1941 at the age of 36 after a mysterious ailment. Some observers attributed her death to an earlier roadside injury when a passing vehicle had hooked her sweater and dragged her for a quarter of a mile, ending the career of Cajun music's only female superstar.

THE BEST

A Cajun Music Classic

i. 1983/Jadfel 101 LP

A historic LP devoted to the queen of early Cajun music. On first hearing, her voice sounds strange to today's listener with its nasal, piercing quality, but she was a talented singer. She was also a songwriter of note, credited with eight of the 12 songs here. Her husband, Joe Falcon, provides good accompaniment on accordion, while Cleoma's guitar locks in a solid beat. The song selection is great, especially "Ma Meilleure Valse," "Prends Donc Courage," "Ils Ont Vole Mon Traineau," "Mes Yeux Bleus" and "Leve Tes Fenetres Haut."

EXCELLENT

Le Gran Mamou: A Cajun Music Anthology, Vol. 1 (The Historic Victor-Bluebird Sessions 1928-1941)

i. 1990/Country Music Foundation 013 CD

The Falcon Trio's "La Valse J'aime" (r. 1936) backs Cleoma's powerful voice with a full instrumental sound provided by only a fiddle, Joe Falcon's accordion and Cleoma's guitar.

Raise Your Window: A Cajun Music Anthology, Vol. 2 (The Historic Victor-Bluebird Sessions 1928-1941)

i. 1993/Country Music Foundation 017 CD

Cleoma's singing is wonderful on the Falcon Trio's "Raise Your Window" (r. 1936). She also plays guitar along with her husband Joe on accordion and a fiddle player.

Louisiana Cajun Music, Vol. 3: The String Bands of the 1930s

(collection) i. 1971/Old Timey 110 LP

Cleoma sings "Hand Me Down My Walking Cane" (r. c. 1938) in English, backed by her guitar and a fiddle. Joe Falcon is listed as accordion player, but he cannot be heard.

GOOD

Cajun Dance Party: Fais Do-Do

(collection) i. 1994/Columbia/Legacy CK 46784 CD

Four cuts feature Cleoma Falcon. The songs are good, as is her voice, but the recordings are marred by the poor instrumental mix. The accordion and fiddle have an echo chamber effect, and there is a loud hiss throughout most of two cuts. That said, they are worth hearing.

OTHER RECORDINGS

Cajun, Vol. 1: Abbeville Breakdown 1929-1939

(collection) i. 1990/Columbia/CBS Records CK 46220 LP

Cajun Music: The First Recordings 1928-1934

(collection) Arhoolie 213 CS (contains Old Timey LPs 108 & 109) (unreviewed)

JOSEPH FALCON

Vocals/accordion

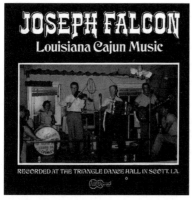

Arhoolie LP 5005

Joe Falcon was the most popular Cajun musician of his day and one of the most influential. With his wife, **Cleoma Breaux Falcon**, he made the first Cajun recording, "Allons a Lafayette," backed with "The Waltz That Carried Me to My Grave," in a hotel room in New Orleans in 1928. The overnight success of these traditional Cajun records opened up the recording industry to other Cajun musicians and spread Falcon's fame throughout the Gulf Coast.

Falcon played the accordion during a time when it was becoming dominant over the fiddle. He sang with a high, crying intensity while his wife accompanied on rhythm guitar. Often they traded vocal duties, and together they produced a voluminous sound that shocked Columbia Records chiefs when they first heard it. Aided by the novelty of an attractive female performer, the duo drew crowds in the thousands when they appeared at dance halls from Lafayette to east Texas.

Born in 1900 near Rayne, Falcon grew up on a cotton and sugarcane farm. Although poor, his father bought him an accordion at age seven, and Falcon taught himself how to play in the barn. His career began when he sat in one night for an accordion player who didn't show up at a local dance. A frequent visitor to the home of **Amedee Breaux**, Falcon often played triangle while Amedee played accordion and his sister Cleoma played guitar. After Joe and Cleoma married, they performed with Falcon's brother Ulysses and two nieces, playing traditional tunes, popular western songs translated into French and blues numbers. They held forth in steamy, gas-lit country halls on platforms surrounded by chicken wire to protect them from rowdy dancers and flying beer bottles. They sometimes performed and recorded with Cleoma's brothers, Breaux Freres.

The Falcons made many recordings during the 1930s, for Bluebird, Columbia, Decca and Okeh, helping establish today's core Cajun repertoire. They often wrote their own lyrics to old tunes they heard growing up. After Cleoma's untimely death in 1941, Falcon's performances dwindled and he stopped recording. Disheartened to see big string bands overtaking his simple, accordion-based style, he nevertheless formed a new band that included his second wife, Theresa, playing drums. Joe's Silver Bell String Band was recorded once, in 1963, two years before his death.

Falcon's early records are still listened to in Louisiana, where the accordionist with the smooth style and emotional singing was known as "the famous Columbia Record King." Recalling family stories of mob scenes at Falcon's appearances, Lafayette singer Johnnie Allan, a relative of Falcon's, told author John Broven, "If all of the United States had been French-speaking he would have been an Elvis Presley in his day."

THE BEST

Joseph Falcon and His Silver Bell String Band (Live at a Cajun Dance)

r. 1963; i. 1968/Arhoolie 5005 CS, LP

Recorded live at the Triangle Dance Hall in Scott, this was Falcon's only album and his final recording, made without thought of publication. While some of the lyrics may be hard to hear, the LP captures the flavor of a 1960s dance hall. The Silver Bell String Band was a quartet that included Falcon's second wife, Theresa Meaux Falcon, on drums, with Lionel Leleux on fiddle and Allen Richard on guitar.

The first three songs on side one stand as some of the best of Falcon's recordings. His accordion and vocal work are excellent, with only "Allons a Lafayette" marred by poor sound quality. Side two is disappointing—his vocals are weaker, the sound balance is off and Theresa Falcon is too heavy-handed with the drums. Hearing Falcon play and sing on the good songs, it is easy to see why he and Cleoma Falcon were such stars. "Lacassine Special" is the album's best song, with "Les Flambes d'Enfer" and "Le Tortillage" nearly as good.

EXCELLENT

Cajun, Vol. 1: Abbeville Breakdown 1929-1939

(collection) i. 1990/Columbia/CBS Records CK 46220 CD

Although this CD only has two songs by Joe Falcon, they are outstanding. The uptempo waltz "Poche-Town" features a dramatic vocal and good accordion work, while Falcon handles the complicated "Aimer et Perdre" well.

Pioneers of Cajun Accordion 1926-1936

(collection) i. 1989/Old Timey 128 CS, LP

The sound is not quite as good as on *Abbeville Breakdown*, but the catchy songs demonstrate why the Falcons were so popular. Their music was entertaining and very danceable. Joe Falcon's vocal on "La Jolie Fille N'en Veut Plus de Moi" is particularly strong. Cleoma sets a steady rhythm with her guitar.

Le Gran Mamou: A Cajun Music Anthology, Vol. 1 (The Historic Victor-Bluebird Sessions 1928-1941)

i. 1990/Country Music Foundation 013 CD

Falcon has a great vocal on "Mon Vieux d'Autrefois," with good guitar backing from Cleoma. Much of the time, Joe's accordion is lost in the poor instrumental sound quality. Joe's accordion backs Cleoma's vocal on "La Valse J'aime," but again his playing is lost in the poor sound mix.

GOOD

J'ai Ete au Bal, Vol. 1

(film soundtrack) i. 1990/Arhoolie 331 CD, CS

The success of "Allons a Lafayette" set off a flurry of Cajun music recordings. Falcon's vocal on the 1928 recording is not quite up to those on some of his later recordings, but it is still good.

Cajun Dance Party: Fais Do-Do

(collection) i. 1994/Columbia/Legacy CK 46784 CD

Although Falcon doesn't sing, he provides fine accordion backing and solos between Cleoma's vocals.

OTHER RECORDINGS

Cajun Music: The First Recordings 1928-1934

(collection) Arhoolie 213 CS (contains Old Timey LPs 108 & 109) (unreviewed)

Raise Your Window: A Cajun Music Anthology, Vol. 2 (The Historic Bluebird Sessions 1928-1941)

i. 1993/The Country Music Foundation 017 CD

FILE
Group

The Lafayette-based File (pronounced *fee-lay*) offers reliably good accordion-based dance music. Starting out in the 1980s as traditionalists, they developed a reputation as a good-humored honky-tonk band. Over the years, they have grown more eclectic and started to attract attention beyond Louisiana.

The bearded ensemble took a promising new direction in 1993 when they formed a close association with the late legendary Creole fiddler Canray Fontenot. Together they toured Europe, played gigs in New Orleans and had a recording session scheduled at the time of Fontenot's death in 1995. With a recent reorganization adding the songwriting skills of fiddler D'Jalma Garnier and R&B pianist David Egan (who used to play with Cajun/country's Jo-El Sonnier), File now offers a richer platter of traditional and original tunes than ever before.

Among traditional Cajun dance bands, File is unique in having a piano player. Besides Egan and Garnier, the band's roster as of 1996 included Ward Lormand, accordion/ vocals; Kevin Shearin, bass/vocals; and Peter Stevens, drums. Only Egan and Lorman are from Louisiana, where File maintains a heavy touring schedule and attracts a growing fan base.

Lorman grew up in a French-speaking family that played only Cajun music, and gained appreciation of both Cajun and zydeco traditions as a young man. In 1985, he forged his friendship with Fontenot at the Smithsonian Folklife Festival and was later instrumental in getting a Texas Folklife grant for Garnier (a Creole originally from Minnesota but with family ties to New Orleans) to study with Fontenot. In a Louisiana music scene still marked by racial divisions, File's partnership with Fontenot made the group a rarity: a modern-day Cajun/Creole band.

THE BEST

La Vie Marron (The Runaway Life)

i. 1996/Green Linnet 2124 CD

On their latest album, File has a depth and strength lacking in its earlier incarnations. While Lormand, Shearin and Stevens have been with the band since its first recording in 1987, other members have changed dramatically along with the band's sound. The best tune here is the title track, a flat-out great Cajun song. Another superb one is "Loup Garou Mange Pas Mes Enfants" (Loup Garou Don't Eat My Children), a quasi-novelty number about a werewolf—an example of the band's willingness to experiment where it pays off. Other outstanding tunes are Egan's honky-tonk influenced "I Just Can't Do Right" and "Cheroquis."

EXCELLENT

Two Left Feet

i. 1989/Flying Fish 70507 CD, 90507 CS, 507 LP

File accurately bill themselves as a Cajun dance band. Besides their hard-driving songs, they do Cajun waltzes and even a rhumba on this release. "Perrodin Two-Step" is a good instrumental with a bluesy fiddle and strong accordion work. "Two Left Feet" is a catchy tune by Richard Thompson that has become a favorite of concert- and festival-goers, and Darren Wallace's singing and fiddle do it justice. " 'Tit Gallop Pour Mamou," which has become a theme song for the evergrowing Mardi Gras celebration in Mamou, again features Wallace's fiddle backing good vocal harmony. Another fine tune is "Les Blues a Cleoma" (also known as "Raise Your Window High"), popularized by pioneer Cajun artist Cleoma Falcon. It is done here with a rocking beat and a good sax solo by guest Richard Landry.

Cajun Dance Band

i. 1987/Flying Fish 70418 CD, 90418 CS, 418 LP

Two waltzes star: Shirley Bergeron's "J'ai Fait Mon Idee" and "La Valse de Kaplan," which shows off Darren Wallace's fiddle skills. Dewey Balfa's "T'en As Eu, T'en Auras Plus" and Michael Doucet's "Z'haricots Gris Gris" demonstrate the band's vocal and instrumental strengths on uptempo numbers.

ALLEN FONTENOT
Fiddle

Fiddler Allen Fontenot has played Cajun music in the New Orleans area for a long time with his Country Cajuns band. He is also a radio host on the local community radio station, WWOZ-FM. He and his band have appeared in the Charles Bronson movie *Hard Times* and on the TV programs "Good Morning America," "Real People" and "Austin City Limits."

Fontenot was born in 1932 in Plaisance and raised in Ville Platte. When he was seven, he fashioned a homemade fiddle, later getting his first real one from his musician grandfather when he was 14. He formed his first band, the American Aces, when he was still a teenager. After Army duty in the early 1950s, he moved to New Orleans and played the country music popular at the time until organizing the Country Cajuns in 1969. They were the first Cajun band to play in the Crescent City at the spot where Tipitina's is now.

Fontenot pioneered Cajun music in New Orleans. In 1974, he opened his own club just outside the city, Cajun Bandstand, the only Cajun music club in the area until 1982. The popular group's repertoire included old and new Cajun tunes, hillbilly music and some swamp pop. In the early 1990s, Fontenot was performing on Bourbon Street at the Cajun Cabin. The versatile fiddler has also toured with zydeco artists **Rockin' Sidney** and **Al Rapone**. Most recently, he and the Country Cajuns performed at the 1996 New Orleans Jazz & Heritage Festival.

Jole Blon (Pretty Blond) and Other Cajun Honky Tonk Songs

i. 1992/Great Southern 11012 CD (same as Delta 1118 LP/i. 1980)

It is difficult to keep an instrumental recording interesting. Fontenot and his Country Cajuns are clearly up to the task, although a few arrangements here could be stronger. Fontenot's fiddle is a delight, and the band gives him solid backing. The rhythm section consists of Darrell Brasseaux on drums, Dallas Bourque on steel guitar and John Scott on bass and banjo. Accordionist Gaynor Soileau also makes a solid contribution. "Roving Cajun Waltz," "Kaplan Waltz" and some blazing fiddle on "Big Mamou" are the standouts.

CANRAY FONTENOT
Fiddle, vocals

Arboolie CD 381

The last of the great Creole fiddlers, Canray Fontenot performed until his death at 72 in 1995. As he often told audiences, he did *not* play zydeco music. Rather, his highly personal songs reached back to the last century, when African-Americans in southwest Louisiana played a Cajun-based *musique Creole*. With an uncanny ability to make his fiddle cry or laugh like a human voice, he was revered for his virtuosity and phenomenal musical memory– he was said to know thousands of tunes by heart. The engaging Fontenot had a profound influence on many musicians such as **Michael Doucet** of **Beausoleil**.

Fontenot's father, Adam Fontenot (known as Nonc Adam), was a renowned accordionist who performed with **Amedee Ardoin** for both black and white dances. (Unfortunately, Fontenot left no recordings, believing his music should die with him.) Among those who studied with Nonc Adam when Canray was a child were the great Cajun musicians **Leo Soileau** and Mayeuse

LaFleur. Fontenot's mother also played the accordion, but not in public.

In 1922, Fontenot was born into this musical household in L'Anse aux Vaches, near Basile. By the age of nine he took a liking to the fiddle over the accordion and made a cigar-box fiddle using screen-door wire for strings. A few years later, his uncle gave him a real fiddle, and soon father and son were playing together. Fontenot also played twin fiddles with his mother's father, who urged the boy to carry on the family's string-music tradition. Another influence was their neighbor, fiddler Douglas Bellard, the first Creole to record.

When Fontenot was 14, his parents died, whereupon he quit school to support himself and his younger sister by cutting sugar cane. He continued to play French dances, and in the late 1930s started a string band that played boogie-woogie, western swing and jazz, in addition to French tunes.

Fontenot also joined his boyhood friend, accordionist **Alphonse "Bois Sec" Ardoin**, in a musical partnership that continued for half a century until Fontenot's death. In 1948 they formed their first band, the Duralde Ramblers, playing songs of Amedee Ardoin, Adam Fontenot and Douglas Bellard, whose haunting "Les Barres de la Prison" (The Prison Bars) became Fontenot's signature tune. Fontenot and Ardoin played hundreds of dances for white and black groups throughout southwest Louisiana; they also made live radio broadcasts from KEUN in Eunice into the late 1950s. They often played at the club run by Ardoin's son, next to the Ardoin family house in Duralde.

Discovered by musicologists such as Alan Lomax and Ralph Rinzler in the 1960s, the pair became the most widely known purveyors of authentic Creole music. After appearing at the Newport Festival in 1966 (and recording an album on the way home), their fame spread. They traveled worldwide to play at festivals, including regular slots at the New Orleans Jazz & Heritage Festival.

In 1986, Fontenot won a National Heritage fellowship from the National Endowment for the Arts, and the following year he and Cajun fiddling master **Dewey Balfa** were appointed adjunct professors at the University of Southwestern Louisiana. In 1994, Fontenot played a command performance for Queen Elizabeth of England. Everywhere he went, audiences responded to his good humor and engaging personality as much as his music.

In his 70s, Fontenot joined the Cajun band **File** for a European tour in 1993 and several appearances at the Maple Leaf Bar in New Orleans, still drawing on his enormous repertoire of French tunes, Texas swing, ragtime, and even Mexican and Haitian songs. At the time of his death, recording sessions were scheduled with File and zydeco artist **Geno Delafose**.

During his final years, Fontenot found recognition as a Louisiana treasure. His infectious smile appeared on festival posters, travel brochures and in *Newsweek*. He also appeared in many documentaries on Cajun-Creole culture. Yet he never worked as a professional musician. He was a rice farmer for 30 years and held a longtime laborer's job at Marcantel's Feed Store in Welsh. He and his wife Artille raised six children, sending all of them to college. Never driven to play music over other pleasures in life, Fontenot once told author/musician Ann Savoy, "I just play 'cause I *can* play," adding, "I like to fish better than I like to play dances."

Only one album featuring Fontenot's huge legacy is available: *Louisiana Hot Sauce,*

Creole Style. However, selections can be found on other albums as well.

THE BEST

Louisiana Hot Sauce, Creole Style 🎵

(collection) r. 1971-1991; i. 1992/Arhoolie 381 CD, CS (contains 4 tracks from Boisec: La Musique Creole/Arhoolie 1070 LP, 9 tracks from Cajun Fiddle Styles, Vol. 1: The Creole Tradition/Arhoolie 5031 LP & 3 tracks from Beausoleil's Allons a Lafayette/Arhoolie 308 CD + 11 previously unissued tracks)

A TOP 10 CAJUN ALBUM

A superb collection by one of the greats, this CD samples various recording sessions from Fontenot's last two decades. Fiddler Michael Doucet has said that watching Canray play was to see a musical genius at work. You don't have to know anything about music to recognize his genius; his playing had a sureness that comes to only the gifted, after years of experience. That sometimes scratchy fiddle sound has undeniable force on these exceptional 27 songs.

EXCELLENT

La Musique Creole

(collection) r. 1966, 1971, 1973; i. 1996/Arhoolie 445 CD (contains Les Blues du Bayou/Melodeon 7330 LP, 8 tracks from Boisec: La Musique Creole/Arhoolie 1070 LP + 1 previously unissued track)

This recent CD featuring "Bois Sec" Ardoin with Fontenot contains in its entirety one of the best LPs of Cajun music ever recorded, *Les Blues du Bayou*. Fontenot and Ardoin recorded this historic 1966 album in Virginia, on their return from a successful performance at the Newport Folk Festival. Their excitement over their great reception at the festival comes out in their spirited accordion/fiddle playing and shared vocals. The final songs from the 1974 LP *Boisec: La Musique Creole* feature Fontenot on fiddle. It's hard to believe that only two musicians can create the amount of music heard on "La Valse de la Misere." Fontenot's vocal on "La Valse de la Prison" and "Bon Soir, Moreau" are some of his best.

Cajun & Creole Masters

(collection) r. 1987; i. 1996/Music of the World 138 CD

The other "masters" besides Fontenot include accordionist Alphonse "Bois Sec" Ardoin and fiddlers Sady Courville and Dennis McGee, along with Beausoleil's Michael Doucet and Billy Ware. Doucet and the World Music Institute assembled this 1987 gathering, recorded at the Washington Square Church in New York City. Fontenot and Ardoin are featured on 16 songs. Fontenot also talks about their determination to play music, regardless of the difficulties they encountered. "Les Barres de la Prison" is Fontenot's outstanding song.

GOOD

Louisiana Cajun French Music From the Southwest Prairies, Vol. 2

(collection) i. 1989/Rounder 6002 LP

With five tunes by the Ardoin/Fontenot duo, this LP is not up to the other recordings in quality, but "Hack a 'Tit Moreau" and "Jug au Plombeau" are excellent.

BLACKIE FORESTIER

Accordion, vocals

Blackie Forestier and the Cajun Aces began their long musical association in 1962. They had been playing for 33 years as of their 1995 CD, *Back in Time*. This well-liked group has played throughout south Louisiana and east Texas, as well as outside the state, and recorded 17 singles and five albums since their first single, "Big Pine Waltz," in 1967. They have also done a weekly TV show in Lake Charles.

Bandleader Forestier was born in 1928 in Cankton. He has composed many Cajun songs, and was still active in music in the mid-1990s. The local label La Louisianne has put out several cassettes by Forestier and a recent CD.

THE BEST

Back in Time

i. 1995/La Louisianne 1014 CD

Forestier's accordion playing distinguishes this collection drawn from earlier LPs together with some new material. He is a decent–not great–singer. Other vocalists help out, although without a list of personnel in the liner notes, they cannot be credited. Vocal duets on several songs are effective. The band is solid, and nearly all the arrangements are good. It is easy to hear why this is a popular Cajun dance band, especially on "Tu Vas Pas Pleurer a Ce Soir," Iry LeJeune's "J'ai Fait une Grosse Erreur" and Forestier's "La Valse du Lac" and "La Valse d'Evangeline."

GOOD

Cajun French Music

La Louisianne 128 LP

Forestier's vocals sound strained at times, but he's better on "Cajun Two-Step," which also features his accordion. This album is helped by the fiddle work of guest artist Rufus Thibodeaux.

OTHER RECORDINGS

Cajun Music

La Louisianne 135 LP (unreviewed)

LES FRERES MICHOT
(The Michot Brothers)
Group

The five Michot Brothers play a traditional acoustic "bal de maison" (house dance) style Cajun music. They were raised in Pillette, between Lafayette and Broussard–hence the name of their LP, "Eleves a Pillette." Several of the brothers still lived in the same spot at the time of their 1987 album. Cajun fiddling master **Dewey Balfa** pays tribute to the power of musical families such as the Michots in his liner notes for the album, put out by **Zachary Richard**'s Ar-Zed label.

THE BEST

Eleves a Pillette

i. 1987/LFM Records 0002 CD, Ar-Zed 1014 LP

This is one of the best, if obscure, LPs drifting around the used vinyl stores. The Michot brothers are exceptionally talented. Fiddler/singer Rick Michot wrote five of the songs, and all five brothers collaborated on the arrangements for the traditional numbers. With Dewey Balfa sitting in on four songs and production by Zachary Richard, there's quality here. The family band has three gifted vocalists in Rick, Tommy and Bobby Michot. This LP should be put out on CD; the group warrants more recording. Their best songs are "Two-step de Ste. Marie," "La Danse de Mardi Gras," "Two-step de Pillette," "La Valse de Platain," "Breakdown de la Pointe de l'Eglise" and the short but haunting "Reprise de Mardi Gras."

EXCELLENT

Escale en Louisiane/ A Journey to Louisiana

i. 1995/Playasound (France) 66511 CD (contains 7 tracks from Louisiana Cajun Memories/PS 65049 LP, 9 tracks from Co Co Colinda/PS 65086 LP + 1 track from Musique Cajun/PS 65024 LP)

Bobby Michot plays guitar and does a great job with the vocals on seven songs, but sounds more flat than plaintive on "Jolie Blonde." Gerard Dole leads the back-up band.

WADE FRUGE
Fiddle

Arhoolie LP 5044

Fruge was one of the last of the old-style Cajun fiddlers until his death in 1992. He figured the standards he played were about 200 years old, handed down to him through his grandfather, Napolean "Babe" Fruge. He called his style "yokery-yokery"–a simple, strong rendering made up of piercing chords, grace notes and rocking the bow from treble to bass strings and back.

Born in 1916 in Tasso, near Eunice, Fruge first played dances with his grandfather and two uncles at the age of 14. He also played with Creole musicians **Amedee Ardoin** and Douglas Bellard, who exposed him to a bluesier style. Fruge, who thought of himself as a cowboy, farmed and trained wild horses throughout his life, playing house parties just for fun. In later years, he played occasionally with accordionist **Marc Savoy**, with whom he made his only recording, *Old Style Cajun Music*, in 1989.

Old Style Cajun Music

i. 1989/Arboolie 5044 CS, LP

Fruge had a good, simple, Cajun fiddle style. The quiet "La Vielle Chanson de Mardi Gras" is haunting, and his fiddle swings on "Wade's Blues." The double fiddle sound from Fruge and Tina Pilione on "Grandfather's Tune" is uncomplicated musically, but very effective. Fruge sings only on "La Valse a Wade Fruge." A group of accomplished musicians joins him. Most of the vocals are by Vorance Barzas, who sings in the old Cajun manner, plaintively and dramatically, as best demonstrated in older tunes such as "La Valse de Coupique" and " ' Tit Mamou." Ann Savoy's guitar work is excellent, and she sings "La Valse de Bayou Teche" well. Her husband, Marc Savoy, provides a strong accordion sound, best heard on "Port Arthur Blues."

"DOC" GUIDRY (Oran Guidry)
Fiddle

Guidry was one of the best Cajun fiddlers in his day. Born in 1918 in Lafayette, he started playing professionally at the age of 13 and went on to play with many well-known Cajun musicians, including **Aldus Roger** and **Vin Bruce**. An early recording artist, he cut singles with Happy Fats and the Rayne-Bo Ramblers for Bluebird in 1936. Later, he formed the Sons of the Acadians with his brother and a cousin and recorded in 1939 for Decca in Houston. As was its practice, Decca had sent him a list of hillbilly songs to be translated into French.

After World War II, Guidry again teamed up with guitarist Happy Fats. In 1946, Guidry and Happy Fats and a few other musicians–billed as Happy, Doc and the Boys–cut the first release for Louisiana producer Jay Miller's fledgling Fais Do Do label: "Colinda." They went on to become Miller's first stars. After a hiatus, Happy Fats and Guidry paired up again, recording and broadcasting popular radio shows throughout Cajun country. Although their acoustical Cajun-country style had become passe by the mid-1950s, the pair exerted a strong influence on later Cajun musicians.

Guidry recorded with a variety of other musicians, including hillbilly recordings for Miller's Feature label in 1947–for example, Bill Hutto's "Some of These Days," with Guidry and his Sons of the South. He also recorded as a vocalist; his 1953 "Chere Cherie"/"The Little Fat Man" was popular locally. Starting in 1961, he served as Vin Bruce's fiddler on most of his albums, becoming a major factor in Bruce's success. In the 1960s, Guidry cut his only solo album, *King of the Cajun Fiddlers*, with his reorganized Sons of the Acadians, a five-piece group.

Guidry's fiddle and mandolin mastery won him considerable local fame, enhancing Louisiana Governor Jimmie Davis' successful 1943 and 1959 campaigns, as well as an unsuccessful 1971 campaign. Guidry also appeared at folk festivals outside Louisiana and made a 1980 tour of southeast Asia with **D. L. Menard**. Around that time, Guidry was living in Houma and working as a deputy sheriff. He died in 1992.

THE BEST

King of the Cajun Fiddlers

La Louisianne 115 LP

With the regal billing, one expects something special, and Guidry doesn't disappoint. A warm, clean sound characterizes his fiddling style. He dubbed an effective second fiddle on "Bayou Lafourche" and "La Valse d'Bosco." A Cajun Perry Como, Guidry handles all the laid-back vocals. His fiddle sings on "Chere Cherie" and the pretty waltz, "La Valse d'Amite." The piano is rare in Cajun music, but here Glynn Himel fits well with the session's low-key approach.

EXCELLENT

Vin Bruce's Cajun Country

i. c. mid-1970s/Swallow 6015 CS, LP

Guidry played on Bruce's first LP, *Jolie Blon*, and returns to a featured role on this album, where he has a substantial solo on every song. His playing is a little more forceful here than on his own album. His fiddle solo on "Veuve de la Coulee" and his great swing fiddle on "Made a Big Mistake" stand out.

OTHER RECORDINGS

Aldus Roger: A Cajun Legend

i. 1993/La Louisianne 1007 CD, CS

CHUCK GUILLORY (Murphy Guillory)
Fiddle, vocals

Arhoolie LP 5039

In the 1940s-1950s, Chuck Guillory & the Rhythm Boys were a big name in Cajun music. Guillory was born in 1919 in Mamou, and learned to play fiddle from his father, a farmer. At seven, he played with his father at a Eunice bar; by eight, he played his first dance; and by 10, he formed his own band. The precocious Guillory beat out **Harry Choates** and **Leo Soileau** (two of Cajun's greatest) in a fiddling contest in the late 1930s.

Guillory's seven-piece Cajun-country string band performed regularly at clubs in Cajun country and worked with the young George Jones and **Jimmy Newman**. Guillory's first recordings, for Modern Records in 1949, included the hit "Tolan Waltz" (on Colonial, a subsidiary label), and a song by Julius Lamperez, known as Papa Cairo, called "You Just Wait and See." Papa Cairo claimed the tune was stolen from him by Marty Robbins, who worked with the Rhythm Boys briefly and recorded the song later as "Pretty Words." In French, Papa Cairo sang another tune that became a regional hit, "Grand Texas" (Big Texas), later stolen, he said, by Hank Williams and turned into the hit "Jambalaya."

Chapter 1 • Cajun & Creole

Guillory also recorded for Feature, a Louisiana label. He retired in 1958 and went into the grocery business, but continued to play for special occasions. In the 1980s, he reformed his band and was recorded by Arhoolie Records.

Grand Texas

r. 1982, 1987; i. 1988/Arhoolie 5039 CS, LP

Nearly all the songs begin and end with Guillory's excellent fiddling. He doesn't sing, but has an outstanding vocalist in Preston Manuel. The other vocals by second fiddler Gervis Stanford and steel guitar notable Papa Cairo are also good. On one side, Michael Doucet adds to the musical richness with his mandolin solos, and David Doucet's full-sounding rhythm guitar carries the bass line. On the other side, Papa Cairo plays steel guitar, but without that strong twang that countrified Cajun music during Guillory's heyday. Marc Savoy plays backing fiddle, and Tina Pilione, who played on Steve Riley's first recording, adds a strong bottom to the rhythm with her bass. "Louisiana Waltz" and "The Last Waltz" stand out.

KRISTI GUILLORY

Accordion, vocals

Swallow CD 6136

Like their album title, *Reveille*, Kristi Guillory and her band are helping awaken the younger generation to the revival of Cajun music, language and culture. Born in 1978 in New Orleans, Guillory was a junior at Lafayette High School at the time the 1994 CD was made, and the other group members were under 20, as well. She is self-taught on accordion and guitar, starting at the age of 11; she also sings and plays fiddle. In 1992, she won Mulate's Accordion Contest.

Fiddler Bill Grass, who shares billing with Guillory on the CD cover, studied classical violin before switching to fiddling. In 1994, he was named Louisiana's Grand Champion Fiddler. Guillory and Grass began playing together in 1991. Kristi's brother, Craig Guillory, plays bass guitar with the group. Rounding out the roster are Horace Trahan on vocals and guitar, Jamey Bearb on fiddle and Doug Belote on drums. The band appeared at the 1996 New Orleans Jazz & Heritage Festival as Kristi Guillory & Reveille and have won the respect of older Cajun musicians.

THE BEST

Reveille

i. 1994/Swallow 6119 CD, CS

It's hard to believe Reveille hasn't spent thousands of nights in smoky dance halls perfecting their skills instead of in high school classrooms. Kristi Guillory and Horace Trahan are outstanding vocalists. Trahan does an exemplary job on the difficult "T'en a Eu, t'en Auras Plus." Guillory is a talented accordion player and wrote two songs on this release. Annette Huval, who usually writes for Jambalaya, also contributed two good songs, and the group thanks Terry and Annette Huval for their support in the liner notes. Bill Grass provides fine solos and back-up, shining especially on "Lake Arthur Stomp" and his own "Sweetheart Shuffle." Other good songs are "Les Veuves de la Coulee," "J'ai Passe Devant ta Porte" and "Reno Waltz," with a superb vocal by Trahan and accordion work by Guillory.

EXCELLENT

La Dance des Ancetres

r. & i. 1996/Swallow 6136 CD

On this second release, Guillory sings with more assurance. The six cuts on which she has the vocal lead are some of the best, for example, on Dewey Balfa's "Orphan Waltz." Fiddler Jamey Bearb's vocals are also good, as in the classic "Kaplan Waltz," and the Harry Choates instrumental "Draggin' the Bow" shows off his exceptional fiddling. Guillory's seven original compositions, a traditional Cajun tune and popular songs fill out the program. The loss of Bill Grass and Horace Trahan, both prominent on the band's first recording, shows; but it may not over time, with such a talented group of players.

THE HACKBERRY RAMBLERS
Group

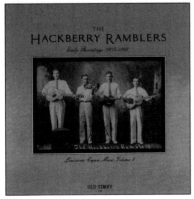

Old Timey LP 127

The Hackberry Ramblers were the most popular Cajun string band of the 1930s. Six decades later, they are still playing. One of the first to adopt a western swing style, this pioneer group also introduced amplification into Cajun music. A happy-go-lucky ensemble of mostly elderly Cajuns and non-Cajuns, they play Cajun tunes with a Texas swing, along with some swamp pop, blues and rock. Over the years, some 70 musicians have played with the band, but bandleader/fiddler Luderin Darbone and guitarist Edwin Duhon have remained its core since founding it as teenagers.

Darbone was born in 1913 in Evangeline. He learned to play the fiddle from a correspondence course, at his mother's urging. Raised in east Texas, he soaked up the Texas swing style of the day at house parties and brought hillbilly songs with him to Louisiana when his family moved in 1930 to the small oil town of Hackberry, near the Texas border. There he met Duhon, who was learning to play accordion and guitar. Born in 1910 in Broussard, Duhon had learned Cajun tunes at house parties. The two boys got together and performed for local dances after adding a second guitar player, Lennis Sonnier. In 1933, they named their band the Hackberry Ramblers, although two years later they moved to Crowley to be more centrally located.

Until this time, Cajun dance bands were made up of accordion, fiddle, guitar and triangle and played in an intense, unsophisticated style. But the Americanization of Cajun music via radio and records had begun, and the smooth, all-string style the Ramblers imported from Texas caught on. Crowds responded enthusiastically when they began using a sound system—a microphone, amplifier and speaker powered by the battery of Darbone's Model-A Ford. Amplification also made possible a lighter, more refined fiddling style and solos by various instruments, as heard on live radio shows. As regulars on such shows, the band's fame spread. They performed throughout southwest Louisiana and east Texas.

In 1939, Darbone gave up music and worked for an oil company, but reorganized the band a year later, adding more members (including for a time Goldband Records owner Eddie Shuler and longtime Ramblers member Crawford Vincent) and broadening its repertoire. Duhon dropped out of the band a few times to work in the oil fields and as an electrician and city marshal. On his return, he filled whatever position was vacant at the time, using his versatility on piano, guitar, bass, accordion, French harp and fiddle. The band sometimes added dobro, saxophone and trumpet. They worked at the Silver Star club near Lake Charles for 10 years after World War II, drawing huge crowds, then played mainly in east Texas.

The Ramblers recorded for many labels, starting with more than 100 singles for RCA's Bluebird, for which they made the first hit out of the Cajun anthem, "Jolie Blonde," in 1935. One of their famous tunes was "Un Piastre ici, une Piastre la Bas" (A Dollar Here, a Dollar There), about the Depression. Their biggest seller was the haunting "Wondering," with Joe Werner. They recorded such English songs under the name Riverside Ramblers, after the Riverside tires made by Montgomery Ward, their main radio sponsor. The band did live shows in the store three days a week, broadcast by remote facilities over a radio station. Their numerous singles from the 1930s were popular throughout the South, not to be matched by those from the 1940s.

The band almost retired several times, particularly in the early 1960s when Cajun music sank in popularity. But in 1963, Arhoolie Records producer Chris Strachwitz showed up on Darbone's doorstep and invited the band to record an album, triggering a revival that continues. Octogenarians Darbone and Duhon

were still leading the six-member band in the mid-1990s. Glen Croker has been with the group for more than 30 years, his lead guitar-playing lending a honky-tonk atmosphere. Johnny Faulk on upright bass and Johnny Farque on acoustic guitar have played with them roughly half that time. The newest member is drummer/producer/music writer Ben Sandmel, who joined them in 1987.

Today the band play regularly in their home base of Lake Charles, entertain at dances and festivals, and tour major cities across the U.S. They have drawn national attention with features on National Public Radio and "Entertainment Tonight." The Ramblers' adaptability and consistent good sound are the secret of their longevity.

THE BEST

Early Recordings 1935-1948: Louisiana Cajun Music Vol. 8

(collection) i. 1988/Old Timey 127 CS, LP

This album captures the Ramblers during their heyday. Darbone swings, getting a sweet or forceful sound from his fiddle as the tune requires. His vocal on "One Step de l'Amour" is one of the album's best. Early band member Lennis Sonnier excelled on vocals. His high-pitched voice is reminiscent of a less nasal Cleoma Falcon, with the same captivating power. The Ramblers lay down a good beat, and their banter and yelps are entertaining. The best songs are "J'ai Pres Parley," "Fais Pas Ca" (better known as "Trouble in Mind") and "Hippitiyo."

EXCELLENT

Cajun Boogie

r. 1992; i. 1993/Flying Fish 70629 CD; 90629 CS

This zesty CD came out 28 years after the Ramblers recorded their first album. Only drummer/music writer Ben Sandmel was new to the group. With Sonnier gone, Croker carries the vocals capably. Guest artists include country singer/songwriter Rodney Crowell, swapping verses with Croker on "Old Pipeliner"; Michael Doucet, adding tasty fiddle solos on four songs; and longtime band member Crawford Vincent, handling two vocals. Duhon sings a nice "Turtle Tail," and Darbone's fiddling is sharp. The voices may not always be great, but the *joie de vivre* makes up for it. Good tunes are "Crowley Waltz," "Les Gens de la Coulee" and the uptempo instrumental, "Beaumont Rag," with great fiddling by Darbone and Doucet.

Jolie Blonde

r. 1963-65; i. 1993/Arhoolie 399 CD (contains 17 tracks from Louisiana Cajun Music/Arhoolie 5003 LP [same as CS 5003] + 9 previously unissued tracks)

This disc collects two sessions resulting from Arhoolie producer Chris Strachwitz's surprise visit to Darbone in 1963–one at Darbone's home in Sulphur, the other at Eddie Shuler's Goldband Studio in Lake Charles. The resulting LP revived the Ramblers' career. The bonus tracks include seven live recordings from the 1965 Berkeley Folk Festival unearthed from Arhoolie's vaults, plus two tracks recorded at the 1963 sessions.

"Jolie Blonde" is the Cajun classic the Ramblers turned into a hit by recording it in western swing style. Lennis Sonnier's singing and Darbone's fiddle are the group's outstanding features, but sound for the fiddle could be better. Duhon's accordion is another Ramblers asset, and his vocals are fine as well. He also plays the harmonica on "J'ai Passe" and "French Harp Stomp." Other outstanding songs are "Black Bayou Rag," "Louisiana Waltz" and "Fais Pas Ca."

ADAM HEBERT
Vocals, fiddle

Hebert is best known for his songwriting, with such classics as "For the Last Time," "I'd Like to Know" and "Cette la J'aime" (The One I Love is Like a Little Bird). Countless Cajun artists have recorded his songs. Born in 1923 near Church Point, he first played the fiddle on a cigar box, with hair from his horse's tail. By 13, he was playing house parties.

Hebert joined the service as a young man. Later, he formed a band called the Veteran Playboys, so-called because two of its members were war veterans. The group played throughout the 1940s and recorded one single on the Fais Do-Do label. Personnel included Alphee and **Shirley Bergeron**, Raymond LaFleur, Wallace LaFleur and Bill Matte.

In the mid-1950s, he formed a new band, Adam Hebert and the Country Playboys, made up of Cleby Richard on accordion, Dick Richard on steel guitar, Hebert and John "Boy" Miller on fiddle, Wilfred Labbe on guitar and Willard Matte on electric mandolin. They recorded 12 singles for Swallow Records during the 1960s–all of them regional hits. His biggest hit, "La Valse de Ma Cherie," provided background music in a 1975 Charles Bronson movie, *Hard Times*. At last report, Hebert was living in Lafayette and performing only on rare occasions.

The Best of Adam Hebert

r. 1960-1967; i. 1987/Swallow 6065 CS, LP

Hebert has a strong, plaintive voice with a slight nasal quality. He is also a good fiddler. The band features strong accordion work by Cleby Richard and good steel guitar playing by Dick Richard. Some top tunes include "You'll Never Break My Heart," "Homesick Waltz," "For the Last Time" and "I'd Like to Know."

"SLEEPY" HOFFPAUIR
(Walden Hoffpauir)
Fiddle

Despite his German name, Hoffpauir is a traditional Cajun fiddler; his mixed-ancestry family goes back two centuries in south Louisiana. He was born in 1931 in Crowley and taught himself to play when he was 10 by listening to old records and the radio. Hoffpauir started off performing as a teenager with his cousin, "Happy Fats" LeBlanc, at a club in Rayne. He went on to play with several different bands, except for two years of Army service in Korea. For a 12-year period, he served as fiddler with **Belton Richard** and his Musical Aces band.

Fiddles Traditional Cajun Music

i. 1976/Swallow 6027 LP

This is a find—an entire LP of fiddle solos with an excellent mix of waltzes and uptempo songs. Hoffpauir plays all the fiddle parts. The liner notes don't mention a bass player, but one can be heard. Just credit is given to the exceptional triangle player, Savy Augustine. Hoffpauir's pride in his culture comes through in this spirited offering. He wrote one of the prettiest songs on the LP, "Tammy's Waltz." That plus "Blue Lake Widow Waltz," "Jolie Blonde" and "Madame Sostan" are the picks.

JAMBALAYA CAJUN BAND
Group

Swallow LP 6085

Like the trademark dish, this band of five seasoned musicians has simmered just long enough to blend their mix of Cajun-based styles into a satisfying offering. Since the late 1970s, they have maintained a growing following in south Louisiana with their easygoing, updated-Cajun acoustic sound. Terry Huval on fiddle and vocals, Reggie Matte on accordion and vocals, Tony Huval on drums and Bobby Dumatrait on guitar have made up the core of Jambalaya since the mid-1980s. Rick Benoit plays electric bass, having replaced Kenneth David recently.

Bandleader Terry Huval (b. 1956) has many talents, playing fiddle, dobro, steel guitar, mandolin and acoustic guitar. In 1988, he was named "Up and Coming Musician" in the *Times of Acadiana* Music Poll. Accordionist Matte, formerly with the Church Point Playboys, has played professionally since he was 13 and has won several regional accordion contests. In 1991, the Cajun French Music Association of Louisiana nominated him "Male Vocalist of the Year" and nominated as "Song of the Year" his tune "Gone, Gone, Gone." Tony Huval, Terry's brother, was named "Best Cajun Drummer" by the

Times of Acadiana Music Poll in 1988 and 1990. Dumatrait won "Best Cajun Guitarist" distinction by the same poll in 1989.

The Huval brothers, from Pont Breaux, started the original band Jambalaya (all of whom were from the Breaux Bridge area), which played from 1977 until the mid-80s. The brothers then played with **Michael Doucet**, **Jo-El Sonnier** and other Cajun performers in the Lafayette area. Dumatrait joined the Huvals after a career in regional country and rock. Matte came from the Pointe Noire area and played originally with Bee Cormier's Church Point Playboys and other local dance bands.

THE BEST

Laisse les Jeunes Jouer! (Let the Young Ones Play!)

r. & i. 1994/Swallow 6115 CD, CS

Jambalaya produces a full sound for a five-piece band, their collective experience showing. Over the years, they have developed richness, learned to arrange better and acquired better sound production. All the players are strong instrumentalists, and Matte and Terry Huval are good vocalists. For this recording, the band produced a wealth of good Cajun songs, most of them original. "Merci M. Dewey," a tribute to Dewey Balfa, is beautiful. Other good tunes are "Notre Petit Ange," a waltz by Tony and Kathie Huval about their daughter, and the instrumental "Swallow Two-Step."

EXCELLENT

Le Nouvel Esprit de la Musique Cadien
(The New Spirit of Cajun Music)

i. 1988/Swallow 6075 CS, LP

This is the first recording by the group that makes up Jambalaya today. Outstanding songs and arrangements are grounded in impressive musical abilities. Terry Huval handles most of the vocals, but Matte does a good job, as well, particularly on "Mon Tour Va Venir un Jour." Other great songs are "L'Accordeon qui a Fait le Monde Danser," "Bon Whisky" and the beautiful waltz, "La Belle de la Campagne," with a wonderful vocal by Terry Huval.

Instrumental Collection

r. 1991; i. 1992/Swallow 6094 CD, CS

Instrumental recordings are risky—they require excellent musicians and a varied repertoire. This CD succeeds, maintaining a lively pace with a good musical mix. However, more ensemble work augmenting the string of solos would have created even better variety. The best tunes are the fast-paced "Ossun Two-Step" and "Quoi Faire," together with the waltz, "Madame Sosthene."

C'Est Fun! (It's Fun!)

r. & i. 1990/Swallow 6085 CD, CS, LP (contains 10 of 12 songs from the Swallow LP Le Nouvel Esprit de la Musique Cadien)

This aptly-named disc offers a generous 23 songs. "La Coulee Rodaire" has a good vocal by Matte. The instrumental "The Jambalaya Hot Step" features Matte's great accordion, and Terry Huval does a superb vocal on Lawrence Walker's "Les 'Tites Yeux Noirs."

GOOD

Buggy Full of Cajun Music

i. 1979/Swallow 6035 LP

This early recording has different instrumentation—accordion, bass, steel guitar and drums—from the band's current one. Terry Huval's vocals are excellent, as are the sound and mixing, especially for 1979. Two waltzes, "Madame Sostan" and "Valse de Tete Dur," stand out.

Joyeux Noel

i. 1992/Swallow 6100 CD, CS

A mixture of quiet Christmas carols and lively seasonal pop numbers. The band is at its usual high performance level, with vocals by both Terry Huval and Reggie Matte. "La Nuit Silente" (Silent Night), "Cette Veille de Christmas" (This Christmas Eve), "Si Loin Dans un Creche" (Away in a Manger) and an instrumental version of "Joy to the World" all do justice to the holiday.

JOHNNY JANOT

Vocals, rhythm guitar, harmonica, piano

Janot's main melieu was radio. He was the longtime host of the popular Sunday morning "Cajun Bandstand" show on KLVI Beaumont, heard from Corpus Christi, Tx., to New Orleans. Previously, he worked for radio stations in Eunice and Lake Charles and played Cajun and Cajun-country music on weekends.

He was born in Eunice in 1933. The first music he played was Cajun and country music; later he turned to rockabilly with his band, the Jumpin' Jacks. His "Havin' a Whole Lot of Fun" was local record producer J. D. Miller's first rockabilly recording leased to Excello. Although the 1956 tune faded for lack of promotion, it won appreciation 20 years later when the session's warm-up tapes were released as an album by Flyright. Janot also recorded a 1957 rock 'n' roll tune, "Mabel's Gone," for Goldband and some country songs, mainly for the Jador label.

Finally, he returned to his Cajun roots and cut a series of albums before his death in 1984. These musical identity shifts are reflected in how he spelled his name over the years: from Janot to Jano and back again to Janot.

THE BEST

I'm Proud to be a Cajun

i. 1980/Delta 1006 LP

Janot could certainly deliver a song, although he sometimes squandered his talents on questionable material—for instance, he talks throughout the title track. Phil Menard and the Louisiana Travelers are pros who provide strong back-up, and Janot excells on two traditional Cajun songs, Nathan Abshire's "Pine Grove Blues" and "Big Mamou." Also good are "Blues Stay Away From Me" and Janot's own "The Ways of a Cajun" and "Girls Love Cowboys."

GOOD

Expose Yourself to Cajun Music and Johnny Janot

i. 1983/Swallow 6050 CS, LP

Again, the song quality is not up to Janot's vocals. He favors his own compositions, some of which are good and some are not. The only truly fine song is "Kaplan Waltz."

OTHER RECORDINGS

Sings Cajun Pure

Goldband 7775 LP

ROBERT JARDELL

Accordion, vocals

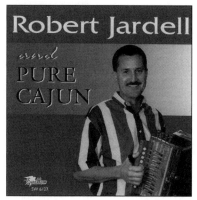

Swallow CD 6127

When traditionalist Robert Jardell plays his accordion, the spirit of his idol, **Nathan Abshire**, hovers. Jardell (b. 1957, Morse) began playing at eight, taught by a family friend. While playing dances in Basile, he encountered Abshire and became influenced by his music. In 1975, he started playing with **Dewey Balfa**; he can be heard on Balfa's recordings *Souvenirs* and *Fait a la Main*.

A trucking accident forced Jardell to stop playing for a number of years, but now he's back with his own group, Pure Cajun. The band includes fiddler Milton Joseph Melancon Sr., who has toured with the Balfas; brothers Edwin Guidry on rhythm guitar and Edmond Guidry on drums; and Jody Viator on bass. They appeared at the 1996 New Orleans Jazz & Heritage Festival and have cut one CD.

Robert Jardell and Pure Cajun

i. 1995/Swallow 6127 CD, CS

An overdue debut, this strong CD stars Jardell's assured and faultless accordion playing. He has a good mid-range voice, but he strains on high notes, as on "Manuel Bar Waltz," and low ones, as on "Bad News." Fiddler Melancon is excellent, and the rhythm section is so good that they go unnoticed, which is generally as it should be. "Waltz of Regret" and "Eunice Two Step" bring out Jardell's voice best, while "Amedee Two Step" does the same for his accordion playing.

DOUG KERSHAW

(Douglas James Kershaw)
Fiddle, vocals

The first modern Cajun-country superstar, Doug Kershaw single-handedly represented Cajun music to a national audience for a long period before it was fashionable. A flamboyant performer and a wild man with a fiddle, he is also a talented songwriter who pioneered bending Cajun to new pop styles to reach mainstream America. His country-rock style resulted in such hits as his signature song, "Louisiana Man."

Despite his Nashville persona, Kershaw is the real thing—a Cajun born in 1936 on a houseboat on the Gulf Coast island of Tiel Ridge, where his father trapped, fished and hunted alligators in the swamps and bayous. His father shot himself when Doug was only seven, whereupon the family moved to Lake Arthur. There Kershaw learned English and earned money by shining shoes and playing fiddle on street corners. At eight, he performed with his mother, Rita, in a local club called the Bucket of Blood. In 1947, he moved to Jennings and at the age of 15 was playing with two of his three brothers, **Rusty** and Nelson (Pee-Wee), in their band, the Continental Playboys.

Kershaw cut his first single, the self-penned "When Will I Learn," in English, with Jay Miller's Feature Records in Crowley. Then Kershaw teamed up with his guitar-playing brother, Rusty, for more country recordings and broadcasts on Miller's own radio show.

Miller's promotions of the brothers led to a recording contract in 1955 with Hickory Records in Nashville; Doug was 18, and Rusty was 16. Doug's tune "So Lovely Baby" kicked off their career as "Rusty and Doug."

The duo recorded extensively but took three years to make a mark on the country charts, with "Hey Sheriff." (Meanwhile, Doug picked up a math degree at McNeese State University.) However, in 1956 their career got a boost when they became regulars on the Wheeling Jamboree, a popular country show out of Wheeling, W.Va. The next year, the Everly Brothers-style pair hit the big time when they were invited to join Grand Ole Opry.

Their developing career as regional stars was interrupted the following year when they were drafted into the Army. On their return to Nashville in 1960 they recorded two Cajun songs for Hickory–"Louisiana Man" by Doug and "Diggy Liggy Lo" by Jay Miller–which rose to No. 10 and No. 14, respectively, on the country charts. They remain the songs most closely identified with Kershaw. After one more successful recording, "Cajun Stripper" in 1963, the brothers split up and Doug set out on his own.

In the late 1960s, Kershaw adopted a new persona–"the Cajun Hippie"– and his solo career took flight. He gave manic performances in brightly colored velvet suits and flowing hair on various TV variety shows, including Johnny Cash's. He also began a long partnership with Warner Brothers Records upon the 1969 release of the album *The Cajun Way* and became a favorite of many rock critics charmed by his bayou-steeped country-rock. Kershaw also appeared in a few movies and caught a moment of fame when his "Louisiana Man" was played during the Apollo 12 moonshot.

For the next decade Kershaw symbolized Cajun music to Americans in that he was all

they were likely to hear. While Cajun maestro **Dewey Balfa** and zydeco king **Clifton Chenier** toiled in a small niche market, Kershaw sawed his fiddle on national TV and enjoyed record sales with a major label –achievements other Louisiana musicians couldn't imagine. Irrepressible, he tossed off stunts like getting married onstage at the Houston Astrodome. But by the time pure Cajun music started its revival in the 1980s, Kershaw had burned out. Like other teen stars, he was unable to maintain success in the face of the rigors of touring and lack of good management. His recording output on CBS in 1979 and 1981 does not approach the quality of his earlier work for Warner, and he has not released anything in years. His live performances can also be uneven.

In 1994, Kershaw returned to Lake Arthur to settle down and write his autobiography. Although Cajun audiences have never warmed to his Nashville style, Kershaw has nevertheless won respect among musicians for his songwriting and fiddling prowess and for pioneering a new sound. For example, he was one of the first Cajun musicians to use a drum kit and bass fiddle. He explained to author John Broven, "With rhythm and blues coming up so big in the fifties it was so obvious: you either had that rhythm or you were in trouble. That changed the whole thing."

THE BEST

The Best of Doug Kershaw

i. 1989/Warner Bros. 25964 CD, CS

These selections from the Warner Brothers vaults represent some of Kershaw's best work, compiled from a series of LPs beginning with Kershaw's first Warner album, *The Cajun Way*, released in 1969, up to the 1977 *Flip Flop & Fly*. The CD features his characteristic romping songs with a strong beat, although his great fiddling comes through from time to time. The disc has only one instrumental, "Mamou Two-Step." Known for his songwriting, Kershaw wrote six of the 10 tunes here.

EXCELLENT

The Louisiana Man

i. 1978/Warner Bros. 3166 CS, LP

Although Warner's Buddy Killen produced Kershaw's excellent first six albums, in 1978 producer Bob Johnston was the right man at the right time. Side one is nearly perfect, starting off with Hank Williams' classic "Jambalaya." This version of "Louisiana Man" is one of the best recorded, with a strong bass drum beat and an excellent mix polishing the infectious tune. Randy Newman's beautiful "Marie," splendidly arranged by Jim Ed Norman (who also arranged "Jambalaya") features Kershaw's vocal, backed by piano to good effect. Side two doesn't quite match side one, but the pretty waltz "The Sooner I Go" is a high point.

Alive & Pickin'

r. & i. 1975/Warner Bros. 2851 CS, LP

The spontaneity of Kershaw's live performance at Great South East Music Hall in Atlanta carries the day. Nicely produced by Warner's Buddy Killen with strong musicians and back-up vocalists, Kershaw is well-supported. Applause and crowd noise add to the excitement, which begins with a rousing rendition of "Diggy Liggy Lo" and continues with a stand-out version of "Louisiana Man." "Battle of New Orleans" and "Orange Blossom Special/You Are My Sunshine" capture Kershaw's spectacular fiddle, which is downplayed on most of his other recordings.

The Cajun Way

i. 1969/Warner Bros. 1820 CS, LP

Kershaw's first effort for Warner was a

notable beginning, with all but one of the excellent tunes self-penned. This "Diggy Diggy Lo" features his wonderful fiddle abilities; other highlights are the waltz "If We Don't Stop Running" and the uptempo "Come Kiss Your Man." Side two is pure gold, the best nuggets being "Rita, Put Your Black Shoes On," "Sweet Jole Blon' " and a slower-than-usual "Louisiana Man."

Hot Diggity Doug

i. 1989/BGM 011589 CD

Despite the fact that this release was recorded in four different cities (Nashville, San Antonio, New Orleans and Bogalusa) with four different producers, it is one of Kershaw's more even recordings. It boasts high-quality arrangements, good musicianship and a strong beat. Outstanding tunes are "Jambalaya", "Louisiana Man" and "Cajun Stripper."

Spanish Moss

i. c. 1970/Warner Bros. 1861 LP

Kershaw wrote all but one of the 11 songs. His "I've Got Mine" contains some of his most interesting lyrics and a dramatic delivery. Also welcome is his great fiddle playing (all too scarce on his recordings) on "Orange Blossom Special." Other good tunes are "My Uncle Able" and "Swamp Rat," which features yells, growls and great fiddling.

GOOD

Devil's Elbow

i. 1972/Warner Bros. 2649 LP

This album has a country & western feel, probably due to the country music writers producer Buddy Killen chose: Roger Miller, Don Wayne and Harlan Howard. Kershaw delivers forceful vocals on the title track and his own "Louisiana Sun," while the steel guitar, prominent on Miller's "You Don't Want

My Love," adds to the country sound. These good tunes are complemented by the offbeat "I Like Babies."

Flip Flop & Fly

i. 1977/Warner Bros. 3025 LP

A strong front side with five good songs including Jo-El Sonnier's "Louisiana Blues" and Kershaw's "Twenty-Three" and "You Won't Let Me" is matched with a weaker back side containing one good tune, Fats Domino's "I'm Walking."

Doug Kershaw

i. 1971/Warner Bros. 1906 LP

This early release is worth tracking down just to hear the wild version of "Battle of New Orleans." Kershaw wrote nine of the 11 songs, and his uptempo "Trying to Live" and the very fast "You'll Never Catch Me Walking in Your Tracks" are excellent.

Mama Kershaw's Boy

i. 1974/Warner Bros. 2793 LP

"Hippie Ti Yo" and "Mama's Got the Know How" are the only well-known songs on the LP, but there are several other good ones: "Nickel in My Pocket," "Can't Be All Bad" and "Colorado."

OTHER RECORDINGS

The Best of Doug Kershaw and Rusty Kershaw

i. 1991/Curb D2-77456 CD, CS

Instant Hero

i. 1981/CBS FZ 37428

Ragin' Cajun

i. 1976/Warner Bros. 2910 LP

Rusty and Doug and Wiley and Friends

i. 1989/Flyright (England) 619 LP

Rusty and Doug with Wiley Barkdull

i. 1991/Flyright (England) 35 CD

Rusty and Doug Kershaw with Wiley Barkdull

i. 1982/Flyright (England) 571 LP

Swamp Grass

i. 1972/Warner Bros. 2581 LP

Wichita Wildcat

i. 1979/CBS Q16035 LP

RUSTY KERSHAW
(Russell Lee Kershaw)
Guitar, vocals

Born on a houseboat in a Louisiana bayou in 1938, Rusty Kershaw to date has not achieved the success of his older brother, **Doug Kershaw,** although the duo gained popularity during the 1950s and early 1960s as "Rusty and Doug." Singing in an Everly Brothers style on their unique brand of Cajun-country tunes, with Rusty on guitar and Doug on fiddle, the two recorded fairly extensively. They were broadcast on regional radio stations, became regulars on the Wheeling Jamboree, a prominent country show from Wheeling, W.Va., and even appeared on Grand Ole Opry. They first recorded for Jay Miller's local Feature Records, then signed with Warner Bros. Records in Nashville in 1955, when Rusty was just 16.

After a string of recordings, the duo split in 1963. While Doug's solo career took off, Rusty—the less sophisticated musician of the two—found work as an electrician with a national pipeline company. However, he continued to play music, and the two brothers still play together for live shows on occasion. Kershaw cut a solo album produced by Doug for Cotillion Records in 1969, and another, for Domino, in 1992. The latter CD features an older and presumably wiser Kersaw, who in one tune refuses a pact with the devil to turn away from Cajun music and become a Nashville country star.

THE BEST

Now and Then

i. 1992/Domino 8002 CD

You love it or hate it—few listeners are indifferent to this CD. In spite of the all-star lineup of Neil Young, Art Neville and the subdudes, this is Kershaw's recording. He wrote all but one song, sings lead vocals and plays guitar. The CD has echoes of the Band, with Kershaw sounding a little like Levon Helm. Kershaw's low voice has a Bourbon-Street-bar-band-for-too-many-years sound well-suited to his songs of bayous and backrooms. "Don't Make an Outlaw Outta Me" and the country-flavored "Boys in the Band" are excellent. So are three other rock-oriented tunes: "The Circle Song," "This is Rock & Roll" and "I Don't Like the Feeling." Not exactly Cajun music, and a radical departure from the Rusty and Doug material, but great music.

OTHER RECORDINGS

The Best of Doug Kershaw and Rusty Kershaw

i. 1991/Curb 77456 CD, CS

Cajun in Blues Country

i. 1970/Cotillion 9030

Rusty and Doug and Wiley and Friends

i. 1989/Flyright (England) 619 LP

Rusty and Doug with Wiley Barkdull

i. 1991/Flyright (England) 35 CD

Rusty and Doug Kershaw with Wiley Barkdull

i. 1982/Flyright (England) 571 LP

HARRY LAFLEUR (Harry Lee LaFleur)
Fiddle, vocals

LaFleur (b. 1934, Sword) grew up with Cajun music, as played by his fiddler father and his brother Raymond, who played with the great **Iry LeJeune**. After playing guitar for many years, Harry switched to fiddle. He has performed with LeJeune himself, as well as with **Dennis McGee**, **Nathan Abshire** and **Wallace "Cheese" Reed**. He had a radio show in Opelousas in the 1950s and led his own band, Harry and the Louisiana Aces.

During the next decade, LaFleur dropped music to run a body repair shop, but returned at the urging of his wife. He has since performed throughout the U.S. and founded the Cajun French Music Association. The other members of his band, Harry and the Cajuns, are accordionist Mark Meier, guitarist/vocalist Claudia Wood, drummer Eston Bellow, bass player Vincent Fontenot and triangle player/vocalist Ricky Duhon.

Harry and the Cajuns

i. 1988/La Louisianne 146 LP

The band focuses on instrumental Cajun music. LaFleur shows off his great fiddling abilities on nearly every song, of which the waltzes with beautiful fiddle/accordion duets are the high point. Unfortunately, the vocals don't measure up; LaFleur has an untrained voice more interesting than good. Otherwise, quality arrangements and instrumental performances produce some great Cajun songs, particularly "La Reel a Harry," "Island Blues," "A Tribute to a Musician" and "La Derniere Minuit."

Chapter 1 • Cajun & Creole

MITCH LANDRY
Accordion, vocals

Mitch Landry (b. 1958, Jennings) started out in Cajun music as a guitar player in 1985. The next year, he switched to accordion and formed the Cajun Ramblers, a band from the Baton Rouge area. At the time of his 1989 album, he was also learning to play the fiddle. He lives in Baker and works for Amoco Production Co.

Pays Des Cajuns (Homeland of the Cajuns)

i. 1990/Bedrock (England) 12 CD; Lanor 1009 LP

This is a good band in need of a good singer. Landry plays a nice accordion, and he is backed capably by steel guitarist Dallas Bourque, fiddler Donald LeJeune and a solid rhythm section. But Landry's pleasant vocals stray off key, strain at high notes and lack richness. Still, there is worthwhile music here, especially "La Valse de la Metave," "J'aimerais Oublier" and "Ensemble Encore."

SHORTY LEBLANC (Vorris LeBlanc)
Accordion

Born in 1922 in Lake Arthur, Vorris "Shorty" LeBlanc worked as a welder in an Orange, Tx., shipyard. But he is remembered as a musician's musician—a distinctive accordionist who could help turn a recording into a hit.

LeBlanc became the first Cajun accordionist to record for a major label in Nashville when Cajun-country singer **Jimmy C. Newman** invited him to play on his first Cajun album for Decca, *Folksongs of the Bayous*. LeBlanc also lent his inventiveness to "Sugar Bee" by Cleveland Crochet, his accordion wailing like a blues harmonica. The first Cajun record to crack the Billboard Hot 100, the English-lyric Cajun rock 'n' roll tune made it to No. 80 in 1961. Along with singer/steel guitar player Jay Stutes, LeBlanc added a modern sound to

fiddler Crochet's band, the Hillbilly Ramblers, renamed the Sugar Bees after Stutes became leader, and veered it back toward traditional Cajun music. The group split up when LeBlanc died in 1965.

The Best of Two Cajun Greats

(with Sidney Brown) i. 1987/Swallow 6067 CS, LP

LeBlanc had one of the most distinctive accordion sounds of any player—clear, sharp and powerful. Although a good singer, he realized he had a better vocalist in Jay Stutes, his steel guitar player. Here Stutes sings four of the seven songs, with LeBlanc taking one and guitarist Ivy Vanicor singing on two. Rufus Thibodeaux and Cleveland Crochet both play fiddle. Crochet's hit "Sugar Bee" is the premier song, but "Drunkard's Dream" and "Forgot I Was Married" are good, too.

OTHER RECORDINGS

Great Shorty LeBlanc

i. 1979/Goldband 7742 (unreviewed)

EDDIE LEJEUNE
Accordion, vocals

Rounder CD 6013

One of the most soulful purists performing today, accordionist Eddie LeJeune sings in a piercing, crying style that expresses the anguish and joy of the Cajun people. A musician since childhood, he did not record until the age of 37. It was then he emerged from the shadow of his father, accordionist/singer **Iry LeJeune**, the most influential Cajun musician of the postwar period. Although steeped in Iry's tradition, Eddie is widely respected for his own musicianship.

"It makes me feel like I've done something when I hear, 'Well, you're almost as good as your father.' That, I've heard all my life. But I'm not trying to be my father. I'm trying to be myself," LeJeune said in liner notes for his 1991 CD, *It's in the Blood.* Often discouraged over the years by comparisons with his father, he considered giving up the accordion at times, but persisted with support from his father's friends and other musicians.

He was born in Ardoin Cove, near Lacassine, in 1951, at the height of Iry's fame following his seminal 1948 recording of "Love Bridge Waltz." LeJeune barely remembers his father, who was killed when Eddie was five, but he listened intently to his records and to his mother and maternal grandmother's stories of him. His grandmother, Adelina Blanchard, also played accordion, and young Eddie learned how to play it at the age of six by watching her and trying out tunes from local Cajun radio and TV shows. Despite his father's fame, Eddie grew up in rural obscurity because his family (his mother, four siblings and grandmother) were poor and isolated by lack of transportation. To amuse themselves, the children sang Iry's songs and beat on cans with sticks for accompaniment.

As a young child, LeJeune entertained at neighborhood barbeques and house dances, partly for fun and partly dreaming of becoming as great as his father. He also played accordion and sang by himself in restaurants to pick up money for the struggling family. School was

difficult since he arrived without knowing English, and in eighth grade his mother signed a minor's work release so he could help support the family. He has worked at rice mills, roughnecked in the oil fields and been a tenant farmer—all the while playing accordion at bars for extra cash on his days off. Sometimes, he and his brother Ervin played together at house parties and local restaurants.

LeJeune performs today with various bands, including his own Morse Playboys—fiddler Lionel Leleux and guitarist Hubert Maitre, who played earlier with **Lawrence Walker**. He also plays with singer/guitarist **D. L. Menard** and fiddler Ken Smith. LeJeune prefers a small ensemble and traditional, acoustic sound. Like musicians from an earlier era, he plays his button accordion sitting down, fervently singing in the high-pitched vocal style of old. At festivals such as New Orleans Jazz & Heritage Festival, LeJeune's unadorned performances from the heart move new listeners every year. Also, his recordings have helped win him a reputation as one of the most respected Cajun musicians playing today.

THE BEST

It's in the Blood

i. 1991/Rounder 6043 CD, CS

You can hear an echo of Iry LeJeune's soulful voice here, but Eddie's individual sound comes through. Fiddler Lionel Leleux, guitarist Hubert Maitre and LeJeune's son Eddie Jr. on triangle provide a solid base for LeJeune. His command of the accordion is impressive and melancholy vocals always on the mark. Like his father's, his songs convey the Cajun people's years of hardship and his own family's struggle to survive. Among the 15 songs are four by Eddie and traditional tunes he arranged or added new lyrics to, as well as two by Iry LeJeune. The best are Iry's "Duralde Waltz," the smooth-flowing "J'aimerais tu Viens me Chercher," (Please Come Get Me) and Eddie's own "Les Conseil's J'ai Ecoute" (The Advice I Took).

EXCELLENT

Cajun Soul

i. 1988/Rounder 6013 CD, CS, LP

This debut disc showcases LeJeune, with back-up from two masters–singer/guitarist D. L. Menard and fiddler Ken Smith. The unamplified sound Eddie prefers enhances the fine songs. LeJeune shows he can handle any song, from the fast, swing-style "Grand Bosco" to the Cajun waltzes. His emotional voice brings the lyrics to life, and he demonstrates his accordion mastery. His own "Little Broken Heart," plus "La Valse de Samedi au Soir" and "Cher 'Ti Monde" are a few of the finest tunes.

Le Trio Cadien

(with D. L. Menard & Ken Smith) i. 1992/Rounder 6049 CD, CS

This Grammy-nominated CD offers mostly traditional Cajun songs done by three virtuosos. Menard shares vocals with LeJeune, whose accordion provides strong support for the other players and captivates on his solos. Menard's vocals and rhythm guitar are rock-steady, while Ken Smith–one of the best young fiddlers today–is in top form here. LeJeune's unpolished, emotive voice is perfect for Cajun classics such as "Chere Tout-Toute" and Amedee Ardoin's "Eunice Two Step."

IRY LEJEUNE

Accordion, vocals

Iry LeJeune is considered one of the two greatest Cajun accordion players of all time,

along with **Amedee Ardoin**. He is also one of the most loved–for putting soul back into southwest Louisiana music during the slick western string-band era. His 1948 hit recording "Love Bridge Waltz" returned Cajun music to its raw, accordion-based roots. Following World War II, homesick veterans and other Cajuns sought out the kind of music popular more than a decade before, and no one captured that early, poignant style better than LeJeune.

LeJeune's inspiration came from Ardoin, the legendary black Creole singer/accordionist, whose recordings from the 1920s-1930s he devoured as a youngster at the home of his uncle, Angelas LeJeune. Angelas himself played accordion and had recorded 78s that Iry listened to, along with those of **Amedee Breaux**; it was Angelas' accordion on which Iry learned. The youngster, born in 1928 outside Church Point to poor tenant farmers, was nearly blind. Unable to work in the fields, he turned to music. Whether by way of Ardoin or of his own hard experience, LeJeune's spine-chilling songs of pain and desolation stand as the ultimate expression of the Cajun voice.

Like Ardoin, LeJeune walked and hitchhiked with his accordion in a flour sack to wherever he could find people to listen to him. Sometimes he joined other musicians at dances. In the late 1940s, he moved to Lacassine, near Lake Charles, where he had trouble breaking into the music scene because the accordion was out of favor. But he met a fiddler named Floyd LeBlanc who took him to Houston in 1948 to cut "Love Bridge Waltz"/"Evangeline Special" for the Opera label. The record's popularity boosted his career and triggered renewed interest by record companies in traditional Cajun music sung in French.

LeJeune played first in Houston clubs, then back in Louisiana. But not everyone bought the Cajun revival sound. Goldband Records producer Eddie Shuler almost got fired for having LeJeune on his Lake Charles radio show to play what the station manager regarded as ungodly music. Shuler stuck by LeJeune, recording him often in LeJeune's tiny prairie home with enough cracks in the walls that on one song, the family dog can be heard barking outside. Today, these piercingly beautiful recordings are as well-loved as they were in his lifetime, despite their rough quality. All his songs were hits, making LeJeune the most popular Cajun musician of his day and kicking off Shuler's Cajun recording enterprise, which greatly influenced the spread of the genre.

As the biggest-selling Cajun artist, the young musician with the bottle-thick glasses supported his wife and five children by playing at southwest Louisiana clubs and dance halls, with a strong and distinctly unslick band consisting of Duckhead Cormier (and occasionally Eddie Shuler) on guitar, Wilson Granger on fiddle and Robert Bertrand on drums. LeJeune's genius dominated, with his imaginative interpretations of simple two-steps and waltzes, dazzlingly complicated accordion style and heart-wrenching singing.

"When you hear Iry LeJeune's voice it makes you want to cry. It makes you feel like you got the blues," Lake Charles musician Crawford Vincent said in liner notes for *Cajun's Greatest–The Definitive Collection*. Vincent played with LeJeune early on. Along with his plain, scruffy appearance and French singing, LeJeune's truly Cajun voice and repertoire almost single-handedly restored Cajun music to its roots after years of string bands dressed up in cowboy outfits and singing in English.

LeJeune's rising star fell in 1955 when he was killed by a passing car while stopping to change a tire on his way home from a dance in Eunice. An obituary revealing public ignorance about Cajuns described the 27-year-old musical giant as "a well-known hillbilly musician." His son, **Eddie LeJeune**, carries on his legacy.

THE BEST

Cajun's Greatest–The Definitive Collection 🎻

r. 1948-1955; i. 1992/Ace (England) 428 CD (also available as Sire 26312 CD, CS)

A TOP 10 CAJUN ALBUM

This aptly-titled CD collects 25 songs recorded over the seven-year period before LeJeune's death, including his 1948 hit "Love Bridge Waltz" and "Evangeline Special" for the Opera label in Houston and the many tunes recorded thereafter for Eddie Shuler's Goldband label. The CD restores the historic recordings to their pure form, without a bass guitar overdub that appeared on the Goldband albums. Despite rough sound quality, the selections show why LeJeune's powerful performances changed Cajun music forever. His intense singing and skillful accordion playing were rivaled only by those of Amedee Ardoin.

In fact, many of the songs here are reworkings of Ardoin's earlier recordings. An example is "La Valse a Abe," which LeJeune turned into "Convict Waltz," one of his greats. Other outstanding cuts include "Grand Bosco," "Waltz of the Mulberry Limb", "La Valse du Grande Chemin" and "Evangeline Special". The CD has informative liner notes by author/musician Ann Savoy.

EXCELLENT

The Legendary Iry LeJune

i. 1991/Goldband 7741 CD (contains CS/LP 7740 & 7741)

The songs are the same as on *Cajun's Greatest*. The two LPs from which the CD is made–*The Legendary Iry LeJune, Vol. 1 & 2*– were assembled from the original Goldband 78s.

THE MAGNOLIA SISTERS
Group

Arhoolie CD 439

Guitarist Ann Savoy and fiddler Jane Vidrine provide the core of this band, which on their CD also adds guest "sisters" Lisa McCauley, Tina Pilione and Deborah Helen Viator. (One of the group's original members, New Orleans Jazz & Heritage Festival co-founder Allison Miner, died in 1995.)

Savoy also plays guitar with the esteemed **Savoy-Doucet Cajun Band**, along with her husband, **Marc Savoy**, and **Beausoleil**'s **Michael Doucet**. The inspiration for the Magnolia Sisters was born when Ann Savoy and Vidrine sang together informally at a crawfish boil at the Savoys in the early 1990s and found their voices blended. Indeed, their vocal duets–unusual in Cajun music–are the main feature of the group.

Sharing the common experience of having left distant homes to move to Louisiana, the Magnolia Sisters named their album after early Cajun recording star **Cleoma Falcon's** lament about leaving loved ones, "Prends Courage" (Take Courage).

Prends Courage

i. 1995/Arhoolie 439 CD, CS

Some tunes from this collection of old favorites get a reworking to reflect a woman's perspective, for example Amedee Breaux's "Les Fils a Nonc Hilaire" and D. L. Menard's "Il Savait Pas J'etais Mariee." Savoy's and Vidrine's voices blend superbly, with arrangements bringing out the beauty of both the voices and the old songs. The instrumental work is not always perfect, but the weak spots don't detract from the music as a whole. The swapping of leads, such as with the twin fiddles and the accordion, creates interest, as do the contributions by the guest "sisters." The title song, the catchy "Tasso" and "La Robe Barree" are beautifully performed.

MAMOU
Group

Rounder CD 6050

Once hard-edged Cajun rockers, Steve LaFleur and his merry band of musicians can turn traditional when they want to. In the late 1970s, a teen-aged LaFleur formed a psychedelic rock band called Fantasia, followed by a punk group called the Movie Stars, who occasionally backed traditional Cajun musicians. Then he dipped into punk/new wave for several years, moving to Atlanta and New York in the mid-1980s.

LaFleur returned to Louisiana when homesickness brought on a new appreciation of his roots. After attending a Cajun fiddle festival, he bought a fiddle and began to study recordings of the **Balfa Brothers** and **Marc Savoy**; he also taught himself French. Eventually, his opposing musical influences merged in Mamou, named after his Louisiana hometown.

Mamou's recording history has bounced from a 1988 rock-influenced album to an acoustic Cajun album in 1992. Whether this demonstrates simply pinball wizardry or a maturing evolution remains to be seen.

THE BEST

Ugly Day

r. 1991; i. 1992/Rounder 6050 CD, CS

The excellence of this straight-ahead acoustic Cajun album should encourage Mamou to continue in this direction. The recording captures the spirit of "Ugly Day," the anarchic pre-Mardi Gras celebration in the band's hometown of Mamou. A weak vocal mars "It's Raining," but that is the only low point on the release. Hints of LaFleur's rock and new wave background appear but don't distract on this CD, which represents modern Cajun music near its best. Good songs, great musicianship and imaginative arrangements abound. The eerie "Ugly Day Stomp" opens bucolically with crickets and other swamp sounds as background for four wild Cajun fiddles that build to a frenetic climax, then fade into the swamp for the finish. Another outstanding

arrangement is the Balfa Brothers' "La Danse de Mardi Gras." Other highlights are three hard-driving tunes–"Opelousas Sostan," "Joli Coeur" and "Homme a Pitier"–and LaFleur's pretty waltz, "Big Mamou." All feature LaFleur's forceful vocals.

GOOD

Mamou

i. 1988/MCA Records 10124 CD

More rock than Cajun, with distorted sound and shades of punk (as on "Between the Lines"), this album demonstrates the problem with combining disparate types of music. On "Bebe Catin" the blended approach works; on "La Valse de Balfa," it doesn't. The best songs are those on which Cajun prevails, as on the slightly Cajun "Les Flammes d'en Fer" and the definitely Cajun "La Louisiane" and "La Danse de Mardi Gras." On the latter, Steve LaFleur's vocal opens and is soon joined by a hard-driving back-up to create an exciting song.

MAMOU PRAIRIE BAND
Group

This ultra-traditional Cajun band sticks to waltzes and two-steps in the old manner. Their sound is full–the group's first recording featured nine musicians; their second had seven. Influences ranging from **Iry LeJeune** to **Nathan Abshire** to **Austin Pitre** echo in their albums.

THE BEST

Oh, Yaille!

i. 1996/Swallow 6129 CD, CS

The pared-down band on this latest recording retains their full sound and strong beat. Bob Reed's fine accordion takes a back seat to the fiddles. Carl Fontenot's voice is somewhat reminiscent of D. L. Menard's, and all his vocals are excellent, especially on "Chameaux One Step" and "Chere Be-Be Creole." Guitarist and fiddler Faren Serrette also sings well. The arrangements are tight, as can be heard on the nice instrumental "Blue Runner," featuring Mitch Reed's fiddle.

EXCELLENT

Catch My Hat

i. 1993/Swallow 6109 CD, CS

Bob Reed's accordion takes center stage, along with the fiddles. Carl Fontenot and Randy Vidrine provide strong vocals; and Mitch Reed, who later became lead fiddler, does an excellent job on the instrumental "Blue Runner." Other outstanding numbers are the Cajun waltz "Valse de Criminelle" and the uptempo "Two-Step de Lac Charles," both featuring Fontenot's vocals.

MCCAULEY, REED, VIDRINE
(Cory McCauley, Mitchell Reed, Randy Vidrine)
Group

This traditional young Cajun trio is an early version of **Tasso**, another trio made up of fiddler Mitchell Reed and guitarist Randy Vidrine, with a different accordionist. Cory McCauley was a student at the University of Southwestern Louisiana in Lafayette when he joined Reed and Vidrine to perform the old-time Cajun songs in French that he had learned growing up. The group plays acoustic music in the old manner.

Accordionist McCauley was born in 1968 on the Soileau Prairie and started playing music at 16, influenced by Hadley Fontenot, **Marc Savoy** and **Octa Clark**. Reed (b. 1971, Bayou Vista) plays fiddle and cello. He learned from **Wade Fruge** and others.

Vidrine (b. 1954, Ville Platte) studied guitar and violin with George Fontenot.

1929 and Back

r. 1990; i. 1991/Swallow 6090 CS, LP

These three quality musicians pull off fine instrumentals like "Old Crowley Two-Step" and "Midland Two-Step." The vocals pose a problem, however. McCauley is a sterling accordion player, but a poor singer. Vidrine, who sings well on **Tasso**'s recordings, doesn't measure up here. Two exceptions are "Pistache a Tante Nana" and "Valse a Austin Ardoin." Uneven sound quality doesn't help.

DENNIS MCGEE
Fiddle, vocals

McGee was the dean of Cajun fiddlers until his death in 1989 at the age of 96, after a career stretching over six decades. With a store of dance tunes reaching back almost two centuries, McGee was a link to the culture's pre-accordion past and a key influence on its modern development. Through a unique musical partnership, he and black Creole accordionist/singer **Amedee Ardoin** created a great deal of the Cajun repertoire. Equally as important was his collaboration of more than 70 years with **Sady Courville**; they were the most famous Cajun twin fiddlers.

McGee was born in 1893 in Bayou Marron, near Eunice, to a father of Irish descent and a half-French, half-Seminole Indian mother. When he was two his mother died, and he and a brother were left on the family farm in the care of their eight-year-old brother. Later, McGee was passed to his grandmother, at whose house the boy first heard his father play fiddle. At 10, he was sent to live with an older cousin, Ben Courville, a farmer. McGee worked miserably there until running away four years later and finding a loving home at last with another cousin, Theodore McGee.

Theodore bought Dennis his first fiddle, when he was 14. Six months later, he was playing house dances. Despite the boy's unstable upbringing, he had learned to play fiddle from his father (whence Irish traces in his music) and other relatives. When McGee met his younger neighbor, Sady Courville, he learned old songs from Sady's father and uncle, popular twin fiddlers. At the house dances of 90-year-old accordionist Gustave Ardoin, he learned contradanses, gigues, reels, mazurkas and other music harking back to the 1700s.

McGee married twice and fathered five children whom he left in others' care when his second wife died. Always poor, he worked here and there as a tenant farmer. He played music on the side, traveling with Courville to country dances in a horse and buggy. He also performed with Amedee Ardoin, with whom he sharecropped for various farmers. In a musical collaboration lasting more than two decades, the close friends performed for both black and white audiences, reflecting the synthesis of Cajun and Creole music at that time. Toward the end of his life, McGee mentioned missing Ardoin, whose emotional singing made him shake when Ardoin cried out.

In 1927, McGee married his third wife, Sady Courville's sister Gladys, and had 10 more children. He worked at a series of jobs to support the family, who were always poor and on the move. Often food and fuel were scarce in winter, when the children went to school barefoot. Still, McGee played dances and honky-tonked.

In 1928, McGee and Courville put their fiddles in flour sacks and headed to New Orleans in Courville's new Model T to cut their first records. Subsequently, McGee also recorded with Ardoin, accordionist Angelas LeJeune and fiddler Ernest Fruge. By 1934, McGee had recorded 53 times, half on his own and half accompanying other artists.

By the 1950s, he was living in Eunice and working on the farm of Louis Savoy, accordionist **Marc Savoy**'s grandfather. Later, McGee worked as a barber. He gave up music for a time in the belief that it had brought bad luck to his family, but resumed it in 1970 when the Cajun music renaissance got underway. Then followed a late-in-life career of national tours with Courville and appearances at the Washington, D.C., national folk festival. He also taught many young musicians like **Michael Doucet**. In his 90s, he still performed regularly with such luminaries as Doucet, **Dewey Balfa** and **Canray Fontenot**.

In 1972, Morning Star Records put out two albums, one solo and the other with Courville. Five years later, the local Swallow label recorded an album of Courville and McGee, who was 84 at the time. McGee recorded only a fraction of the many dances he knew from the days when dancers demanded greater variety than the waltzes and two-steps of today. Many of his recorded tunes gained widespread popularity; for example, "Adieu, Rosa," now known as "Les Flammes d'Enfer."

The albums reveal a forceful, decorative fiddling technique, along with a piercing singing style. His playing was complex in tuning, timing and melody line. Although McGee drew on multiple influences, he never bent to modern trends. As he said in liner notes for *The Complete Early Recordings*, "I play *French*! I play my tunes *plain*! I don't mix them up with nothing."

Chapter 1 • Cajun & Creole

THE BEST

The Complete Early Recordings of Dennis McGee 1929-1930 🪗

i. 1994/Shanachie/Yazoo 2012 CD

A TOP 10 CAJUN ALBUM

We are fortunate to have these splendid early recordings featuring McGee's fiddling and singing, formerly available only on rare 78s. McGee created catchy songs, many with a hint of swing. Here they range from turn-of-the-century reels to Creole-based songs such as the wonderful "Adieu, Rosa." Other great tunes are "Mon Chere Bebe Creole," "La Valse de Vacher" and "La Valse des Reids." With his enormous command of the fiddle, McGee tries variations others wouldn't dare to. He also had two superb second fiddlers in Sady Courville and Ernest Fruge. Courville seconds on about two-thirds of the recordings, revealing a sensitive grasp of what best augments McGee. Fruge drove McGee harder, with his more dramatic style.

Musician/author Ann Savoy co-produced the album. As she says in the thorough liner notes, the recording captures "a strong, virile, accomplished young Cajun musician crying his life and tunes onto shellac." The album's remastering is meticulous, with preserving the music in its entirety a priority over total elimination of noise. Generally, the sound is no problem. Forget the occasional scratches and the hiss, and be swept away by the music.

EXCELLENT

La Vielle Musique Acadienne

r. & i. 1977/Swallow 6030 LP

Eighty-four and 71 respectively at the time, Dennis McGee and Sady Courville showed no diminution of their musical gifts; their twin fiddling was still fresh and vibrant. McGee's vocals are still powerfully soulful, though his fiddling is less adventuresome here than in his early years. Courville's perceptive backing anticipates McGee's every move. The six decades they had played together by this time shows in their relaxed musical relationship. Outstanding songs include "Kathleen's Waltz," "Courville Breakdown," "Rosa, Tomorrow is Not Sunday" and "Tante Aleene's Waltz."

Cajun & Creole Masters

r. 1986; i. 1995/Music of the World 138 CD

McGee and Courville share this CD with two Creole masters, fiddler Canray Fontenot and accordionist "Bois Sec" Ardoin. McGee (93 at the time) and Courville (80), together with Michael Doucet on guitar, create nine beautiful tracks. McGee's voice hints at his age, but he could be taken for a singer decades younger. Courville's second fiddling powers are undiminished. Good sound quality enhances the recording, which includes seven fine songs by Fontenot and Ardoin and interesting interviews with the artists. "Ville Platte Two-Step" and "La Valse Qui Finit Dans le Coin de la Maison," featuring McGee's soaring fiddle, stand out.

GOOD

Amede Ardoin: I'm Never Comin' Back

r. 1930, 1934/i. 1995/Folklyric 7007 CD

McGee backed Creole accordionist Amedee Ardoin, his musical partner and friend, for a 1930 New Orleans session and a 1934 session in San Antonio. Although his fiddling can scarcely be heard on tracks featuring Ardoin's accordion, he can be heard well behind Ardoin's vocals on "Les Blues Crowley" and "Oberlin."

Amede Ardoin: Louisiana Cajun Music, Vol. 6

r. 1929, 1930; i. c. 1981/Old Timey 124 LP

McGee backs accordionist/vocalist Ardoin. Although Ardoin's accordion dominates, McGee's fiddle is pronounced on "I'm Never

Coming Back," particularly behind Ardoin's vocals. On "Madame Etienne," McGee provides strong backing and is featured briefly.

Pioneers of Cajun Accordion 1929-1935

(collection) i. 1989/Old Timey 128 CS, LP

McGee backs Amedee Ardoin on five songs, but his playing is faint; he is best heard on "Valse de Opelousas." In terms of McGee, the record is best suited for students of Cajun fiddle. However, it has other excellent Cajun and early zydeco music.

OTHER RECORDINGS

The Early Recordings of Dennis McGee

r. 1928-1930; i. 1972/Morning Star 45002 LP (unreviewed)

Traditional Cajun Fiddling

(McGee & Courville) i. 1972/Morning Star 16001 LP (unreviewed)

D. L. MENARD (Doris Leon Menard)
Vocals, guitar

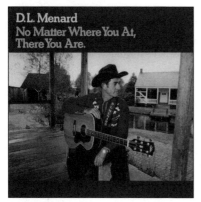

Rounder LP 6021

Nicknamed "The Cajun Hank Williams," D.L. Menard brings a soulful vocal style to his country-tinged tunes. He sings largely in French, with the traditional Cajun nasal "holler." Surprisingly for a Cajun musician, he plays guitar—not fiddle or accordion—and is

perhaps the best rhythm guitarist in the business. Menard's outstanding songwriting makes him a major force in Cajun music, while his warmth makes him one of the most loved.

Menard has written some of the best-known Cajun songs, including the 1962 hit, "La Porte dans Arriere" (The Back Door), a satire on the Cajun stereotype that has been called the second Cajun anthem after "Jolie Blonde." It is an exuberant song, complete with Cajun yells, about a hard-drinking, brawling, honky-tonking Cajun who creeps home in disgrace through the back door.

Menard was born to a farming family in 1932 in Erath. He was not exposed to Cajun bands growing up, although his father played harmonica. His major influence was country music he heard on the radio. He was working the sugarcane fields at 16 when he bought his first guitar from Montgomery Ward after hearing his uncle's Cajun band. Learning quickly, he played regularly with the band that same year in Abbeville.

In 1952, he joined the Louisiana Aces, a popular local Cajun-country band led by accordionist Elias Badeaux. Menard eventually took over the group, with whom he played for 18 years. During the 1960s, the band recorded for the Louisiana-based Swallow label, landing their first big seller with "Valse de Jolly Rogers." They topped that success with their smash hit "The Back Door." The band didn't like the song, but Menard wanted to record it because it was his seven children's favorite. The tune he had composed while pumping gas as a gas station attendant turned him into a star.

In those years, Menard composed many Cajun songs reflecting the everyday life of south Louisiana with wit and feeling. He based some of them, like "The Back Door," on tunes by Hank Williams. Williams was profoundly influencing Cajun music, and Menard had met him in 1951 at a club in New Iberia.

The Aces broke up in the late 1960s, but Menard remained active, playing dance halls and recording with various other musicians. Although his first recordings were in French, he has recorded in English, as well. The press named him "the Cajun Hank Williams" in 1973, when he was invited to play at the National Folk Festival in Vienna, Va., the first time he had played outside Louisiana. By now, he has toured dozens of countries with his current band, also called the Louisiana Aces. In 1994, he was honored for his "intense musicality" by the National Endowment for the Arts and awarded a Folk Heritage Fellowship.

When home in Erath, Menard makes handcrafted chairs and rockers at the Menard Chair Factory, located next to his house. He still thinks of himself as a chairmaker who happens to play music. Like most musicians from the prairies of southwest Louisiana, Menard has always worked hard. In a 1988 *Smithsonian* article, he is quoted as saying, "Most of us was raised poor and worked hard. We had to amuse ourselves with things that didn't cost too much, and music was one way of letting loose."

THE BEST

Cajun Memories

r. & i. 1995/Swallow 6125 CD, CS

Menard's most recent work is among his best. This CD is bouncy and fresh compared to his previous recordings, perhaps due to the abundance of new material. Only "The Back Door" is from Menard's old repertoire. All but three songs are written or cowritten by Menard, three of them with his wife, Louella Menard, who wrote the uptempo waltz "Sound of the Night." Menard's vocals are better than ever. Fiddler/producer Terry

Huval (of the Cajun band Jambalaya) plays good fiddle and steel guitar, with Horace Trahan providing strong accordion back-up. Great new Cajun music in the older tradition.

EXCELLENT

The Swallow Recordings 🪗

r. 1961-1976; i. 1991/Ace (England) 327 CD (contains 13 cuts from "The Back Door" and Other Cajun Hits/i. 1980/Swallow 6038 CS, LP + 14 tracks by Austin Pitre and the Evangeline Playboys)

A TOP 10 CAJUN ALBUM

Original analogue tapes have been remastered to produce a richer sound. This version of Menard's hit "The Back Door" with his heavy western twang is a classic. He wrote all but one of the tunes, including great renditions of "Bachelor's Life" and "The Water Pump." Menard's catchy lyrics tell a story, with a country and western flavor. Most of the songs were recorded in the early 1960s, with Menard's voice strong and musicians well chosen.

Le Trio Cadien

(with Eddie LeJeune & Ken Smith) r. & i. 1992/Rounder 6049 CD, CS

This Grammy-nominated disc features three Cajun virtuosos. Menard swaps lead vocals with accordionist Eddie LeJeune, whose singing fits perfectly with Menard's guitar and fiddling by the album's co-producer, Ken Smith. There's a a nice, lively feel to the album.

Under a Green Oak Tree

(with Dewey Balfa & Marc Savoy) r. 1976; i 1989/ Arhoolie 312 CD, CS (contains Arhoolie LP 5019 + 6 previously unissued cuts)

Three of the most respected Cajun musicians, Balfa, Menard and Savoy were also friends who fit well together as a trio. Menard takes turns with fiddler Balfa on lead vocals, with Jerry Whiten's bass adding depth. However, it is Savoy's astonishing accordion playing that sets this recording apart.

No Matter Where You At, There You Are

i. 1988/Rounder 6021 CD, CS, LP

This CD sticks more closely to traditional Cajun than Menard's others, but he does sing a few country tunes: "The Little Black Eyes" and "I Went to the Dance Last Night." According to the liner notes, co-producer Ken Irwin took special care to balance Menard's guitar in the acoustic mix so his strong rhythm contribution would come through, and it shows. Complementing him nicely are fiddler Ken Smith and accordionists Eddie LeJeune and Blackie Forestier.

OTHER RECORDINGS

"The Back Door" and Other Cajun Hits

i. 1980/Swallow 6038 CS, LP

Cajun Saturday Night

i. 1984/Rounder 0198/CD, CS, LP

D. L. Menard and the Louisiana Aces

r. 1974; i. 1988/Rounder 6003 CS, LP

JIMMY C. NEWMAN
Vocals, guitar

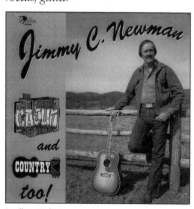

Swallow LP 6052

Country music star Jimmy C. Newman is that rarity—a Cajun musician who made it big. The first Cajun to join Grand Ole Opry, he made his fortune in Nashville, near where he lives

on a 670-acre spread called Singing Hill Ranch. Back home, the Louisiana legislature honored him as "one of Louisiana's Foremost Goodwill Ambassadors." He has dozens of Top 100 country singles. He was also the first Cajun to earn a gold record in Canada, with the 1973 French-lyric song, "Lache Pas la Patate" (Don't Drop the Potato), an exhortation to "hang in there" through hard times that has become a Cajun classic.

Hard times were no stranger to Newman, a country boy from High Point, outside Big Mamou. Born in 1927 to humble farmers, he grew up during the Depression listening to records by Jimmie Rodgers, the Carter Family and Bob Wills, and watched Gene Autry and Roy Rogers movies in town on Saturday nights. Of mixed ancestry (German, Irish, Spanish, French and Indian), he is related to fiddler **Dennis McGee** on his mother's side. His first music job, in 1946 in the Lake Charles area, was with **Chuck Guillory's** Rhythm Boys, with whom Newman sang hillbilly songs as well as some French-lyric Cajun songs. He made his first recordings with the band.

Starting in 1949, Newman cut his own first records in English for J. D. Miller's local label, Feature: "Wondering" and "I Made a Big Mistake." "Darling," a local hit co-written by Miller and Newman and recorded for Khoury, another local label, soon followed. Miller and Newman wrote more songs together, and Miller's Nashville contacts paid off in a recording session yielding a new version of "Darling," under the name "Cry Cry Darling," which hit the *Billboard* country Top 20 chart in 1954. The hits "Daydreamin'" and "Blue Darlin'" followed.

These successes led to TV appearances and a stint with Shreveport's Louisiana Hayride. In 1956 he graduated to the Opry, where he still performed as of 1995. The versatile Newman has also recorded country-rock and rockabilly. His biggest hit, "A Fallen Star," was a rock ballad. He has recorded for many labels, including Dot, MGM and Decca, where he produced such 1960s Cajun-country hits as "Alligator Man" and "Bayou Talk." He has also cut some traditional Cajun albums, such as the 1963 *Folk Songs of the Bayou Country*.

Two traditional musicians have lent Cajun authenticity to Newman's performances over the years: fiddler **Rufus Thibodeaux**, who played with him from 1951 to 1980, and accordionist Bessyl Duhon, who co-founded **Beausoleil** with **Michael Doucet**. The band also includes steel guitar, bass and piano. Proud of his Cajun heritage, Newman performs in a suit studded with rhinestone alligators and has kept the middle name once created for him by a Nashville D.J.: the "C" stands for "Cajun."

THE BEST

The Alligator Man

i. 1991/Rounder 6039 CD, CS

This CD takes Newman back to his Louisiana origins with Cajun songs sung mostly in French. He has a rich, pleasant voice and an easy way with a song. The band is enriched by such Louisiana stalwarts as fiddler Rufus Thibodeaux and accordionist Bessyl Duhon. A long overdue Cajun recording by a Louisiana artist who never lost the connection with his roots, its best tunes are "J'ai Fait une Grosse Erreur," "La Porte d'en Arriere" and the instrumental "Vieux Chance."

EXCELLENT

Louisiana Saturday Night

r. 1977-1980; i. 1987/Charly (England) 71 CD

The best of several CDs and LPs originating from Newman's stint with Plantation Records in Nashville. Fiddler Rufus Thibodeaux and

accordion player Bessyl Duhon add a Louisiana touch. "Thibodeaux and His Cajun Band," "Sweet Suzannah," "Big Mamou" and "Grand Chenier" are the best of 23 consistently good, well-produced songs.

Cajun Country Classics

i. 1992/Charly (England) 1068 CD

Same as *Louisiana Saturday Night* (above), with four songs dropped and a fair version of "Louisiana Man" added.

Lache Pas la Patate (Don't Drop the Potato)

La Louisianne 140 LP

More Cajun than country, this recording features beautiful performances of old Cajun tunes sung in French. Newman's strong, clear vocals are boosted by fiddle great Rufus Thibodeaux and an unnamed steel guitar player. The title track, "La Valse de Grand Basile," "Grand Mamou," "La Valse du Grand Chenier" and "Allons a Lafayette" stand out.

Whatever Boils Your Crawfish

i. 1995/Swallow 6122 CD, CS

Newman's vocals and his band are reliably good, but song quality doesn't hold up on his latest CD. After the first four catchy new tunes, it's hit or miss. The high points are the classics "Colinda" and "Jambalaya," as well as Bessyl Duhon's instrumental "Bessyl's Two Step." Given his vocal gifts, Newman could top the *Alligator Man* and *Saturday Night* albums if he put his mind to it.

GOOD

Cajun and Country Too!

i. 1983/Swallow 6052 CS, LP

With a country side far superior to its reverse Cajun side of mostly novelty tunes, this recording fails in its intention to display

Newman's dual talents. Even the country vocals are better, and Newman seems more at ease with them. The better tunes are "You're so Easy to Love," "Hanging the Clouds Out to Dry" and the Cajun song "Lache Pas la Patate."

Cajun Classics

i. 1995/Sun Entertainment 7018 CD

Twelve good–if not best–tunes from the Plantation sessions in Nashville. They can all be found on the CD Louisiana *Saturday Night*, along with 11 others.

Cajun Country

i. 1985/Charly/Topline (England) 131 LP

Another dozen Plantation recordings, also found on the CD *Louisiana Saturday Night*.

The Happy Cajun

i. 1979/Charly (England) 30177 LP

Yet another 12 Plantation recordings found on the CD *Louisiana Saturday Night*.

OTHER RECORDINGS

Artificial Rose

i. 1966/Decca 74748 (unreviewed)

Bop a Hula

i. 1990/Bear Family 15469 CD (unreviewed)

Cajun Cowboy

i. 1978/Plantation 530 (unreviewed)

Cajun Music

MCA 206 (unreviewed)

Country Crossroads

i. 1966/Dot 2573 (unreviewed)

Fallen Star

i. 1966/Dot 2539 (unreviewed)

Folk Songs of the Bayou Country

i. 1963/Stetson/Hat (England) 3013 LP

Greatest Hits

i. 1981/Plantation 501 (unreviewed)

Jimmy Newman

i. 1961/Stetson/Hat (England) 3060 LP

Jimmy Newman

i. 1962/Decca 4221 (unreviewed)

Jimmy Newman & Al Terry

r. 1949-1952; i. 1981/Flyright (England) 573 LP

Jimmy C. Newman & Cajun Country

i. 1986/Dot/MCA 39047 CS, LP

Jole Blon

PL 229 (unreviewed)

Louisiana Love

Playback 34001 CD (unreviewed)

More Cajun Music

i. 1986, 1995/MCA 20855 CD, CS

Progressive C. C.

i. 1977/Charly (England) 5005 LP (unreviewed)

Sings Country Songs

i. 1966/Decca 74781 (unreviewed)

16 Best of Cajun Country

PL 406 (unreviewed)

Songs by Jimmy Newman

i. 1962/MGM 4045 (unreviewed)

This is Jimmy Newman

i. 1959/MGM 3777 (unreviewed)

20 Cajun Country Classics

PL 2011 (unreviewed)

Wild 'n' Cajun

i. 1984/RCA 70437 (unreviewed)

JIM OLIVIER
Vocals

Swallow LP 6059

Olivier is best known as the host of a popular Cajun music show on KLFY-TV in Lafayette called "Passe Partout," which Louisiana and Texas Cajuns are said to turn on in the morning even before starting the coffee brewing. Since 1970, the program has showcased local Cajun bands and shown video clips of early artists, between farm prices, weather forecasts and the news.

Less impressive, but also popular in Cajun country, is Olivier's singing. Since 1980, he has turned out five Cajun-country recordings for Louisiana's Swallow label and produced several videos to promote songs from his albums. Because of his smooth vocals, his fans call him "the Cajun Jim Reeves."

Olivier was born in Arnaudville in 1951. His lucky musical career can perhaps be credited to his mother's aunt, who followed Cajun custom for producing a singer by burying his umbilical cord under a rose bush when he was born.

THE BEST

Cajun Music for Everyone

i. 1981/Swallow 6042 CS, LP

Olivier's voice fits the songs here, whereas on other recordings, the tunes are not always suited to his smooth style. Good arrangements produce a full instrumental sound, and both vocals and the band sound rich due to excellent recording at Jay Miller's Master Trak Studio in Crowley. The outstanding song selection includes the uptempo "Allons au Fais-Do-Do," "Grand Texas" and two nice waltzes—"La Valse du Malchanceaux" and "La Valse 1-2-3." Also, "Le Cajin de la Rue Bourbon" has a winning arrangement with Dixieland back-up.

GOOD

I Love Cajun Music

i. 1980/Swallow 6039 CS, LP

Compared to *Cajun Music for Everyone*, this album lacks drive and excitement, but it has the best song Olivier ever recorded. The catchy "J'aime Mes Samedis Soirs" (I Love My Saturday Night) boasts a sparkling arrangement and ranks up there with the swamp pop classic "Mathilda" by Cookie and the Cupcakes. "Si Tu Me Donnes une Autre Chance" and "Tout les Soirs" are also outstanding.

La Musique de Jim Olivier

i. 1985/Swallow 6059 CS, LP

A strong side one is countered by a weaker side two, but the album has a nice vocal duet by Jim and Monica Le Roi on "Pourquoi On Rest Dans L'enfer" and good swamp pop flavor on "Pour Toujour Ma Chere."

OTHER RECORDINGS

Let's Keep it Cajun

i. 1982/Swallow 6048 CS, LP

Sings the Cajun Way

i. 1981/Swallow 6044 CS, LP

AUSTIN PITRE
Accordion, fiddle, vocals

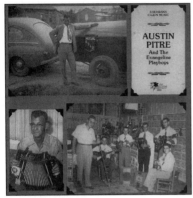

Swallow LP 6041

Besides leading a popular band, the Evangeline Playboys, Austin Pitre is remembered for being the first Cajun accordionist to play standing up. He showed off for the crowd by playing the instrument over his head, behind his back and between his legs. He was also known for his 1959 hit rendition of the classic two-step "Flumes Dans Faires" (better known as "Les Flammes d'Enfer," or The Flames of Hell). His style was pure Cajun, influenced by the great Creole accordionist/singer **Amedee Ardoin**.

Born near Ville Platte in 1918 to poor sharecroppers, Pitre played both the accordion and fiddle at rural dances by the time he was 11. Never attending school, he worked as a car mechanic to support his family of seven and played music at night. His greatest prominence came during the postwar Cajun music revival in the 1940s, when he recorded for Feature and played for six years at the Chinaball Club in Bristol. Between 1949 and 1955, the band performed in a popular show on radio KLSO in Opelousas.

During the 1960s, Pitre recorded for the Swallow label in Ville Platte. He appeared at the Smithsonian Festival of American Folk Life in Washington, D. C., in 1973 and 1976.

In 1980, a year before his death, he received a Louisiana Freedom Festival award for 50 years of contributions to Cajun music.

THE BEST

The Swallow Recordings: D. L. Menard and Austin Pitre

r. 1959-1971; i. 1991/Ace (England) 327 CD (contains Austin Pitre and the Evangeline Playboys: Louisiana Cajun Music/Swallow 6041 LP + 3 other tracks)

The CD's sound is crisper, without losing the warmth of the LP. Pitre sings and plays both accordion and fiddle. On the uptempo songs in particular, his singing is reminiscent of Amedee Ardoin in its straining, powerful style. "Pretty Rosie Cheeks" is an outstanding double fiddle song, and fine accordion work and mournful vocals create a great "Opelousas Waltz." "Two Step de Bayou Teche" and "Le Pauvre Hobo" have a lively feel, full accordion sound and good old-fashioned Cajun vocals. The last of the three added songs is a waltz featuring a good steel guitar and dramatic singing by Austin. The CD also offers excellent material by D. L. Menard.

EXCELLENT

Folksongs of the Louisiana Acadians

(collection) r. 1959; i. 1994/Arhoolie 359 CD, CS

The best available recording by Pitre in terms of performance, material and sound quality is "The Prison Song" on this CD. He sings and plays accordion, with guitar backup by Lurlin LeJeune. Unfortunately, there is only one other song by him here, "Contredanse." But this disc is an excellent value, with 34 songs by important artists. One of the best collections of historic 1950s field recordings of Cajun music by Dr. Harry Oster, it includes selections from two previous Arhoolie LPs.

Cajun Folk Music

(collection) Prestige International 25015 LP

The songs recommended above ("The Prison Song" and "Contredanse") come from this LP, which contains four additional songs by Pitre and six by Milton Molitor, another accordionist and singer. In spite of poorer sound quality, this album is worthwhile, notably for Pitre's "The Marriage March" and "Ninety Nine Year Waltz." Molitor provides good accordion backing for Pitre's vocals.

OTHER RECORDINGS

Back to the Bayou

r. & i. 1979/Sonet (England) 815 LP

WALLACE "CHEESE" READ
Vocals, fiddle

If Read is not well known, it is only because he shunned the professional musician's life, playing instead for family and friends. In fact, the big, jovial "Cheese" was a top-notch fiddler with a powerful voice harking back to the days of dance halls before amplification when a singer had to have strong lungs to carry over the band and crowd noise. His style was drawn from many influences: traditional musicians such as the Breaux family, Mayeus Lafleur and **Dennis McGee**, as well as Texas swing artists like **Harry Choates** and the **Hackberry Ramblers**' Luderin Darbone.

Born in Eunice in 1924, Read got his fiddle from his grandfather, a German immigrant; his other ancesters originally came from France. Growing up in the 1930s, he often accompanied his father to Creole dances, where he heard jazz, blues and French music. There he met accordionist Adam Fontenot, father of the famous Creole fiddler **Canray Fontenot**. Read's style of playing reflects the syncopated sounds he heard during this period.

Read's first instrument, at the age of 12, was a harmonica, but soon thereafter he began playing the fiddle. In his teens, he formed a band. When he was in the service in Amarillo, he was in another group with some of Bob Wills' musicians. But Read, a cotton grower for most of his life, only played at parties and dances in the Eunice area in later life.

Read made two recordings which have been released. One is a field recording by Dr. Harry Oster in the late 1950s. The other is by Arhoolie producer Chris Strachwitz at Read's home and at Marc Savoy's Music Center near Eunice in 1979, two years before Read's death.

THE BEST

Cajun House Party

r. late 1950s, 1979; i. 1994/Arhoolie 415 CD; 5021 CS, LP

In her excellent liner notes, Ann Savoy mentions that Read absorbed jazz, blues and swing in addition to Cajun music while growing up, and it is evident in his playing. You can hear the swing style of Harry Choates and Luderin Darbone of the Hackberry Ramblers in several songs, especially "Tu M'as Quitte Dans La Louisiane" and "Battle of New Orleans." Read was an accomplished Cajun fiddler, but it was his voice that set him apart: he had a clear, shouting style of singing going back to early dance hall days.

The first 17 cuts of this CD are from two 1979 sessions produced by Chris Strachwitz of Arhoolie. Marc Savoy's accordion shines on the first seven songs as the instrumental lead and backing Read's and John Stelly's vocals. Savoy plays fiddle in a beautiful blend with Read on " 'Tit Canard Mulet" and "Mamou Two-Step." Some of the late 1950s field recordings made by Harry Oster are not as strong, but there are two gems: the instrumental "Mamou

Breakdown" and "Valse de l'Anse Maigre." Fourteen of the CD's songs had been unissued previously, and the others were available only on various LPs and cassettes. It is good to have so much of Read's work from different periods available here.

EXCELLENT

Folksongs of the Louisiana Acadians

(recorded by Dr. Harry Oster) r. 1956-1959; i. 1994/Arhoolie 359 CD, CS

This compilation contains nine early recordings by Read. His fiddle work and vocals glow on "Fiddle Stomp" and "French Jig." "Mamou Breakdown" is the same version as on *Cajun House Party*, but the other tunes are new to this CD.

BELTON RICHARD
Vocals, accordion

Swallow CD 6135

Jukebox king Belton Richard was the most popular Cajun musician of the 1960s and 1970s. Unfashionable thereafter, the Cajun crooner earned respect nevertheless for modernizing his native music in the 1960s, when it was in danger of dying out. Taking advantage of amplification unavailable to earlier bands, Richard offered a bigger sound and sang in the smooth-as-honey, detached style then favored in mainstream music. He is considered the first in the modern era to mount a seven-piece band, and the first to include bass guitar. Meanwhile, he stayed true to tradition by featuring his capable accordion playing and reviving the use of twin fiddles.

Richard was born in 1939 near Rayne, where his father, accordionist Claby Richard, taught him to play the instrument when he was seven years old. By 12, Richard was performing at dances and bars, and starting at 18 he sang in his own rock 'n' roll band, the French Rockers, for three years. But in 1959 he "went back to French" by picking up the accordion again and forming the Musical Aces. Richard's romantic baritone and Elvis-like physical appearance to the fore, the popular group played clubs throughout Louisiana and east Texas.

A poetic songwriter, Richard drew on swamp pop for tunes he usually sang in French. After his mid-1960s hit "Just Un Reve," (Just a Dream) for Chamo Records in Crowley, he enjoyed solid success with recordings for Swallow in Ville Platte until 1987, when he tired of fame and retired. "Un Autre Soir d'Ennui" (Another Sleepless Night) and "The Cajun Streak," a novelty song, were his biggest hits. Recently Richard has been honored with several Cajun awards, and the 1995 Festivals Acadiens in Lafayette was dedicated to him. There are signs of a comeback, starting with a new CD in 1996 and local festival appearances.

Richard believes Cajun music almost died out because it got stale. He told Ann Savoy, author of *Cajun Music: A Reflection of a People*, "All your songs that were made were 'You left me to go with another'... Rock 'n' roll was strong, they had stories and our French music didn't have any stories. It was always the same words, man, always the same thing. So, I figured I was going to do something about it and it worked."

THE BEST

At His Best

r. & i. 1981/Swallow 6043 CS, LP

This is Richard's most Cajun recording, although some songs and the steel guitar add a country flavor. The band's strong lineup includes Allen Ardoin on fiddle and Johnny Credeur on guitar, both constants in Richard's Musical Aces. Richard wrote six of 10 songs, including some of the LP's best: "Il Fait Chaud" and "I Like Cajun French Music," done in swing style, plus his pretty "Let Me Talk to Your Heart." Some of Richard's earlier Swallow recordings lacked clarity, but this one, recorded at Master Trak Studios in Crowley, has excellent sound—superior in fact to the later Ace collection on CD.

EXCELLENT

Modern Sounds in Cajun Music

r. 1966-1974; i. 1993/Ace (England) 378 CD (contains Modern Sounds in Cajun Music, Vol. 1/Swallow 6010 LP & Vol. 2/Swallow 6013 CS, LP)

This CD is a great value, with 26 high-quality songs and improved sound. These early recordings cover a wide range of Richard's Cajun, swamp pop and country music. They saw him through a trying period when musicians playing only Cajun music could not find work. He wrote the majority of the songs here, many of which have become modern Cajun standards, like his classic "Cajun Stripper." The country feel to his own "J'ai Pleurer Pour Toi" shows the power of that style in Cajun music in the 1970s. Richard's accomplished accordion playing is heard throughout.

Louisiana Cajun Music

r. & i. 1978/Swallow 6032 CS, LP

Good vocals and accordion work by Richard and strong musicianship are shown on "Home Sick Waltz" and three other cuts:

"Valse de Cankton," "The Lonely Waltz" and "Jamais une Autre Chance."

GOOD

I'm Back

i. 1996/Swallow 6135 CD

After a long break from recording, Richard announces his return. While his singing and accordion-playing seem undiminished, the songs are not up to par. Nevertheless, a worthwhile disc, with some outstanding numbers: "Adalida," Willis Touchet's "Dream of Me" and his own "She's Gone, Gone."

Good n' Cajun

r. & i. 1974/Swallow 6021 CS, LP

A good cover of D. L. Menard's "She Didn't Know I Was Married."

OTHER RECORDINGS

The Essential Belton Richard Cajun Music Collection

i. 1996/Swallow 6117 CD (unreviewed)

ZACHARY RICHARD
(Ralph Zachary Richard)
Vocals, accordion, piano, guitar

Arzed CD 2001

Zachary Richard is one of Cajun music's most colorful and controversial musicians. The

Bob Dylan of south Louisiana music, he's changed his style so often, it's hard to keep track of who he is. His early moves to Canada and France took him out of Acadiana at a crucial time in the Cajun renaissance, and he is still more popular in Canada than in the U.S. But the charismatic Richard has steadily gained American fans with his flamboyant performances and more mainstream recent recordings featuring his songwriting talents.

Richard was born in 1950 to the mayor of Scott and his homemaker wife. Like his childhood friend and relative, **Michael Doucet,** he grew up in Americanized, middle-class surroundings where speaking French was compartmentalized into Sunday visits with grandparents. Musical training included private lessons and singing first soprano in the church choir. His true love was rock music—New Orleans style, then the Rolling Stones, Simon and Garfunkel, and the Byrds. He and Doucet imitated the Stones when they played music together as young teens attending the same high school. Richard also cites **Clifton Chenier** and **Iry LeJeune** as influences.

A gifted student, Richard graduated from Tulane University, where he played guitar, and set off for New York in 1972 as a hippie country rocker. Beginner's luck struck when the folk label Elektra signed him after hearing his demo tape, with Michael Doucet on guitar. No record was ever released, however. Turning to Cajun music, Richard bought an accordion and taught himself to play listening to **Aldus Roger** records. He joined Doucet for a duet gig in 1973 at a folk festival in France, where the crowd's ecstatic reception inspired Richard to take his native music seriously. On their return to Louisiana, they formed a Cajun rock group called the Bayou Drifter Band, but its reception was anything but ecstatic.

Thereupon, Richard and Doucet split—Doucet settling deeper into Cajun music, and Richard heading in 1974 for Montreal, where he became a star in clubs and on TV. Canadian audiences offered a proving grounds for Richard's musical experimentation. During the late 1970s, he hit the big time across French-speaking Canada, with constant touring and recording, and several of his albums became gold records.

Meanwhile, Richard's Cajun identity took on a radical edge after he fully awoke to his heritage at an Acadian festival in New Brunswick. Bouncing back and forth between Canada and Louisiana, he joined the French separatist movement in Quebec, and back home began a one-man campaign to restore the French language by insisting on speaking only French and insulting those who didn't. He failed as *provocateur* (once he publicly wrapped himself in a revolutionary French Louisiana flag)—only years later realizing he was mistaken to try to transplant Canadian French separatism to Louisiana.

Feeling nostalgic, and with his Canadian music career on the wane, Richard returned in 1981 to Louisiana, where Doucet and others were reviving interest in Cajun music. Richard started a band with slide guitarist Sonny Landreth that played throughout Acadiana. He also began to put down roots by building a house in Scott. But he continued to travel, living for long periods in Paris and playing pop music. In 1986, he finally settled in Scott, where he lives today with his longtime companion and manager, a Frenchwoman named Claude Thomas. Partly responsible for the Cajun mania of the last decade, Richard remains an outspoken activist on behalf of Cajun culture and preserving French.

Richard is an incendiary performer, ego irrepressibly out front. Articulate, moody and versatile, he seeks acceptance today as a

Chapter 1 • Cajun & Creole

"Louisiana singer-songwriter who also happens to be Cajun." Still playing an Acadian button accordion (in more quirky than gifted fashion, he admits) and venturing occasionally into traditional Cajun and zydeco, he primarily plays the rock and R&B he loved as a teenager.

Richard has made 12 albums in his zig-zag career. The first eight, spanning his decade on the road from 1976 to 1986, were recorded in French on the Arzed label (a reference to his initials, ZR, in reverse) in Louisiana, Montreal and Paris, and released abroad. His first two American albums, on Rounder, focused on south Louisiana dance hall music, sung mostly in English. Signed to a major label, A&M, Richard made two mainstream pop albums with a Cajun tinge, and struggled to redefine himself after years of identification with Cajun music. In a 1993 *Offbeat* interview, Richard reflected on what he called his "weird career," careening from rejecting being an American artist to "discovering that who I really was was not a French pop singer but wanting to be a guy from Louisiana who plays in a band."

THE BEST

Women in the Room 📖

r. 1989; i. 1990/A&M 5302 CD, CS

A TOP 10 CAJUN ALBUM

Recorded at Richard's small studio in Scott, his major-label debut is an incredibly even release with a great variety of music featuring Richard's best songs yet. He wrote or co-wrote 10 of the 11 tunes, which are more rock than Cajun or zydeco, along with R&B and soul. The waltzes and ballads best show off his pleasing voice, while "No French, No More" carries the Francophone banner. Outstanding songs are "Give Me Back My Wings," "Zack's Zydeco," "La Ballade de Howard Hebert" and "Take Me Away." A powerful beat is produced by Brian Stoltz,

guitar; Didier Alexandre, bass; and Craig Lege, keyboards; with Joe Hammer and Cruz Fruge swapping drum duties.

EXCELLENT

Cap Enrage

i. 1996/Initial/Audiogram 10093 CD

Polish up your French and dive right into this newest release with all lyrics and liner notes in that language (perhaps signifying Richard's belief in the power of French to ensure the survival of the Cajun identity). It is a strong contender for Richard's best. He has never been in better voice, the songs are uniformly excellent, and most of them are originals. With a more restrained performance than on earlier recordings, this is a quality addition to the impressive output by a multi-talented artist who deserves greater recognition.

Looking Back

r. 1976-1986; i. 1986/Arzed RZ 1011 CD

This CD is a treasure chest of Richard's best music over a decade of recordings. As the liner notes point out, it is not a "greatest hits" package because Richard's biggest-selling sides, his French and Canadian hits, aren't included. Of the 17 cuts, only four were previously released on albums available in the U.S. More Cajun-zydeco based than his recent albums, the excellent songs include an early studio version of "Dear Darling" plus the previously unreleased, spontaneous "Zack Attack Rap," recorded at the La Louisianne studio with zydeco's Rockin' Dopsie Jr. on rubboard. Other good tunes are "Travailler C'est Trop Dur," "Ma Louisiane," "Les Ailes des Hirondelles" and "La Berceuse Creole."

Snake Bite Love

i. 1992/A&M 5387 CD, CS

On this grab-bag album, Richard wrote or co-wrote all 12 songs. The most successful are uptempo rock numbers with a Cajun/zydeco influence and ballads like "Cote Blanche Bay" and "Sunset on Louisianne," whose haunting accordion back-up and arrangements conjure a bayou atmosphere. The catchy "Down in Congo Square" and "One Kiss" also stand out.

Live in Montreal

r. 1980/Arzed RZ 1003 CD

Recorded live at the Club Montreal, this disc captures the excitement of a Richard performance. Although fast numbers usually star in live recordings, in this case the ballads do: "Les Ailes des Hirondelles," "Travailler C'est Trop Dur" and "La Berceuse Creole." There is also a great version of "Antibon Legbo."

Mardi Gras Mambo

i. 1989/Rounder 6037 CD, CS, LP

A collection of quality songs celebrating Carnival, most with a rock or New Orleans R&B feel. The classic "Handa Wanda" and "Big Chief" are excellent, as are the slow ballad "Creole Lullaby" and "Ton Ton Gris-Gris," both written by Richard.

Zack's Bon Ton

i. 1988/Rounder 6027 CD, CS, LP

Richard sings mostly in English on this first American album, which has a more Cajun/zydeco feel than some of his other recordings. A strong band features Craig Lege on keyboards, Tommy Shreve on guitar, Cruz Fruge on drums and Rufus Thibodeaux on fiddle. Richard's "Big River" and the Cajun classic "Jolie Blonde" are fine, along with the uptempo "Ma Louisianne" and "Bayou Pon Pon."

Migration

r. 1977; i. 1978, 1992/Arzed RZ 2001 CD

Two outstanding songs make this worth buying–"Les Ailes des Hirondelles" and "La Berceuse Creole"–but Richard's "Son Premier Bal" is also a winner.

OTHER RECORDINGS

Allons Danser

r. 1979; i. 1979, 1989 Arzed RZ 1007 CD

Bayou des Mysteres

i. 1976/Arzed RZ 1017 CD

Mardi Gras

i. 1977/Arzed RZ 1005 CD

Vent d'Ete

i. 1981, 1992 Arzed RZ 1019 CD

Zack Attack

r. 1984; i. 1984, 1989/Arzed RZ 1009 CD

STEVE RILEY & THE MAMOU PLAYBOYS
Group

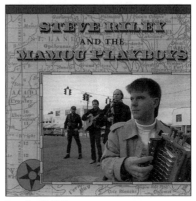

Rounder CD 6038

This is the best young Cajun band in the country, hot on the heels of **Beausoleil**. Formed in 1988, they exploded on the scene in front of the toughest critics: Cajuns attending the annual Festivals Acadiens in Lafayette, where they have headlined several times since. Now, five albums and many tours later, they have cemented their reputation as innovative traditionalists whose musical finesse sets them apart. They have a polished, rich sound, with two- and three-part harmonies (most Cajun bands feature solo singing) and full instrumentation that includes several fiddles, accordion, guitar, bass, drums and triangle.

Accordionist/fiddler/vocalist Steve Riley and two other band members are in their 20s, while another two are in their 40s. Riley and fiddlers David Greely and Peter Schwarz shared mentoring by the band's guiding spirit, the late fiddler and Cajun music revival godfather **Dewey Balfa**. The group adheres to Balfa's mission of progressivism within the Cajun tradition.

Riley (b. 1969, Mamou) grew up with Cajun music, playing triangle and singing with the great fiddler **Dennis McGee** at age five and learning accordion at seven. He was encouraged to play by his grandfather, who emceed Mardi Gras dances in Mamou and threw parties attended by McGee, accordionist **Marc Savoy** and other musicians.

Riley started studying Cajun music after listening to **Balfa Brothers** recordings, then sought out Balfa as a teacher. By 16, he was touring with Balfa, who groomed him to be a bandleader.

"People long to belong to a group. But when I was born, it was automatic for me. I was a Cajun, with the food, the culture, the music and the festivals," Riley told *Offbeat* in 1992. David Greely, Riley's fellow frontman and close musical partner, also jammed with McGee as a young man, although he grew up in Baton Rouge amid popular, not Cajun,

culture. Now the band's chief songwriter, researcher of old Cajun songs and translater of liner notes, Greely is drawn to the old masters who pushed Cajun music into new directions, like Creole accordionist **Amedee Ardoin**. That adventurous edge is very much a part of the Playboys' style

Fiddler/bassist/vocalist Peter Schwarz (the band's arranger and manager) is the son of a famous folk musician, **Tracy Schwarz** of the New Lost City Ramblers, and grew up on the road with the family band. In 1964, his father befriended Dewey Balfa, and the younger Schwarz eventually wound up Balfa's star fiddling pupil. He even lived with the Balfas in Basile under a National Endowment for the Arts apprenticeship at 15. Before his death in 1992, Balfa gave Schwarz his favorite fiddle, "The Old Man." Schwarz first met Riley when they were teenagers playing music on the back of a wagon in the Mamou Mardi Gras. After picking up an anthropology degree from Harvard University, Schwarz joined the Playboys.

The newest band member, guitarist Jimmy Domengeaux, is a seasoned musician who grew up accompanying his grandfather's fiddle and accordion playing and later worked with many Cajun and swamp pop bands. Drummer Kevin Dugas is another veteran of Cajun dance halls. Rounding out the ensemble on many occasions is guest Christine Balfa (Dewey's daughter) on triangle.

Like one of Riley's favorite musicians, zydeco king **Clifton Chenier**, they push the parameters of their genre by fusing Cajun with other styles (lately they've been trying zydeco), revitalizing old tunes with new arrangements and–as of their most recent album–writing their own material. All their recordings boast exceptionally high quality.

THE BEST

La Toussaint 🪗

r. & i. 1995/Rounder 6068 CD, CS

A TOP 10 CAJUN ALBUM

This band just gets stronger and stronger. With the addition in 1993 of Peter Schwarz on fiddle, bass and vocals, the Playboys expanded their line-up to three fiddlers, three vocalists and a solid rhythm section backing Steve Riley's great accordion. Furthermore, as of this CD, they have started writing original songs to expand their repertoire of Cajun standards. The band's strength is still beautiful Cajun waltzes, but their own new material in the same vein is an excellent addition. The title track, by Schwarz and David Greely and sung by Greely, is one of the highlights. Another is a lovely rendition of "Doc" Guidry's "La Valse d'Amitie." The zydeco tunes are quite new to the band–another example of their continued musical growth. After almost a decade together, the Playboys still sound as fresh as on their first recording.

EXCELLENT

Live!

r. 1993; i. 1994/Rounder 6058 CD, CS

Back home after extensive touring, the Playboys recorded this release live with a crowd of dancers at a VFW dance hall in Eunice. The band was in fine fettle, with uptempo numbers showing off its flawless musicianship. "Bosco Stomp/Zarico Est Pas Sale" (their first step into zydeco) has a driving beat and an excellent fiddle solo. The waltzes "Elle Savait Pas J'etais Marie" and "J'aimerais te Pardonner" are beautiful songs beautifully done.

'Tit Galop Pour Mamou

r. 1991; i. 1992/Rounder 6048 CD, CS

This second release features songs with a strong beat, even the waltzes. The swing feeling in some of the fast numbers like "Jongle a Moi" is reminiscent of 1930s Cajun string bands. The waltzes, especially "J'aimerais te Pardonner" and "Les Barres de la Prison," are outstanding.

Trace of Time

r. & i. 1993/Rounder 6053 CD, CS

This disc is the Playboys' first after fiddler/bassist/pianist/vocalist Peter Schwarz joined them, enriching their sound. Also, Riley and Greely sound better with each release. "La Valse du Regret" is a great song, as are "Mon Vieux Wagon," "Sur le Courtableau" and the Quebec reel "La Pointe-au-Pic." With great variety in song selection and stellar musicianship, this CD was justifiably nominated for a Grammy in 1993.

Steve Riley and the Mamou Playboys

r. 1989; i. 1990/Rounder 6038 CD, CS

Produced by Zachary Richard in his home studio, this CD of traditional Cajun tunes is amazingly polished for a debut album. A strong beat propels the uptempo "La Pointe aux Pins," "Indien Sur le Chicot" and "High Point Two Step." Waltzes like "Valse de la Belle" feature good accordion and vocal work by Riley and a strong fiddle solo by Greely, while "La Valse des Vachers" shows the entire ensemble's strength.

GENE RODRIGUE (Eugene Rodrigue)
Guitar, vocals

Rodrigue was a Cajun-country singer from southeast Louisiana whose career spanned the 1940s to1980s. Born in 1926 in Larose, near Cut Off, he learned music from his father, a fiddler who earned his living by trapping. The young Rodrigue started his career in 1946 by accompanying his father on guitar. He cut his first record, "Dan le Coeur de la Ville" (In the Heart of the Town), in 1953 with his Hillbilly Swing Kings for the local Folk-Star label. He later recorded in English and French for

Meladee, finding success with the catchy "Jolie Fille." Meanwhile, he won local fame by broadcasting shows over several radio stations and appearing with country stars like Hank Williams and Jim Reeves.

Rodrigue dropped out of music during the rock 'n' roll years, but resumed after opening a lounge in Lockport. His "Little Cajun Girl," recorded in New Orleans, made a splash in 1960, but after a few more successes, Rodrique dropped out again and worked as an oil field roughneck for a period. He continued recording, for the Houma label, but in later years put his energy into a successful sales career until his death in 1988.

The Bayou Cajun Music of Gene Rodrigue

i. 1986/Swallow 6062 CS, LP

A good collection of original songs featuring solid vocals and rhythm guitar work by Rodrigue. The slower songs bring out the richness in his deep voice. Rodrigue wrote the tunes, the best of which are "Dan le Coeur de la Ville," "Mon Desire" and "J'apre Rire."

ALDUS ROGER
Accordion

Aldus Roger was one of the most popular accordionists of the 1950s, along with **Lawrence Walker**. Many traditional Cajun dance bands playing today bear the stamp of his Lafayette Playboys, who exerted a wide influence on dance hall bands from the 1950s through the 1970s.

He was born in Carencro, near Lafayette, in 1916 and started sneaking behind the barn to play his father's accordion when he was eight. Early influences were his cousin, Ivy Roger, as well as **Amedee Breaux** and **Lawrence Walker**. He attended Walker's dances and copied his accordion playing.

Later, Roger perfected his own style of "playing double" (two notes at the same time). He formed his band, Aldus Roger and the Lafayette Playboys, in the mid-1940s and played dances throughout Cajun country.

With a smooth, precise style, the band was highly danceable, emphasizing professionalism and good musicianship over performance tricks. Roger always chose top-quality musicians of the calibre of fiddler **"Doc" Guidry** to play with him. Roger composed several of the band's most popular tunes, including "Johnny Can't Dance," "The Lafayette Playboy Waltz" and "The Mardi Gras Dance." While he didn't sing, he featured popular vocalists of the day. The Playboys won a wide following with a Saturday afternoon TV show in Lafayette 1955-1970. Their career peaked in the 1960s, when Roger had his best band and best-selling records. In 1962, he was invited to appear at the National Folklore Festival in Washington, D.C.

In the 1950s, Roger became one of the first recording artists with two Louisiana record companies, Eddie Shuler's Folkstar/Goldband Records and Jay Miller's Feature and Cajun Classics labels. Recordings for another two local labels, La Louisianne and Swallow, followed. He worked all his life as a carpenter when he wasn't on the bandstand. Living in Scott, he continued to perform occasionally into his 70s.

THE BEST

A Cajun Legend

i. 1993/La Louisianne 1007 CD, CS

This CD provides a 22-track cross section of Roger's best recordings (12 tracks in the case of the cassette). He attracted superb musicians to his bands and maintained extraordinary quality over a wide range of material. He has a strong attack on the accordion and hits the notes in even the fastest runs dead on. One of the greats, "Doc" Guidry, is featured, along with another excellent fiddler, Tony Thibodeaux. Steel guitarist Phillip Alleman also appears, and rhythm is provided by guitarist Johnny Credeur and drummer Fernice "Man" Abshire. Roger's own "Lafayette Playboy Waltz," "Hicks Wagon Wheel," "Mamou Two-Step" and "Creole Stomp" are a few of the outstanding songs.

EXCELLENT

Plays the French Music of South Louisiana

La Louisianne 107 CS, LP

Seven of the 12 best songs on this album can be found on the CD *A Cajun Legend.* Two good songs not on the CD, however, are "Grand Mamou" and "I Passed by Your Door," which shows off Roger's accordion skills.

RODDIE ROMERO
Accordion, vocals

When Romero recorded his first album in 1991 at the age of 15, he was one of south Louisiana's youngest Cajun musicians to do so. From the start, he placed himself squarely in the **Wayne Toups**-style zydecajun camp, with a little country thrown in. Indeed, *The New Kid In Town* was produced by Rick Lagneaux, Toups' keyboard player. Romero acknowledges Toups as an influence, along with **Buckwheat Zydeco**, **Zachary Richard**, Sonny Landreth and Warren Storm.

Growing up in Lafayette, Romero has played accordion since he was 10, encouraged primarily by his grandfather. Along with his older brother, drummer Jeff Romero, he formed his first band in 1988, Roddie Romero and the Rockin' Cajuns. The versatile Romero plays accordion and other instruments, as well as sings.

THE BEST

State of Louisiana

i. 1995/Habana (England) HABCD 2 CD

Romero has come quite a way since his 1991 debut album. This latest CD showcases a young talent who is beginning to find his niche. The best tunes are the rockers, especially his driving version of "Zydeco Son Pas Sa Les." Other toe-tappers are "Allons a Lafayette," the intense "Went to the Dance" and a Louisiana-ized version of "Kansas City." Romero does a credible version of "Promised Land," although he doesn't threaten Chuck Berry or Johnnie Allan. Less effective are the Nashville country-style ballads like "Baton Rouge" and "Tired of Going Nowhere." Romero's vocals are improving, and he plays an excellent accordion.

OTHER RECORDINGS

Da' Big Squeeze

r. & i. 1991/Swallow 6093 CD, CS

Lafayette

i. 1993/TechnoZydeco 100 CD

The New Kid in Town

i. 1991/Swallow 6086 CS, LP

PAT SAVANT
Accordion

When not playing music, Savant (b. 1955, Lake Charles) is a junior high school teacher. He began his musical career as a teenager with the **Sundown Playboys**. In 1972, he scored a coup by encouraging the Beatles' Apple Records to issue the Playboys' "Saturday Nite Special," the first British commercial Cajun single, resulting in a wide distribution rare for a Cajun band at the time. As the band's accordionist, he had boldly sent Apple a copy of the 45.

In 1980, Savant started his own group, the Louisiana Playboys. Four years later, the enterprising bandleader got them booked at London's Dingwall's Club in the first performance in England by a Cajun band, who then also became the first to record in Britain, with the album *Saturday Night Special* (JSP Records 1080). Their second JSP album, *Louisiana Playboys*, came from the same session.

The Playboys perform in the 1950s-60s mainstream tradition of **Belton Richard**, **Aldus Roger** and **Lawrence Walker**. Drummer/vocalist Joe Turner's credentials go back to the Happy Fats band; bass guitarist Randy Falcon (replaced on the Playboys' second album by Tim Foreman) is a second cousin of early Cajun recording star **Joseph Falcon**; fiddler Wallace Touchet played with the Sundown Playboys for more than 25 years; and steel guitarist Orsy Vanicor played with such popular early musicians as **Iry LeJeune** and **Lawrence Walker**.

THE BEST

Louisiana Cajun Music

i. 1982/Master-Trak/Kajun 5015 LP

Savant has attracted talented musicians, and they tend to stay with him. In particular, drummer Joe Turner is a very good vocalist (Savant does not generally sing), and Wallace Touchet is a gifted fiddler. The sound is good here, as is usually the case with Mark Miller of Louisiana's Master-Trak at the controls. This album has a notable song selection–the best being "Crowley Two-Step," with great accordion work by Savant. Other good tunes include "Both for the Same Price," "Church Point Breakdown" and "Little Black Eyes."

GOOD

Louisiana Playboys

i. 1985/JSP (England) 1098 LP

This recording is marred by a slight flatness of sound and doesn't measure up in terms of song selection. Savant answers Turner's vocal lead on two songs, but Turner is still primary vocalist. Touchet's excellent fiddling is displayed well, particularly on "Steel Guitar Rag," on which Vanicor's steel guitar also shines. The instrumental star is Savant's accordion, as on "Musicians Waltz." "Zydeco Pas Sale" and the catchy instrumental "Canton Two Step" are the best songs.

MARC SAVOY
Accordion

Arhoolie LP 5023

Marc Savoy is one of the best Cajun musicians around today. A highly accomplished accordionist, member of the purist **Savoy-Doucet Cajun Band**, and world-class accordion builder, he is also a linchpin of the Cajun revival and outspoken warrior against commercialized Cajun music and culture.

Born in 1940 on a rice farm near Eunice, Savoy grew up hearing his grandfather play the fiddle, sometimes with fiddling legend **Dennis McGee**, a onetime tenant farmer on his grandfather's farm. He has played traditional music since he was 12. For a time in the 1950s, he played with the Rambling Aces in east Texas and southwest Louisiana.

Turning his back on a chemical engineering degree, he opened a store in 1966 to build accordions for Cajun musicians. He endured a decade of financial hardship when the musical style sank to a low point in popularity. Today his handmade, top-of-the-line "Acadian" accordions fetch upwards of $1,000. Around the same time he dived into accordion building, Savoy stopped playing the dance halls, disgusted at what he regarded as the "show business" turn performances had taken and the public's lack of taste.

"People listen to this cheap, Nashville music and they lose the beauty of their own Cajun or Creole sound. They replace it with this wimpy, wee-wee sounding, Nashville-type of music," Savoy complained to an Opelousas *Daily World* interviewer in 1995.

Over the years, Savoy has toured the U.S., Canada, Europe and South America. Today, he plays most often with the Savoy-Doucet Cajun Band. Besides Savoy, the popular group includes his wife, singer/guitarist Ann Savoy and Beausoleil's **Michael Doucet**. Appearing at festivals and occasionally at local dances, the group plays only before audiences with an appetite for traditional Cajun music. Marc and Ann Savoy were profiled in Les Blank's PBS documentary, *Marc and Ann*. In 1992, Savoy received a Heritage Award from the National Endowment for the Arts.

At his Savoy Music Center in Eunice, he hosts Cajun jam sessions for local musicians on Saturday mornings. The store is a popular stop for visitors looking for musical equipment, repairs to old instruments or information about where to hear Cajun music. Signs on his

workshop walls express his personal crusade against Americanization—"Some Cajuns are turning their back on a hot bowl of gumbo for a cold, tasteless American hot dog"—and against the inferior, Johnny-come-latelys of Cajun music who jumped on the bandwagon only when it became popular again—"An imitation of something is always more popular than that which is being imitated."

Known for accordion playing marked by a spirited attack and clean execution of even the fastest runs, Savoy has performed with greats such as **Dewey Balfa, D. L. Menard, Wallace "Cheese" Read, Dennis McGee** and **Sady Courville**, and recorded several albums with them. Although he has appeared with other musicians on recordings for Crazy Cajun, Swallow and Arhoolie, he has made just one solo album.

"Oh What a Night"

r. 1980; i. 1981/Arhoolie 5023 CS, LP

Savoy's accordion stars on this fine recording of dance music, reinforcing his reputation as one of Cajun music's best players. One side was recorded in the Savoys' home and store with Michael Doucet, cousin Frank Savoy and a few other musicians joining Marc and Ann. On this side, "Reno Waltz" and "La Valse a Pop" features Marc, Ann and Doucet, while all the other songs except "La Pointe aux Picques" add one or two additional players. Savoy shares vocals with Ann on the opening song, "Reno Waltz," their voices blending to good effect; but he leaves the singing to others on remaining cuts. An excellent band assembled for the second, studio-recorded, side with Frank Savoy singing and "Doc" Guidry turning out some spectacular fiddle solos. Marc's accordion shines brightest on "La Queue de Tortue" and "Traveler Playboy's Special."

THE SAVOY-DOUCET CAJUN BAND

Group

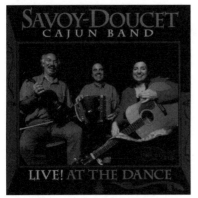

Arboolie CD 418

The Savoy-Doucet Cajun Band is the sterling trio of accordionist **Marc Savoy** (b. 1940), fiddler **Michael Doucet** (b. 1951), and guitarist Ann Savoy (b. 1952). This is a traditional, front-porch-style group without peer. Doucet also heads the world-famous **Beausoleil**, while Cajun accordion virtuoso Savoy is also a master accordion builder and Cajun culture advocate.

Ann Allen Savoy ably supplies rhythm guitar and vocals, drawing on knowledge gained by years of research; she is the author of the exemplary *Cajun Music: A Reflection of a People* (Eunice, La.: Bluebird Press, 1984). Born in St. Louis, Mo., and raised in Richmond, Va., she was drawn to Louisiana after first hearing Cajun music in 1974. Since marrying Marc, she has sung with him and played guitar, which she learned to play at 12. A Cajun by marriage, she studied French for many years, living in Switzerland and France for two years. For her book, she conducted many interviews in French.

The Savoys share a passionate devotion to unadulterated Cajun music. When performing with them, Doucet throws the purist side of himself into the proceedings, reserving experimentation for the more progressive Beausoleil. The trio digs out old tunes from the likes of **Dennis McGee**, **Amedee Ardoin** and **Cleoma Falcon**. In fact, the Savoys and Doucet are responsible for rescuing many old songs from oblivion. Their own new compositions fit well into the Cajun repertoire. The highly selective group tours and plays at festivals and occasionally at local dances, preferring to perform before audiences with an appreciation of the traditional style.

"I've always thought of Cajun music as a social thing, something which best belonged in the intimacy of a home where it was considered a natural and enjoyable part of the family environment. I think that when you get out and start playing commercially you begin to worry too much about trivial things," Savoy wrote in liner notes for the CD *Home Music with Spirits*.

The Savoys are known for their family-style home performances. Also, visitors to the Savoy Music Center outside Eunice may catch a Cajun jam session on a Saturday morning at the store. The trio's reverence for the down-home style is captured in the three CDs they have made since 1988. Since their first recording, the band members have grown beyond simply being three highly accomplished musicians to displaying a familiarity and looseness these days that only time can develop.

THE BEST

Live! at the Dance

r. 1993, 1994; i. 1994/Arboolie 418 CD, CS

The excitement the trio brings to a live performance is captured for the first time on this CD, recorded in 1993 in Berkeley, Ca., and in 1994 in Pittsburgh and Alexandria, Va. In spirited performances reflecting the crowds' enthusiasm, Marc Savoy whoops with delight as he pumps out his syncopated accordion sounds and urges Doucet on to ever headier fiddling flights. Ann Savoy's vocals are sure and relaxed. Almost every song is excellent. Some especially winning tunes include the instrumentals "Amede Two-Step" and "Perrodin Two-Step," as well as "Petite Ou la Grosse," with a vocal by Ann Savoy, and "J'ai Ete-z-au Bal," with vocals by both Savoys. Bassist Billy Wilson joins in on seven numbers.

EXCELLENT

Two-Step d'Amede

r. 1988; i. 1989/Arboolie 316 CD, CS

One of the best tunes on this CD is the title cut, written by Marc Savoy in tribute to the great Creole musician Amedee Ardoin. Recorded here for the first time, the song is by now a favorite of accordionists. Other top songs include the three recorded live at the Great American Music Hall in San Francisco—"Flammes d'Enfer", "La Negress" and "La Queue de Tortue." "The Kaplan Waltz" and "Diggy Liggy Lo," with Ann's vocals, are also excellent. The addition of bass by Elizabeth Weil and Tina Pilione strengthens the bottom line provided by Ann's rhythm guitar.

Home Music with Spirits

r. 1980s; i. 1992/Arboolie 389 CD, CS (contains Home Music/Arboolie 5029 CS, LP & With Spirits/Arboolie 5037 CS, LP)

This 18-track compilation from Savoy-Doucet's 1980s albums is wonderful instrumentally, but on songs not perfectly fitted to their voices, both Ann Savoy and Doucet sound strained. On the other hand, the feeling that comes

through more than compensates. As Marc Savoy says in the liner notes, musicians can lose the essence of the music in a search for the polished act. The two vocal duets by the Savoys, "Reno Waltz" and " 'Tits Yeux Noirs," are outstanding, as is Doucet's fiddling on "Mon Chere Bebe Creole."

TRACY SCHWARZ
Fiddle, accordion, vocals

An eminent fiddler, Schwarz has had a long career with the New Lost City Ramblers and other folk revival groups. He and his son, Peter Schwarz, formed a close friendship with the great fiddler **Dewey Balfa** and recorded three albums with him. Peter is a Balfa disciple who later joined **Steve Riley & the Mamou Playboys**.

Tracy Schwarz has recorded widely with other folk musicians, including many Cajun artists. Ever exploring different kinds of traditional music, this musicologist has recently turned to making Cajun recordings. His Tracy Schwarz Cajun Trio, based in West Virginia, includes himself on fiddle/accordion/vocals, Matt Haney on fiddle and Lee Blackwell on guitar/vocal harmony.

They have put out two albums of authentic Cajun music. Their first, *The Tracy Schwarz Cajun Trio*, won the Cajun French Music Association's 1995 "Prix Dehors de Nous" award, given to artists outside Acadiana who closely emulate the ethnicity of Cajun music.

THE BEST

The Tracy Schwarz Cajun Trio

i. 1993/Swallow 6106 CD, CS

For a trio, these highly accomplished musicians produce a very full sound. The arrangements are tight, with a nice interplay between accordion and fiddle. Schwarz is a good, if not spectacular vocalist. The excitement he shows in "La Valse de Balfa" would benefit some of the other vocals, but he proves himself on the difficult "La Valse de Tout l'Monde." Other good songs include "Les Flammes d'Enfer," "La Valse de Durald" and "Hick's Wagon Wheel Special."

EXCELLENT

Mes Amis! (My Friends!)

i. 1996/Swallow 6131 CD

This latest album doesn't match their earlier one, especially in song selection. Also missed is the interweaving of the accordion and fiddle. No complaints about the musicianship, however.

LEO SOILEAU
Fiddle, vocals

Old Timey LP 125

Leo Soileau was the first Cajun fiddler to record and only the second Cajun musician to do so, after **Joseph Falcon**. Soileau's popular 1928 single, "Mama, Where You At?" (better known as "He, Mom"), with the brilliant accordionist/singer Mayuse LaFleur struck a tragic chord when the young LaFleur was killed by a stray bullet in a barroom brawl just days after the recording was made. At the time, Soileau was on the verge of a major

innovation–the Cajun-country string band music on which his fame rests.

Born in 1904 in Ville Platte, Soileau learned fiddling and old-style tunes from his father and the great **Dennis McGee**. After LaFleur's death, he cut 14 singles with accordionist Moise Robin for Paramount, Victor and Vocalion during the late 1920s, the accordion's heyday. Finding his fancy fiddling outpacing the accordions, however, Soileau made the fiddle lead instrument. In 1934, he formed Leo Soileau's Three Aces, made up of fiddle, two guitars and drums. Inspired by the western swing bands of Texas, he thus created one of the first Cajun string bands and opened up its Cajun repertoire to western swing, country and French-language versions of popular American tunes such as "Let Me Call You Sweetheart."

Later, the band's name changed to Soileau's Four Aces, then Leo Soileau's Rhythm Boys. The smooth, sophisticated-sounding group was likely the first string band to record, cutting nearly 100 singles from 1935 to 1937 for Bluebird and Decca. The accordionless group had the first drummer to record with a Cajun band. They made popular singles of everything from adaptations of pop songs to Cajun classics like "Le Valse de Gueydan" (a version of "Jolie Blonde"), Soileau's biggest hit. He usually sang the French tunes himself.

Soileau's recording tours took him to Atlanta, Richmond, Memphis, New Orleans, San Antonio and Chicago. During World War II, the band played a longstanding gig at the Silver Star Club in Lake Charles and another later at the Showboat Club in Orange, Tx., as well as regular radio broadcasts. Soileau played with such luminaries as Joe Falcon, **Amedee Breaux** and **Harry Choates**. As a longtime bandleader, he influenced the careers of many other musicians.

When the accordion once again replaced the fiddle in popularity, Soileau stopped playing music in 1953 and worked at various jobs in Lake Charles and as a janitor in Ville Platte. He died in 1980, never having owned a single record that he made. Interviewed by the Ville Platte *Gazette* in 1974, he explained: "I was too busy playing music. I was a trooper and letting the good times roll and never gave any thought to collecting records."

THE BEST

Louisiana Cajun Music, Vol. 7: Leo Soileau and His Four Aces—Pioneer Cajun Fiddler: His Original 1930s Recordings

Arhoolie/Old Timey 125 LP (also available as Pioneer Cajun Fiddler/Folklyric 9057 CS, containing 15 tracks from the LP + 5 others)

This album samples Soileau's 1929 fiddle/accordion partnership with Moise Robin, but mostly features the string band sound of the 1930s. Soileau's singing and fiddling range from a soft, smooth sound to a loud, raw, sliding style. He glides through some vocals effortlessly, while singing in a more poignant style with dramatic shouts on others, such as "La Bonne Valse." Other great songs are "Petit ou Gros," "Embrace Moi Encore" and "La Valse de la Rosa."

EXCELLENT

Le Gran Mamou: A Cajun Music Anthology, Vol. 1

i. 1990/Country Music Foundation 013 CD

This disc contains four songs by Soileau—two of them, "Basile" and the title track, equal to anything he has recorded. "Basile" is an uptempo waltz with a dramatic vocal by Mayuse LaFleur sounding reminiscent of Iry LeJeune. LaFleur was Soileau's first and most famous partner, and Soileau provided exciting back-up. On "Le Gran Mamou,"

Soileau fiddles and sings with a Cajun-country influence, with guitar backing by Floyd Shreve and Dennis Landry.

GOOD

Gran Prairie: A Cajun Music Anthology, Vol. 3

i. 1993/Country Music Foundation 018 CD

The CD has one Soileau track: "Hackberry Hop," a variant of "Hip et Taiau."

Louisiana Cajun Music, Vol. 3: The String Bands of the 1930s

i. 1971/Arhoolie/Old Timey 110 LP

Three famous Soileau songs are included: "La Valse de Guedan" (Jolie Fille), "Hackberry Hop" and "La Blues de Port Arthur."

OTHER RECORDINGS

Louisiana Cajun Music, Vol. 1: First Recordings—the 1920s

i. 1970/Old Timey 108 LP (contains 2 Soileau tracks); 213 CS (contains 3 Soileau tracks)

JO-EL SONNIER
Vocals, accordion, guitar, drums

Rounder CD 6059

Like his idol, the legendary **Iry LeJeune**, Jo-El Sonnier is a highly accomplished accordionist and singer. But unlike LeJeune, Sonnier has strayed from his Cajun roots. Best known as a Nashville-style Cajun-country performer, Sonnier has won a measure of fame and respect as "a musician's musician," yet had an uneven career illustrating the risks involved in trying to follow different musical paths.

Born in Rayne in 1946, Sonnier was often handed an accordion as a child to play at family gatherings. He learned so quickly that by the age of seven he was sitting in with bands (even with LeJeune once), and won many accordion contests. At 13, he recorded his first tune, "Tes Yeaux Bleu" (Blue Eyes), on Louisiana's Swallow label. The popular song won him the nickname "the 13-year-old wonder." When he finished school, he moved to Lake Charles and played with Robert Bertrand's Louisiana Ramblers. He went on to record numerous singles for another local label, Goldband, and performed throughout Cajun country. For a time, he donned an Arab headdress and promoted himself as the Cajun Valentino.

In 1972, Sonnier headed to California for a folk festival and wound up staying to do college concerts and workshops, followed by stints as a drummer and bassist in country dance bands throughout the Southwest. Two years later, he was discovered by Mercury Records and brought to Nashville, where for the next few years he cut country singles in English, with French lyric inserts. Influenced by George Jones, Lefty Frizzell and Johnny Cash, the hybrid Cajun-country crossover tunes caused an initial stir in Nashville. But they were eventually regarded as not country enough and didn't lead to an album. Following his autobiographical "Cajun Born," cut later by Johnny Cash with Sonnier on accordion, Mercury dropped Sonnier.

During these heady but eventually disappointing years, Sonnier made a trip to New Orleans, where he cut five tracks with the Cajun-rock band Coteau, led by **Michael Doucet**. He also got introduced to Hollywood director Peter Bogdanovich, who gave him roles in the movies *They All Laughed* and *Mask*. The best product of this period was the well-regarded 1980 Rounder LP *Cajun Life*, sung in French and recorded in Louisiana with Cajun and Nashville musicians.

"I think ethnic music, roots music, will come back in…" Sonnier said in the album's liner notes. "I am proud of my roots and proud to be recording what I believe in."

Nevertheless, Sonnier then moved back to California, where he played with West Coast bands, and label-hopped from RCA to Capitol to Liberty. Blessed with a voice that can sing anything well, Sonnier has turned out more pop/country than Cajun recordings during his long career. In 1994, he came full circle to his *Cajun Roots* on his latest Rounder CD, a tribute to Iry LeJeune.

THE BEST

Cajun Roots

r. 1993; i. 1994/Rounder 6059 CD, CS

Sonnier announces his Cajun intentions by starting off with six Iry LeJeune songs and following up with six others by Austin Pitre, Lawrence Walker and his own arrangements of traditional tunes. The great songs and superb musicianship are augmented by an intensity of feeling. The CD has a relaxed quality that is not often heard except in bands that have been together for many years. Sonnier's voice is in fine fettle, even on the challenging "La Chere Toute-Toute." Fiddler Michael Doucet provides strong backing, but Sonnier's accordion and vocals star on this outing. "Huppes Taiauts" is excellent, as is the instrumental featuring Sonnier and Doucet, "Amedee Two Step."

EXCELLENT

Live in Canada

r. 1995; i. 1996/Stony Plain 1224 CD

Recorded live before 10,000 fans at the Edmonton Folk Music Festival, this recording finds Sonnier near peak form. The Amos Garrett House Band provides excellent back-up. The Cajun songs like "Big Mamou," "Jolie Blon" and "Jambalaya" are best.

Cajun Life

r. 1980; i. 1988/Rounder 3049 CD, CS, LP (CD includes the LP Cajun Life + 2 bonus tracks)

More good Cajun music featuring Sonnier's accordion and outstanding vocals. With a robust voice of exceptional clarity, Sonnier is a joy to hear. Ten of the 12 songs were recorded at Master-Trak Sound Recorders in Crowley, with excellent sound except for a slightly fuzzy quality to the accordion at times, and good backing by Michael Doucet on rhythm guitar and Merlin Fontenot on fiddle. The two Nashville cuts feature Sonnier's vocals, leaving his accordion to blend into the band. A fast-paced "Lacassine Special," and the graceful waltzes "Chere Alice" and "Les Grands Bois" are noteworthy.

Come On Joe

i. 1987/RCA 6374 CD, CS, LP

Lush arrangements and good song selection mark this mostly pop album. Cajun influence is slight, except on a great version of Randy Newman's "Louisiana 1927" and "Come on Joe." It's good music, however, with "No More One More Time" and Richard Thompson's "Tear-Stained Letter" showing off Sonnier's remarkable range and vocal abilities.

The Complete Mercury Sessions

r. mid-1970s; i. 1992/Mercury 324-512645 CD, CS

Popular music with a country flavor and a hint of Cajun, but beautifully done. The simple arrangements bring out Sonnier's vocals, notably on "Cajun Born," "It Don't Hurt Me Half as Bad," "He's Still All Over You" and "Cheatin' Turns Her On."

Hello Happiness Again

i. 1992/Liberty CDP-7-98761 CD

Good songs, clean arrangements featuring Sonnier's singing and accordion, and good back-up mark this recent recording. "Cafe du Monde" and "French Quarter Moon" capture a New Orleans feel. "Cry Like a Baby," "Hole in the Clouds" and the title track also stand out.

GOOD

Cajun Young Blood

i. 1996/Ace (England) 598 CD

Recorded in the late 1960s and early '70s, these songs offer an interesting glimpse into Cajun music of that period. Selections ranging from weak to awful alternate with some quality ballads. Sonnier fans will appreciate the better tunes—"Blue Letter," "Auntie's Peanuts," "I'm Leaving You," "I'd Like to Forget" and "Broken Heart."

Have a Little Faith

i. 1989/RCA 9718-2-R CD, CS

"Evangeline Special" is the only Cajun tune on this release, but some good songs and Sonnier's great voice make it worthwhile. "I'll Never Get Over You" is a classic, and "Walls" is a difficult song that shows off Sonnier's abilities.

Tears of Joy

i. 1991/Capitol 7-95684 CD

A country-flavored recording with a little Cajun spice. "Smile When You Say That" is worth the price of the CD.

OTHER RECORDINGS

The Cajun Valentino

Goldband 7806 CD; The Cajun Troubadour/Goldband 7806 LP

Right Next Door to Texas

Goldband 7805 CS, LP

JOHNNY SONNIER
Vocals, accordion

Besides accordion, Sonnier can play drums, bass guitar and steel guitar. Born in 1960 in Lafayette, he started his career at 13 as a drummer. He had several bands playing Cajun, country and progressive French before forming his present band, Cajun Heritage, in 1988. A strong singer, Sonnier was chosen "Best Male Vocalist" in 1991 by the Cajun French Music Association, which named Cajun Heritage "Band of the Year" the same year. Sonnier has also won several "song of the year" awards from the organization.

Sonnier has cut three albums for Louisiana labels. His second, *Oh Pour les Memoirs*, released in 1990, is no longer available.

THE BEST

Send a Message to My Heart

i. 1992/Vidrine 91004 CD, CS

"In the Barn" and "Till a Tear Becomes a Rose" from this CD were released as a single and won the Cajun French Music Association award for "Best Single of the Year." The steel guitar heightens the C&W feel of some numbers, but the album is more Cajun than country. Steve Burkhammer's fiddle solos enhance several cuts, and the steel guitar fits well. The band backs Sonnier's vocals and accordion well. Top songs include his "Saturday Night Waltz" and Iry LeJeune's "Give Me My Hat."

GOOD

Tous Les Dimance Apres Midi

r. 1988-1989; i. 1989/Lanor 1010 LP

Sonnier's singing and accordion playing are the main attraction; the five-piece band doesn't produce a full sound until the last cut. The steel guitar is weak on some songs, and Russell Quebodeaux's good fiddling is heard too little. "Paul Daigle Sur le Juke Box" is worthy, as are the accordion/steel guitar duet and solos, and fiddle solo on the instrumental "Two Step de Pon Breaux."

THE SUNDOWN PLAYBOYS
Group

The Sundown Playboys are one of the oldest Cajun bands still playing. In 1972, they enjoyed a brush with fame when the Beatles' Apple label leased their Swallow Records single, "Saturday Night Special," after the band's then accordionist, 16-year-old **Pat Savant**, mailed Apple a copy of the 45. Otherwise, the Cajun-country ensemble has remained a local favorite in the Lake Charles area since 1947, when it was formed by the late accordionist Lionel Cormier.

Cormier died of a heart attack while playing "Church Point Two-Step" at the Bamboo Club in Lake Charles in 1971. Since then, his son, drummer Lesa Cormier (b. 1931, Elton), has led the band. The only remaining original member, he bridges the generational gap between his father and his son Danny Cormier, who plays steel guitar and sings with the group.

The band also includes accordionist Homer Lejeune, the group's principal vocalist since its first recording in 1988; Darrell Higginbotham on guitar/vocals; and Wallace Touchet on fiddle. Other personnel have come and gone over the years. The group recorded with Feature and

Goldband before cutting the following Swallow albums in the traditional style.

THE BEST

Hier et Aujourd'hui (Yesterday and Today)

i. 1993/Swallow 6108 CD, CS (contains 4 songs from the Swallow LP Cajun Spirit)

The quality of the vocals varies on this recent CD featuring singing by Homer Lejeune (adequate), Darrell Higginbotham (inadequate) and four young women called Les Amis (good). However, the instrumentals are fine, and the rhythm section creates a good dance beat. Lejeune's accordion is strong, as are the fiddlers. The most delightful instrumentals are "Creole Stomp," "Jealous Heart" and Lejeune's "Homer's Two Step."

GOOD

Saturday Night Cajun Music!

i. 1988/Swallow 6072 CS, LP

The band was 41 years old when it recorded this debut album. The players are talented instrumentalists, as best shown on "Papa Burke Special," the record's high point. LeJeune's vocals work on some tunes, notably "Bayou Que Tortue," but not on others.

Cajun Spirit

i. 1990/Swallow 6083 CS, LP

Good songs by good musicians. LeJeune's vocals are better than on their first album, but Higginbotham's are no help. D. L. Menard's "Back Door" and the instrumental "Homer's Two Step" are the best tunes.

TASSO
Group

Old-time Cajuns remember "tasso" as meat strips hung on a fence to dry and then smoked. The past is hallowed to this trio, as their album *The Old Timey Way* suggests. The CD even sports a cover photo of blood-red beef strips hanging on a barbed-wire fence. Yet the musicians are by no means old-timers.

Fddler Mitchell Reed (b. 1971, Bayou Vista) accompanied his father and brother, both accordionists, when he was young. He met guitarist/vocalist/songwriter Randy Vidrine (b. 1954, Ville Platte) at **Marc Savoy's** Saturday morning jam sessions at his shop in Eunice. They formed the trio along with accordionist/vocalist Philip Allemond (b. 1956 in the Atchafalaya Swamp near Henderson). Playing in a folk music style, the group adds a few original tunes to their strictly traditional repertoire.

THE BEST

The Old Timey Way

i. 1993/Swallow 6103 CD, CS

On Tasso's first CD, their song choice, vocals and unadorned instrumentation all harken back to a time when Cajun music was still unaltered by outside influences. Vidrine's fine vocals enhance every song he sings, but Allemond's do not always measure up. He projects the dramatic style common to the old Cajun singers, but his voice sometimes strays off key. All three players are excellent instrumentalists, creating a full sound. The best songs are "La Valse des Opelousas," Lawrence Walker's great "Laissez les Bons Temps Rouler" and "Pour la Derniere Fois."

EXCELLENT

Viens a ma Maison (Come to My House)

i. 1994/Swallow 6113 CD, CS

Michael Doucet of Beausoleil added his expertise and production skills to this second release by the talented trio. Allemond's three new songs blend well with the traditional numbers, although his singing zeal can't substitute for a better voice. Vidrine, a first-rate vocalist, adds greatly to the songs he sings. The group is strong instrumentally, and their worthy efforts to preserve traditional Cajun music should be applauded.

AMBROSE THIBODEAUX
Accordion

Thibodeaux, born into a musical family in 1903 near Eunice, played solidly traditional Cajun accordion music from the age of 17. As recently as the early 1980s, he performed every Saturday on Revon Reed's "Mamou Hour," a program of Cajun music broadcast by radio KEUN Eunice from a lounge in Mamou, as part of a band led by fiddler **Sady Courville**. He also played at folk music festivals for many years and won accordion contests on his single-row, button accordion.

THE BEST

That French Acadian Sound

La Louisianne 133 LP

This recording is vibrant. Although personnel are not named in the liner notes, the good vocals appear to be by Gervis Quebedeaux; the sound quality here is so superior to the group's other recordings that he sounds better than usual. Thibodeaux himself is a moderately good accordion player. The triangle and guitar provide a strong, steady beat, and the balance between instruments is excellent. "Madam Sostan" stands out for the powerful, dramatic vocal, and "The Cemetery" for song quality and overall performance.

GOOD

Authentic Cajun French Music & Folk Songs

i. 1977/La Louisianne 143 LP

Gervis Quebedeaux is listed in the liner notes as vocalist, and he is a very talented Cajun singer, excelling on "La Valse du Vieux Homme." The fiddle and Thibodeaux's accordion share the limelight.

OTHER RECORDINGS

Authentic French Acadian Music

La Louisianne 112 LP

More Authentic Acadian French Music

La Louisianne 119 LP

RUFUS THIBODEAUX
Fiddle

Best known as a longtime accompanist for Cajun -country's **Jimmy C. Newman**, Thibodeaux is a session player who has appeared on so many recordings that he is sometimes called the "King of the Cajun Fiddlers." Along with **Dewey Balfa** and **"Doc" Guidry**, he is credited with the comeback of the Cajun fiddle.

Born in Ridge in 1934, and raised in Lake Charles, he learned guitar at six and fiddle at 12. He first played music with his accordionist father's band. The youngster left school to play with Papa Cairo, then Newman, with whom he stayed from 1951 to 1980. Thibodeaux was a session man at Jay Miller's studio in Crowley during the 1960s, playing fiddle, guitar, fender bass and electric mandolin on everything from Cajun to hillbilly and blues. He also played with country stars like George Jones and Bob Wills. In 1986, he joined the Neal Young band.

THE BEST

Cajun Fiddle

i. mid-1970s/La Louisianne 137 LP

This all-instrumental release wears well. The songs are lively, and the back-up musicians (unidentified on the album) produce a full sound. Thibodeaux's fine fiddling is looser and more interesting than on his other recordings, and the steel guitar is also good. The uptempo version of the Cajun classic, "Pauvre Clochard" (Poor Hobo) has an outstanding fiddle solo; "La Valse de Meche" (The Waltz of the Marsh) is also nice.

EXCELLENT

A Tribute to Harry Choates and His Cajun Fiddle: The Legendary Jay Miller Sessions, Vol. 23

r. mid-1960s; i. 1981/Flyright (England) 572 LP

Some of Thibodeaux's most fluid fiddling appears on this LP, for which Jay Miller assembled a sterling group of musicians. Thibodeaux shares top billing with Abe Manuel, a fiddler who sings here. The best fiddle work is on "Louisiana Waltz," "Allons a Lafayette" and "Chere Tou Toute."

GOOD

The Cajun Country Fiddle of Rufus Thibodeaux

i. mid-1970s/La Louisianne 129 CS, LP

This all-instrumental LP of Cajun and country music classics showcases Thibodeaux's fiddle. Otherwise similar to the earlier *Cajun Fiddle*, Thibodeaux's playing is less adventuresome. The steel guitar playing is also less interesting. "Lake Arthur Stomp" stomps, and "Maiden's Prayer" offers a taste of country swing.

WAYLON THIBODEAUX
Fiddle, vocals

Billing himself as "Louisiana's Rockin' Fiddler," Waylon Thibodeaux was most recently in residence on Bourbon Street in New Orleans, playing for tourists. He is in fact a French-speaking Cajun from Houma, "down the bayou" south of the Crescent City. He started playing drums in a country band when he was 13, but soon switched to fiddle. At 16, he won the title of Louisiana State Fiddle Champion in 1984 and has since toured in France and Latin America. For a time, Thibodeaux toured with **Jo-el Sonnier**, then played with **Bruce Daigrepont** until the mid-1990s.

Thibodeaux's band plays clubs and festivals. He has recorded three albums for Mardi Gras, a New Orleans label, serving up a gumbo of Cajun and zydeco standards along with crowd-pleasing Louisiana pop-rock and country. However, on his most recent disc, *Dans La Louisiane*, Thibodeaux returns to his acoustic, Cajun roots.

THE BEST

Dans La Louisiane

(with Gina Forsyth) i. 1995/W. G. Records 9501 CD

An exceptional recording by two talented and energetic performers. Thibodeaux handles most of the vocals, his relaxed manner making the difficult seem easy. Singer/songwriter Forsyth has a strong, soulful alto voice and is an outstanding guitarist and fiddler. Top tunes are "Danse Carre," "Branche de Murier" and "Lacassine Special."

Chapter 1 • Cajun & Creole

EXCELLENT

Best of Cajun: The Traditional Songs

i. c. 1995/Mardi Gras 5007 CD, CS

From the opening note, Thibodeaux demands serious attention. With spare backing, his vocals and fiddling control the stage. A relaxed singer with a good range, he can sing anything well–especially the old classics like "Grand Mamou." Other choice cuts include "Grand Texas," "Madame Sosthene," "Jolie Blonde" and "Big Mamou." Unfortunately, the album has no liner notes (a common fault with Mardi Gras recordings), so personnel and recording/issue dates are unknown.

Cajun Festival: Live from the Bayou

i. c. 1995/Mardi Gras 5008 CD, CS

A mix of traditional and newer songs. Again, no liner notes, so the excellent accordion player goes unidentified. Thibodeaux's vocals are good and his strong fiddle work is featured often. Highlights of the top quality song selection are "Blues de Toc Toc," "Bayou Pon Pon" and "Tante Na Na."

GOOD

Like a Real Cajun

i. 1995/Mardi Gras 1023 CD, CS

Thibodeaux sounds less like a real Cajun on this inaptly named disc than on any of his others. The song mix has everything from a Mardi Gras classic and swamp pop to some Cajun and zydeco tunes. The back-up musicians are talented, but Thibodeaux works better with simpler arrangements and more traditional music. Where his singing and fiddling predominate, the songs work, as on the self-penned "Allons Faire une Vie Ensemble" and "Ce N'Est Pas Comme D'Habitude."

THE TOUCHET BROTHERS
Group

An example of a Cajun family band that plays well even though it is not their full-time occupation, the Touchet Brothers consists of about half of the dozen children of a Kaplan farm family whose mother played accordion at house dances. In 1940, three of them –guitarists Arconge "Tee-Coon" and Iday, plus fiddler Willis, began playing for house dances. Later, brother Elier joined, and sister Eva played on and off with the group, which nevertheless remained the Touchet "Brothers".

The band broke up after the death of their mother, Celestine. In 1954, Arconge joined Elias Badeaux's Louisiana Aces and played with them until 1967, when he reformed the Touchet Brothers Band. In the new group, Arconge played steel guitar, and Elier played accordion. Among musicians who played with them was **D. L. Menard**.

The Touchet Bros. Cajun Music Band

i. 1985/Swallow 6055 CS, LP

Though not professional musicians, the Touchets sound good. Eva, who has an attractive voice similar to Sheryl Cormier's, is lead vocalist or shares the vocals on four songs, and Willis is a fair vocalist; but Arconge's singing is the best of the three. Instrumental strengths are Elier's accordion playing and Willis' fiddling. The Touchets (mainly Willis) wrote all but one of the songs, which are pleasing. Highlights are "Poor Man Waltz," "Jolie Fille" and "Lonesome Cajun Waltz."

WAYNE TOUPS & ZYDECAJUN

Accordion, vocals

Swallow CD 6124

Purists may frown on Wayne Toups, but he is one of Cajun music's most popular modernists. He calls his style "a Cajun, R&B, Southern rock sound," and to many, he is the most gifted example of the hybrid. Since he burst on the scene at the 1984 Cajun Music Festival in Lafayette, his flamboyant performances and deft accordion-playing have taken audiences by storm not only in Louisiana, but in Latin America and Southeast Asia, as well. *Offbeat* calls him "the Cajun counterpart to zydeco's **Beau Jocque**."

Raised on traditional Cajun music in Crowley, Toups learned the accordion from his brother and uncle at 13. His tastes were more Motown than Cajun; he idolized rock and R&B artists such as Duane Allman and Otis Redding, along with Cajun musicians Walter Mouton, **Iry LeJeune**, **Amedee Ardoin** and **Belton Richard**. Toups worked in the oil fields before forming a band called Cajun Creole in the late 1970s that was succeeded by Zydecajun.

As the bands' names suggest, Toups has always sought to blend Cajun with Creole styles. For a time, he played with fiddler **Michael Doucet** regularly at Mulate's, a popular dance hall in Breaux Bridge, and began to incorporate more traditional music into his repertoire. It wasn't until his 20s that Toups discovered zydeco king **Clifton Chenier**. Today, Zydecajun's repertoire includes an eclectic blend, but Toups makes sure to include several traditional songs in every performance.

After Toups' smash performance at the 1984 festival, his career took flight with several albums, national touring and an appearance on MTV, where he co-hosted a Mardi Gras special. He earned a reputation as "the Cajun Springsteen" or "Le Boss" for his dynamic live performances. However, his dizzying accordion playing wins higher marks than his singing. His string of recordings–six in10 years–established him as an important Cajun/Southern rock artist. One album, *Blast from the Bayou*, was the first Cajun or zydeco recording to make the *Billboard* pop charts.

THE BEST

Live! Down Home

r. 1987; i. 1992/MTE 5043 CD

Recorded live at the 51st International Rice Festival in Toups' hometown of Crowley, this disc captures the crowd's fervor and boasts exceptional sound quality. The pace is frantic, letting up only for the one slow tune, the traditional "Lafayette Waltz." Standout rockers include "Zydeco Shoes," "Lacassine Special," "I Went to the Dance" and "Sugar Bee." The rest of the band, including Wade Richard on guitar and R. P. Harrell on piano, are given plenty of chances to show their skills, although Toups' accordion virtuosity deservedly gets top billing.

EXCELLENT

Johnnie Can't Dance

i. 1988/Mercury/Polygram 846585 CD, CS

Toups' second release remains one of his most enjoyable. Featuring the same band as on his live album, this disc finds the group in fine form with a varied program including waltzes such as "A Secret Love" and "Calcasieu Waltz/La Valse de Calcasieu," rockers "Zydeco Shoes" and "Madeleine," and two-steps "Two Step Mamou" and "Johnnie Can't Dance." "Ma Pretty/Ma Jolie," Toups' version of the zydeco standard "Ma Negress," rocks along nicely. One small complaint: the CD clocks in at only slightly over 33 minutes.

Back to the Bayou

i. 1995/Swallow 6124 CD, CS

On his most recent release, Toups continues to expand his horizons while remaining true to his Cajun roots. The Southern rock/blues influence is most apparent on the hard-driving rockers "Come on In" and "Ma Belle," while he tries his hand at balladry on "Take My Hand" and "Every Man Needs a Woman." Fiddler Michael Doucet adds Cajun spice in guest appearances.

GOOD

Blast from the Bayou

i. 1989/Mercury/Polygram 836518 CD, CS

Not quite as frantic as most Toups albums, this one features three ballads and one waltz out of 10 tunes, the most effective ballad being his rendition of Van Morrison's "Tupelo Honey." Toups would have been well advised to stay away from "Tell it Like it Is," since his vocals suffer from comparison to Aaron Neville's. However, "Sweet Joline," "Sugar

Bee" and "Going Back to Big Mamou" rock as hard as anything Toups has done.

OTHER RECORDINGS

Fish Out of Water

i. 1991/Mercury/Polygram 848289 CD, CS

ZyDeCajun

i. 1986/Mercury/Polygram 846584 CD, CS

LAWRENCE WALKER
Accordion, vocals, fiddle

One of the best Cajun musicians of this century, Lawrence Walker cut an impressive swath through the 1930s, 1940s and 1950s. Had he left more recordings behind, his legacy would probably be more widely acknowledged. Instead, his reputation as the King of the Accordion Players rests on his huge popularity in the dance halls of his day.

Despite his name, Walker (b. 1907 near Scott) had Cajun blood and spoke perfect French. In 1915, his family moved to Orange, Tx. There, he and his brother Elton teamed up as The Walker Brothers group, with Lawrence on accordion and Elton on fiddle. They joined their father, well-known fiddler Allen Walker, for recordings of traditional Cajun and hillbilly fiddle songs 1928-1932. In the mid-1930s, Lawrence updated his sound, adding pop tunes like "Alberta," his adaptation of "Corinna" honoring his daughter. In 1936, he made a hit appearance with the Broussard Family Band at the National Folk Festival in Dallas.

With string bands dominating the scene during the late 1930s and early 1940s, Walker set aside his accordion, picking it up again after World War II on his return to Louisiana. Along with other giants of the Cajun music revival like **Nathan Abshire** and **Aldus**

Roger, he restored the accordion to center stage and purveyed the simpler, old-time style then in demand. He maintained high standards for his band of strong musicians, among them Johnnie Allan, who played steel guitar with the group 1953-1958 before turning to swamp pop.

Walker reached his peak of popularity during the 1950s with his Wandering Aces Band, performing in dance halls through south Louisiana and east Texas. Famous for his smooth accordion style and exceptional singing, the hugely popular bandleader stuck mainly to a mainstream Cajun repertoire, but proved he had a way with rock 'n' roll and country, as well.

A rice farmer by trade, this important musician had a surprisingly scanty recording career, with no albums by the time of his death in 1968. Along with a few 78s for Victor's Bluebird label in 1936 like the popular "Alberta", he recorded a string of singles for George Khoury's local Lyric label in the early 1950s. Of the Khoury's recordings, he is best remembered for his songs of lost love, like "Reno Waltz" and "Evangeline Waltz." His later recordings for the La Louisianne, Vee-Pee and Swallow labels featured Walker's mainstream Cajun sound plus some Cajun rock 'n' roll. One of the Swallow singles, Walker's "Les Bon Temps Rouler," became that label's first Cajun hit. The year Walker died, 1968, La Louisianne put out a tribute album featuring his Khoury's hits plus "Allons Rock and Roll" and "Lena Mae," two early Cajun rock 'n' roll tunes sung in English.

A Legend at Last

i. 1983/Swallow 6051 LP

This LP is one of the few sources of Walker's music on either LP or CD, other than a few scattered singles on compilations. Since most of the songs are from the original Khoury 78s, the sound is thin on some selections, although remarkably good on others, as on the stellar "Midnight Waltz." Uneven, too, is the balance between instruments and vocals. Walker's talent and spirit always come through, however; just listen to "Osson Two Step" and "Wandering Aces Special." The prolific songwriter composed all 12 songs here, including his hit "Les Bon Temps Rouler." He possessed one of the stronger voices in Cajun music–clear, powerful and pleasingly gravelly.

OTHER RECORDINGS

A Tribute to the Late Great Lawrence Walker

i. 1968/La Louisianne 126 CS (unreviewed)

Chapter 2 • Zydeco

TOP 10 ZYDECO ALBUMS
(in alphabetical order)

We consider these albums essential buys, because of their high quality and/or because they capture the essence of a major performer. Please see artist entries in the book for reviews of the albums, which are highlighted in the text with this symbol:

BEST OF LOUISIANA ZYDECO–BUCKWHEAT ZYDECO
AVI 5011 CD

BOGALUSA BOOGIE–CLIFTON CHENIER
Arhoolie 347 CD

GIT IT, BEAU JOCQUE!–BEAU JOCQUE
Rounder 2134 CD

IT'S LA LA TIME–ZYDECO FORCE
Maison de Soul 1054 CD

LIVE! AT THE HABIBI TEMPLE–BOOZOO CHAVIS
Rounder 2130 CD

LOUISIANA MUSIC–ROCKIN' DOPSIE
Atlantic 82307 CD

MY BABY DON'T WEAR NO SHOES–C.J. CHENIER
Arhoolie 1098 CD

SAUCE PIQUANTE–LYNN AUGUST
Black Top 1092 CD

STEADY ROCK–NATHAN & THE ZYDECO CHA-CHAS
Rounder 2092 CD

ZYDECO DYNAMITE: THE CLIFTON CHENIER ANTHOLOGY
Rhino 71194 CD

CHAPTER 2: ZYDECO

COREY ARCENEAUX
Accordion, vocals

Corey and the Hot Peppers are one of the many promising young zydeco bands sprouting up in southwestern Louisiana. Arceneaux picked up his interest in zydeco at the age of 11 when he heard his uncle, **Fernest Arceneaux**, play accordion. The youngster asked another accordionist he met at a dance, Clayton Sampy, to teach him the instrument. Then, through an uncle who works as a security guard at El Sid O's Club in Lafayette, Arceneaux began attending **Nathan Williams**' rehearsals there. Before long, Williams let Arceneaux sit in.

For a year, Arceneaux played with his uncle Fernest and Rick Williams. Then he joined with his cousin Shane Benard and bassist Russell Benoit (formerly with Nathan Williams' Zydeco Cha Chas) in the Hot Peppers, which debuted at El Sid O's in 1992. Before the age of 20, he had cut his first record, in 1995. Arceneaux plays the piano accordion, like his neighbor **Buckwheat Zydeco**. He points to Buckwheat and Nathan Williams as influences, along with **Clifton Chenier**, at whose funeral he served as altar boy.

Hit and Run

i. 1995 / Jewel/Vidrine 5053 CD

The music here ranges from traditional zydeco to more funkified sounds popularized by Beau Jocque. Arceneaux also tries his hand at covering Solomon Burke's country-soul ballad "Nothing Else Matters." Unfortunately, his youthful-sounding voice can't quite cut Burke's. (But whose can?) The influence of Buckwheat Zydeco can be felt on tunes such as the title track and on "Time After Time," both R&B-type rockers. One can hear Beau

Jocque and the Hi Rollers funk on "Warm Up." The flat-sounding production hampers the impact of this release, but with a little maturity and better sound, Corey and the Hot Peppers could become a force to reckon with.

FERNEST ARCENEAUX
Accordion, vocals

As much as anyone in zydeco today, Fernest Arceneaux carries on the zydeco blues tradition of **Clifton Chenier**. In fact, he learned accordion by watching Chenier and Claude Falk, as well as his father, a rural musician. Born in 1940 near Lafayette into a big French-speaking family of sharecroppers, Arceneaux first played his brother-in-law's accordion when he was out working in the fields. When the youngster was good enough, his father let him sit in with him at house parties, perching him on a chair on top of two soda water cases so people could see him.

In the 1960s, Arceneaux forsook the accordion for the guitar to play in an R&B/rock band that included two saxes, guitar, bass and two drummers. Because the drummers were so loud on the tom-toms, Arceneaux acquired the name "Fernest and the Thunders." However, Chenier persuaded him to pick up the accordion again in 1978 (much the same as Chenier had pulled Buckwheat Zydeco into the zydeco fold two years earlier, also after a short career in R&B), and the zydeco band Fernest and the Thunders was born.

Discovered that year by a Belgian blues enthusiast, Robert Sacre, Arceneaux and his group began touring Europe regularly with their crowd-pleasing mix of zydeco, blues, R&B and rock 'n' roll. The same year, the band began a healthy recording career with a Blues Unlimited release called *Fernest and the Thunders* that featured zydeco and swamp pop. At home, Fernest and the Thunders mainly work the Gulf Coast crawfish circuit.

Arceneaux is a talented accordionist with a full sound, but because of asthma, his vocals lack force. Behind him, the Thunders provide abundant power, largely due to the outstanding drumming of Clarence "Jockey" Etienne, a well-known blues session player, and versatile blues guitar work of Chester Chevalier, Arceneaux's brother-in-law. A tragic loss for the band occurred in the early 1980s, when bassist/vocalist Victor Walker, a gifted blues singer and veteran of the Gulf Coast music scene, was killed in a Louisiana barroom brawl.

THE BEST

Zydeco Stomp!

r. 1981; i. 1995/JSP (England) 220 CD

Recorded in London, this release catches Fernest and the Thunders in top form. Backed by his longtime associates Chester Chevalier on guitar, Clarence "Jockey" Etienne on drums and the late Victor Walker on bass, Arceneaux rocks his way through a solid program of mostly straight zydeco blues, with a few old-time French numbers thrown in. What sets this album above Arceneaux's others is the astounding singing of Walker, who died shortly after this session. Shivers run up and down your spine when he wails on the slow blues "Sweet Little Angel," "Chains of Love" and especially "Mean Woman." Arceneaux himself was in good form vocally here, as witnessed by his renditions of the rocking "Big Mamou" and Little Walter's tough slow blues, "Last Night," also showcasing Arceneaux's excellent accordion playing. The CD's only drawback is

the flat sound on several of the tracks; otherwise, this is a must-have for any lover of zydeco blues.

EXCELLENT

Rockin' Pneumonia

r. 1979; i. 1991/Ornament/CMA (Germany) 8009 CD

Recorded before live audiences in Germany on two different dates in 1979, this release finds Fernest and the Thunders on fire with a solid program of blues, waltzes and French zydeco. Guitarist Chester Chevalier and drummer Clarence "Jockey" Etienne are present, along with bassist and part-time vocalist Wayne Burns. Standout rockers include "Ma Negresse," "Please Don't Leave Me" and "Zydeco Boogaloo," while the moody slow zydeco blues genre is represented by Jimmy Reed's "Honest I Do" and Guitar Slim's "The Things I Used to Do." Another winning classic is the Louisiana swamp ballad "Irene," cutting a swinging, mellow groove.

Zydeco Blues Party

i. 1994/Mardi Gras 1019 CD

This disc could be at the top of the must-buy list were it not for Arceneaux's weak vocals. The band is a collection of zydeco all-stars, including such veterans of Clifton Chenier's and Rockin' Dopsie's bands as John Hart on sax, Paul Senegal on guitar, Alonzo Johnson on bass, Joseph Edwards on drums and Rockin' Dopsie Jr. on rubboard. Well-recorded and produced at Ultrasonic Studios in New Orleans, the album includes such chestnuts as "My Negress," "Choo Choo Cha-Boogie" and "Jolie Blonde." Lowdown zydeco blues like "Last Night" and "I'm On My Way Back Home" allow Hart and Senegal to strut their stuff. A strong zydeco album squarely in the Clifton Chenier tradition.

OTHER RECORDINGS

Fernest and the Thunders

i. 1979/Blues Unlimited 5005 LP

Gumbo Special

r. & i. 1987/Schubert 7865 LP (also available as CMA [Germany] 8016 CD)

Zydeco Thunder

r. & i. 1985/Greybeard GRI-1001 LP

CHRIS ARDOIN (Christopher Ardoin)
Vocals, accordion

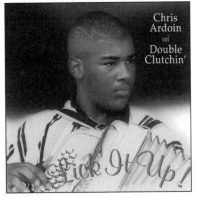

Maison de Soul CD 1058

The best of the young *"nouveau zydeco"* crowd, Chris Ardoin of Lake Charles belongs to the eminent Ardoin musical dynasty. He is the grandson of Creole accordionist and elder statesman **"Bois Sec" Ardoin** (cousin of the legendary Amedee Ardoin) and son of **Lawrence "Black" Ardoin**. Like their predecessors, Chris and his siblings, Sean and Erica, learned accordion–but of them, Chris was recognized as the best early on.

At the age of four, Chris first played in public with his father's band at a gumbo cook-off in Texas attended by 3,000 people. At nine, he played Carnegie Hall with his grandfather and joined his father's band. But just as Lawrence had turned his back on his own

father's old-style Cajun music to form his "French Zydeco Band," Chris resisted his dad's traditional bent, to the point where Lawrence gave up and handed the reins to his son. Today, Lawrence manages Chris' band, Double Clutchin'.

In the mid-1990s, Double Clutchin' excelled at a funk groove a la **Beau Jocque**. In fact, the band's name refers to the repeated bass drum kicks characteristic of this "new zydeco" sound. But the group also pays homage to its ancestors by including some traditional Creole material along with songs written by Chris and his older brother Sean, the band's drummer.

In liner notes for the band's first popular recording, *"That's Da Lick!,"* Sean admits that the album was an attempt to reach the audience that Beau Jocque had created. Sean wrote all the songs on the album, but all three siblings helped with the music and arrangements. By the next album, released in 1995, the band had been together for 10 years, even though Chris was just 14. Most of the other band members were teenagers, too, with a lineup that included cousin Alphonse Ardoin and Peter Jacobs. The oldest was Sean, 26 at the time. Now that his voice has deepened, Chris' vocals are featured along with his seasoned accordion-playing, in what has become the hottest teen zydeco band around.

THE BEST

Lick it Up!

i. 1995/Maison de Soul 1058 CD, CS

Listening to this CD, it is hard to believe the band members are mostly in their teens. The music is good, hard-rockin', double-pumpin' modern zydeco of the Beau Jocque school. There are nods to the past with a slow minor-key blues, "I Wonder," and a funked-up version of "Uncle Bud." But most of the album is squarely

Chapter 2 • Zydeco

in the nouveau, funk zydeco bag popular in Louisiana in the early '90s. Highlights include the nasty title cut, the bouncy "Good Times" and the funky "Play That Thing," a Beau Jocque-type band workout. With youngsters like Chris Ardoin putting out music like this, the future of zydeco is bright indeed.

OTHER RECORDINGS

That's da Lick!

i. 1994/Maison de Soul CD, CS

LAWRENCE "BLACK" ARDOIN
Accordion, drums

The second son of Creole accordionist/singer **Alphonse "Bois Sec" Ardoin**, Lawrence was born in 1946 in Duralde. He played drums with the Ardoin Family Band until his older brother, Gustav, a highly accomplished accordionist, was killed in an auto accident, leaving the accordion seat vacant. The band played old-style Cajun music reflecting Bois Sec's apprenticeship with his cousin, the great **Amedee Ardoin**. When Bois Sec retired in the mid-1970s, Lawrence took over the band.

In the early 1980s, Lawrence traded his father's traditional music for zydeco, forming his own French Zydeco Band. His first album, *Lawrence "Black" Ardoin and His French Zydeco Band*, reflects Ardoin's southwest Louisiana heritage, with his Acadian push-pull accordion style and Cajun sounds mixing with zydeco and even swamp pop. He sings in both French and English.

The latest recording artist in the remarkable Ardoin dynasty is Lawrence's son, **Chris Ardoin**, to whom Lawrence passed the torch in the early 1990s. Today, Lawrence manages Chris' band, Double Clutchin'.

THE BEST

Lawrence "Black" Ardoin and His French Zydeco Band

(with Edward Poulard) r. & i. 1984/Arhoolie 1091 CS, LP

This is Ardoin's first album. It contains a mixture of songs by Amedee Ardoin, Clifton Chenier and others, as well as originals. His vocals sound strained on the first two songs, "Bayou Two-Step" and "You Used to Call Me." He fares better on the later "Haunted House," "I've Been There" and "Every Now and Then." Edward Poulard's fiddle work is exceptional, and his singing on "Talk to Your Daughter" is also good. With good instrumental sound throughout, the result is some good zydeco music.

OTHER RECORDINGS

Hot & Spicy Zydeco

i. 1992/La Louisianne 1041 CS

LYNN AUGUST
Vocals, accordion, keyboards, drums

Black Top CD 1092

Lynn August is one of zydeco's most versatile artists and finest vocalists. Heavily influenced by **Clifton Chenier**, Ray Charles and Fats Domino, Lynn August has played in many styles over a varied career. Intelligence and professionalism shine through his music.

August was born in 1948 in Lafayette and grew up listening to swamp pop, New Orleans rhythm & blues and zydeco. Encouraged by his mother to become a musician, the blind August learned how to play drums on an old washtub. He didn't like the state school for blind children he was sent to because, he said, they wouldn't let kids play the piano. As a French speaker with little English, he also found the school hard. He then attended a private school.

At 12, August was recruited as a drummer by Esquerita, the bandleader who also tutored Little Richard. Esquerita convinced August to switch to piano; a few years later he switched again, to the Hammond B-3 organ. He later rode the crawfish circuit and directed a church choir for a time.

During the 1960s and '70s, August performed solo, played with various swamp pop and zydeco bands (including a stint with **Buckwheat Zydeco** in the early '60s) and performed with his own big band before picking up the accordion in 1988 and starting his zydeco career. He formed the Hot August Knights with his longtime friend, tenor sax player John Hart, who is also blind.

One of the few zydeco musicians who have made a historical study of Creole music tradition, August listened to the 1934 Alan Lomax field recordings and incorporated the original percussive and syncopated unaccompanied Creole style of "jure" singing into his performances. He spices his blues-based zydeco with R&B, pop and gospel.

THE BEST

Sauce Piquante

i. 1993/Black Top 1092 CD, CS

A TOP 10 ZYDECO ALBUM

This blues-oriented CD contains music from all styles, including old-time zydeco, R&B and gospel. Killer cover versions of blues jewels like "It's Too Late" and "Marked Deck" stand alongside originals such as "City Woman" (I'm Not Your Country Boy) and "Did You Have Fun Making Me Cry?" August pays tribute to Clifton Chenier with a lovely version of the blues waltz "You Used to Call Me." Guest appearances by New Orleans guitarist Snooks Eaglin and Fats Domino sax man Fred Kemp add to the appeal.

EXCELLENT

Creole Cruiser

i. 1992/ Black Top 1074 CD, CS

Just a notch in quality below "Sauce Piquante," August's first Black Top release showcases his many styles. Particularly moving is his rendition of Chuck Willis' "That Train Is Gone." He rocks the house with "Undivided Love" and "When I Woke Up This Morning." The cuts "Blind Man" and "Losing Hand" illustrate his adeptness in the minor blues mode. The band for this New Orleans session includes keyboardist Sammy Berfect and bassist George Porter Jr. of the Meters.

OTHER RECORDINGS

It's Party Time!

i. 1988/Maison de Soul 1027 CS, LP

Zydeco Groove

i. 1989/Maison de Soul 1036 CS, LP

BEAU JOCQUE (Andrus Espre)
Accordion, vocals

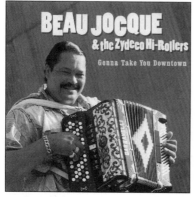

Rounder CD 2150

Beau Jocque is zydeco's overnight sensation. Bursting on the scene in the early 1990s, he quickly became a top draw on the Louisiana dance hall circuit and attracted national and international attention. He is a mighty force in the urban zydeco movement.

A former electrician from Kinder who was once bored by the old-timers' zydeco, Beau Jocque (b. 1957) began playing his father's Cajun accordion in 1987 after a serious back injury at work sidelined him, paralyzing him from the waist down for a year. As a youth he had played various horns in the high school band and listened to ZZ Top and James Brown, avoiding his dad's instrument. During his recuperation, his father "conned" him into learning it by refusing to let him touch it—a challenge the son met.

"Actually, it was an answer to a lot of prayers. Bein' injured and bein' down and knowing that you can't do any more what you trained yourself to do can be very depressing," he told *Offbeat* in 1996. For the next five years, he and his wife Michelle carefully researched what club-goers liked best, and he listened closely to rural zydeco eminence **Boozoo Chavis'**

rhythmic songs. In 1991, he formed a band that made a splash around New Orleans. Two years later, they were so hot that when Beau sang his hit single "Give Him Cornbread" at the Zydeco Festival in Plaisance, fans threw cornbread at him until he sang it again.

A major innovator, Beau Jocque originated the contemporary style of zydeco which blends zydeco's traditional roots with classic rock and urban styles such as rap and hip-hop. His rapping and funky phrasing reflect the influence of James Brown, while his repertoire honors both the blues and his Creole culture. An imposing 6' 6" stage presence, he sings in a primal style reminiscent of the late Howlin' Wolf. Beau Jocque and the Zydeco Hi-Rollers put out one of the funkiest, bass-thumping sounds in zydeco, enticing a new generation of dancers to the Creole dancehalls.

A friendly feud with Boozoo Chavis involving staged zydeco "battles" has boosted Beau Jocque's career. More serious is his ongoing battle with hot young accordionist **Keith Frank**, who trades charges of song theft and other nasty barbs with his rival. With heavy touring, Beau Jocque increasingly is leaving the home field to Frank and setting his sights higher. An acute businessman, he attributes his success partly to his insistence on quality musicians and equipment (he bought the band's drums, guitars and keyboards, as well as a heavy-duty sound system) and the services of a professional sound engineer.

If any of the recent zydeco artists seems destined to make it big nationally, it is the steamrolling Beau Jocque. He hit the ground running with his first Rounder album—*Beau Jocque Boogie* is one of the best-selling zydeco recordings in the last 25 years—and subsequent releases have kept up the beat. As Beau Jocque sings, "The Hi-Rollers play a little harder."

THE BEST

Git it, Beau Jocque!

r. 1994; i. 1995/Rounder 2134 CD, CS

A TOP 10 ZYDECO ALBUM

You'd better have a strong heart for this one, because the intensity is overwhelming. Recorded live in September 1994 at Harry's Lounge in Breaux Bridge and Slim's Y-Ki-Ki Lounge in Opelousas, both classic zydeco dancehalls, this disc captures the excitement and high energy of a Beau Jocque performance in front of hometown Louisiana audiences. Beau's brand of zydeco/funk/rap/blues is best exemplified here by "Shaggy Dog Two Step," "Beau Jocque Run" and "Beau Jocque Boogie." Also included is his smash hit, "Give Him Cornbread."

EXCELLENT

Gonna Take You Downtown

i. 1996/Rounder 2150 CD

On his latest release, Beau Jocque continues his marriage of traditional zydeco, funk and blues, adding Michael Lockett on keyboards and vocals to good effect. His regular working band backs him, and do they cook! The title cut is pure zydeco funk, as is "Boogie Woogie All Nite Long." Beau remakes Clifton Chenier's "I'm on a Wonder," a slow minor blues, and does funked-up Cajun on D. L. Menard's "The Back Door." The rhythm section of "Skeeta" Charlot on drums, "Sly" Dorion on guitar, "Caveman" Pierre on rubboard and especially Chuck Bush on bass makes for the funkiest zydeco heard lately. Beau's best studio effort so far.

Beau Jocque's Nursery Rhyme

r. & i. 1994/Beau Jocque Music 1001 CD

This four-song, self-produced CD features three dance tunes and a killer version of the Clifton Chenier classic "I'm Coming Home." Beau's rhythm section, the best in the business, pushes the music incessantly. Try not to dance!

Pick Up on This!

i. 1994/Rounder 2129 CD, CS

While the song selection here is not as varied as on *Beau Jocque Boogie*, his first Rounder recording, the grooves run much deeper, especially on the eight-minute-long medley, "Hi-Rollers Theme/Low Rider." The band has matured, and Beau's Howlin' Wolf-influenced vocals have improved markedly.

OTHER RECORDINGS

Beau Jocque Boogie

r. & i. 1993/Rounder 2120 CD, CS

My Name is Beau Jocque

i. 1994/Paula 1031 CD, CS

BUCKWHEAT ZYDECO
(Stanley Dural Jr.)
Accordion, piano, organ, vocals

Rounder LP 2045

Stanley "Buckwheat" Dural Jr. is a driving force behind contemporary zydeco and its most visible international star. A protege of **Clifton Chenier**, the late king of zydeco, Dural is a highly accomplished musician who has no rival as the most successful zydeco recording artist, one of the few to record with major labels like Island Records.

Chapter 2 • Zydeco

Dural's career illustrates zydeco's close relationship with rhythm & blues. He was born in 1947 in Lafayette, the fourth of 12 children. His braided hair earned him the childhood nickname of "Buckwheat" after the character on the TV show *The Little Rascals*. A prodigy on the piano at the age of four, Buckwheat heard old-time zydeco at home growing up, but preferred the modern R&B sound. By the time he was nine, he was playing keyboards professionally with drummer **Lynn August** and in his teens continued to play soul and R&B in local nightclubs. Dural scorned the accordion, his father's and great-grandfather's instrument.

"The music my father played wasn't hip enough for me to play. I used to play Fats Domino and Little Richard on the piano, but he felt I should be playing my roots," Dural told *Downbeat* in 1990. His fame as a keyboardist spreading, Dural next became a sideman for Gulf Coast R&B greats such as Joe Tex, Barbara Lynn and Clarence "Gatemouth" Brown. In 1971, he founded his own 16-piece R&B/funk band, Buckwheat and the Hitchhikers, with whom he mined the commercial soul sound for the next five years.

Dural's resistance to zydeco finally crumbled in 1976, when Chenier, a friend of his father, invited him to join his touring ensemble as an organist. Chenier's dynamism and musical genius blew away the young Dural. Two-and-a-half years later, the master had inspired the reluctant pupil to pick up the accordion and return to his zydeco roots.

With a profound new respect for Creole music and keen awareness of its growing popularity, Dural launched his own zydeco career in 1979 with the Ils Sont Partis Band (named after "They're off!"–the cry at the start of the Lafayette horse races). And take off he did, touring Europe and peeling off four excellent recordings for the Blues Unlimited label. When

a Texas zydeco society named him the new "King of Zydeco," he unintentionally ruffled a few of his elders' feathers.

Dural scored a major hit in 1986 when New York music writer Ted Fox (now his producer) got Ils Sont Partis signed to Island Records–the first zydeco band to record for a major label. Their first Island album, *On a Night Like This*, earned a Grammy nomination and was named one of the ten best albums of the year by *The New York Times* and others. The following year, their appearance in the Hollywood film *The Big Easy* brought them national attention. Since then, the band–by now nominated several times for Grammys–has toured North America and the U.K. and recorded with stars such as Eric Clapton, Willie Nelson and David Hidalgo of Los Lobos, opening up zydeco music to new audiences.

Riding high on the Cajun/zydeco revival, Dural is careful to point out that the word "Cajun" should not be applied to African-American music. In his words, Cajun is music "played straight," whereas zydeco is "played wavy." His urban, R&B/soul-drenched zydeco has struck the right chord with mainstream audiences. He modernized the style by adding a trumpet and a synthesizer and, like Chenier, put a zydeco spin on blues, country and rock tunes. He is proud that his mixture of the traditional and the modern beat reaches the younger generation and provides a bridge to the French language.

In recent years, Dural has edged more and more into commercialism, which may eventually hurt him. Sadly, his crowd-pleasing live performances and recordings hold few surprises these days, as reflected in our choice of his best CDs: two recordings of material from more than a decade ago. Keeping to a hectic touring and recording schedule and making commercials on the side, Dural maintains his popularity with an increasingly mainstream pop-zydeco diet that nevertheless allows his immense talents as a musician, arranger and bandleader to shine through.

THE BEST

Best of Louisiana Zydeco 🪗

r. early 1980s; i. 1996/AVI 5011 CD

A TOP 10 ZYDECO ALBUM

For fans of blues-based zydeco, this is a must-have CD. The titles herein were culled from Buckwheat's four Blues Unlimited albums recorded in the early 1980s soon after he left Clifton Chenier, and the zydeco king's influence permeates this release. Hard rockin', fast tunes such as "Buckwheat Music" and "Zydeco Boogie Woogie" alternate with lovely original instrumentals like "One for the Road" and "Tanya." Slow and midtempo straight zydeco blues songs like "Bad Luck," "I Bought a Raccoon" and "You Got Me Walkin' the Floor" showcase Buckwheat and his band as a swinging, integrated blues machine. The sound is wonderful, much improved over the LPs.

Still, this release could have been better if all the Blues Unlimited recordings had been released as a two-CD set. Eight of the 21 songs here came from the LP *One for the Road*, already released as a CD by Paula Records. Why include these tunes and neglect others from the remaining three Blues Unlimited albums? Although the concept here is flawed, the CD still has Buckwheat's best material.

EXCELLENT

Buckwheat's Zydeco Party

r. 1983,1985; i. 1987/Rounder 11528 CD

This exuberant 17-track compilation from Dural's most inventive years is definitely a "best buy." Led by bass player Lee Allen Zeno,

the band cooks–on patented Buckwheat Zydeco covers of R&B classics like "Turning Point" and "Ya Ya," straight blues like "Someone Else is Steppin' In" and traditional zydeco such as "Lach Pas la Patate." Also noteworthy is the blistering version of "Hot Tamale Baby," the sweet classic Fats Domino tune "Walkin' to New Orleans" and a driving Clifton Chenier song, "Tee Nah Nah." Without a clunker on it, this well-produced CD has a great, full band sound. An essential addition to any zydeco collection, buy this instead of the two Grammy-nominated Rounder releases from which it came: *Turning Point* and *Waiting for My Ya Ya*.

One for the Road

r. & i. 1979/Paula 21 CD, CS

The first of four Buckwheat releases originally issued on the Blues Unlimited label, this remains one of his best. Recorded shortly after he left Clifton Chenier's band, this CD is strongly blues-based and reflects Chenier's influence. Dural penned nine of the 12 songs, with "Rock Me Baby," the zydeco standard "Lucille" and "You Got Me Walkin' the Floor" being the only covers. The swinging, midtempo zydeco blues of "I Bought a Raccoon" and "Bim Bam, Thank You Mam" are but two highlights of this fine release, which unfortunately is the only Blues Unlimited production to find its way onto the CD format in its entirety. The other three Blues Unlimited albums are listed below and are well worth searching out, since they are the equal of *One for the Road*. Even though this is a great release, opt for the AVI CD *Best of Louisiana Zydeco*, because it contains eight of the 12 songs heard here plus 13 more from the other three Blues Unlimited LPs.

Menagerie: The Essential Zydeco Collection

r. 1987-90; i. 1993/Mango/Island 162-539-929 CD, CS

While not quite up to the standard of *Buckwheat's Zydeco Party*, this compilation of some of the best 1987-1990 songs from his first three Island releases nevertheless contains some hard-rocking tunes. Listen to "Ma 'Tit Fille" and "What You Gonna Do?" The album is well-produced and accurately represents Dural's current rich, commercial sound, with the addition of guest artists Dwight Yoakam and Los Lobos' David Hidalgo. Choose *Menagerie* rather than any of the Island offerings.

100% Fortified Zydeco

r. 1983; i. 1988/Black Top 1024 CD, CS, LP

A Grammy nominee, this is the only Buckwheat album put out on the New Orleans-based Black Top label. It dates from his peak creative period in the 1980s. With his longtime sidemen Lee Allen Zeno and Nat Jolliviette pushing the beat behind him, Buckwheat slashes his way through rockers like "I'm Ready to Play" and "Jasperoux." The blues creep in with "Is There Something Inside You?" and "I've Had Trouble with the Blues."

OTHER RECORDINGS

Choo Choo Boogaloo

i. 1994/Music for Little People 42556 CD, CS

Five Card Stud

(with David Hidalgo, Willie Nelson & Mavis Staples)/i. 1994/Island 314-524018 CD, CS

Ils Sont Partis

i. 1984/Blues Unlimited 5022 CS, LP

On a Night Like This

i. 1987/Island 422-842739 CD, CS, LP

On Track

i. 1992/Charisma 91822 CD

People's Choice

i. 1982/Blues Unlimited 5017 CS, LP

Take it Easy Baby

i. 1980/Blues Unlimited 5009 CS, LP

Taking it Home

i. 1988/Island A2 90968 CD, CS, LP

Turning Point

r. 1983; i. 1988/Rounder 2045 CD, CS, LP

Waitin' for My Ya Ya

r. 1985; i. 1988/Rounder 2051 CD, CS, LP

Where There's Smoke There's Fire

i. 1990/Island 422-842925 CD, CS

CHUBBY CARRIER (Roy Carrier)
Accordion, vocals

A popular but not original performer, Roy "Chubby" Carrier draws from many influences to form his please-em-all style. Both his father, **Roy Carrier Sr.**, and grandfather played the accordion, in the old Cajun style. Carrier started his musical career with them as a child when he played drums in the family band.

At the age of 12, he taught himself accordion on his father's instrument when his father was away from their Lawtell farm working in the offshore oil fields. Finally his father bought him his own. The young Carrier got turned on to modern-style zydeco by listening to **Clifton Chenier** records and hearing Chenier in a Lawtell club. Chenier became an important influence on his music.

Carrier started his own zydeco band at 18 but left it in 1987 to gain touring experience playing drums with **Terrance Simien** and the Mallet Playboys, who were traveling throughout the U.S. and Europe. In 1990, he regrouped his own Bayou Swamp Band, which includes his brother Troy on drums, cousin Kevin on washboard, **Buckwheat Zydeco**'s nephew Rodney Dural on bass and David LeJeune on guitar. After touring only six months, Carrier was signed by the Flying Fish label. He has produced two recordings.

Smooth-voiced and sure-fingered on the triple-row accordion, Carrier produces zydeco with a rock beat and big arrangements. The combination plays well on stage, but wears somewhat thin on recordings listened to repeatedly.

THE BEST

Dance All Night

r. & i. 1993/Blind Pig 5007 CD, CS

"Dance all night" is what you'll want to do when this buoyant CD hits your player. Clifton Chenier's influence is present in two highlights, "I'm Coming Home" and "Tule Ton Son Ton," both written by Chenier. Rhythm & blues is represented, too, with a frantic rendition of Bobby Bland's "Turn on Your Lovelight"; and Carrier gets down with the zydeco blues "Rock Me Baby." He even zydeco-izes Bob Wills' western swing song "Stay a Little Longer" and returns to his traditional zydeco roots with "Old Time Zydeco," an accordian/drums/rubboard trio. All in all, a well-produced and recorded release.

GOOD

Boogie Woogie Zydeco

r. & i. 1991/Flying Fish 70575 CD; 90575 CS

Although the vocals are less mature and the recording quality poorer than in *Dance All Night*, this disc still has a lot to recommend it. The band cooks, especially on "Hey Barbariba," Rockin' Sidney's "Good for the Goose" and Boozoo Chavis' "Dog Hill." Carrier

slows the pace with the delightful Louisiana ballad "Sherrie." An enjoyable but hardly essential release.

OTHER RECORDINGS

Go Zydeco Go

i. 1989/Lanor/Jewel 5028 CD

Who Stole the Hot Sauce

i. 1996/Blind Pig 5032 CD

ROY CARRIER
Accordion, vocals

Accordionist Roy Carrier is the father of the better-known **Chubby Carrier** (also named Roy Carrier), leader of the Bayou Swamp Band. The longtime leader of the family band where Chubby got his start, Roy Carrier Sr. has supported his family by working at an offshore oil job and running a small farm.

A popular performer at clubs in the region, he began recording for Louisiana producer Lee Lavergne's Lanor Records in the late 1980s; his first two singles, "I Found My Woman Doing the Zydeco" and "I'm Coming Home to Stay," became regional hits. Carrier owns a zydeco club, the Offshore Lounge, in his hometown of Lawtell.

THE BEST

Soulful Side of Zydeco

i. 1991/Zane 1003 CD

Recorded in the down-home Sound Center studios of producer Lee Lavergne in Church Point, one-half of this CD belongs to Roy Carrier, the other half to Joe Walker. Carrier's selections alternate between rural zydeco rave-ups and smooth soul ballads. The band, including family members Troy Carrier on drums and Deran Carrier on rubboard, plus

George Attle on guitar and Paul Newman on bass, provides the funk-influenced backing that propels Carrier and his accordion on the aptly titled "Rocking with Roy" and "Everybody's Picking on Me," with its James Brown-type bass line. The blues is represented by "Same Old Place," a zydeco version of the oft-recorded "Sweet Home Chicago." The soulful side of zydeco is here with a moody interpretation of Wilson Pickett's soul classic "I Found a Love" and Carrier's own composition, "Show Me How to Love." This CD contains the best of both Carrier and Joe Walker.

GOOD

Zydeco Strokin'

i. 1995/Paula 1044 CD

Originally released on Lanor on cassette only and titled *You Better Watch Out*, this album has now been put onto a CD by Paula and retitled. "Strokin' " was the title of the nasty R&B hit for Clarence Carter and is given the rockin' zydeco treatment here. Eight of the 12 cuts are Carrier originals, but Clifton Chenier's influence appears in Carrier's cover of "Baby Do Right" and the straight zydeco blues of "I'm Leaving Town." An enjoyable enough disc, but hardly an essential purchase.

OTHER RECORDINGS

At His Best

i. 1996/Cajun Sound 206-1010 CD (unreviewed)

BOOZOO CHAVIS (Wilson Chavis)
Vocals, accordion

Maison de Soul LP 1017

Zydeco's longest standing artist, Boozoo Chavis is also its most popular rural-style practitioner. He holds two other distinctions: his 1954 recording "Paper in My Shoe" was zydeco's first hit; and after dropping out of sight for 30 years afterwards, he made a spectacular comeback in 1984. The spunky jokester in the cowboy hat who picked up the nickname "Boozoo" as a kid hasn't slowed down since.

Chavis' melodies, lyrics and button-accordion playing are simple—some say "primitive"—but wildly crowd-pleasing. His importance lies in his revival of traditional, highly rhythmic "French" music as it was enjoyed by Creoles in the post-World War II years before zydeco was known by that name. He is a gifted spontaneous performer and prolific songwriter. What Chavis calls his "old-style, natural zydeco" borrows little from mainstream styles except the blues. With its multiple beats, it is more Afro-Caribbean than its urban counterpart.

Chavis grew up playing house parties and dances around Lake Charles in the late 1940s and has been playing the same music ever since. With an unvarying style, his huge appeal comes largely from his clowning, blunt-talking personality and the quirky tunes he pens, for example, "Hamburgers and Popcorn" and "Billy Goat Number Three." A farmer and horse trainer, Chavis slips barnyard sounds, personal references and lots of laughs into his highly informal performances.

Born in 1930 in the Dog Hill section of Lake Charles, Chavis listened as a boy to "French music" at country dances where his accordionist father played. At nine, he played a harmonica, but soon swapped a small horse for an accordion. He played dances on weekends while working as a trainer and jockey, racing quarter horses. His big break came in 1954, when Goldband/Folk-Star producer Eddie Shuler recorded "Paper in My Shoe," Chavis' version of a 19th century Creole song about hard times, when paper was used to patch holes in shoes.

By Shuler's account it was a rocky session, pairing an R&B band who had never played zydeco with Chavis, who had never played with a band; he usually played unaccompanied, banging out time by stomping his foot on a Coke box. The song surprised everyone by becoming a regional hit. It has become a Louisiana standard.

For several years afterward, Chavis toured southern states before disagreeing with Shuler about recording again. The proud son of poor tenant farmers with an entrepreneurial spirit, Chavis had soured on the recording industry after suspecting Shuler of cheating him. His next few recordings in the early 1960s came too late, and when the record companies dropped him as a "one-hit wonder," he returned to training race horses and raising his family.

In 1984, as zydeco started to catch on in Louisiana and east Texas, Chavis' wife, Leona, prompted him to get back into the music business. He dived back in with a vengeance, becoming one of the hottest draws on the Gulf Coast dance hall circuit. Cutting "Dog Hill" for the local Maison de Soul label

propelled him to the tremendous popularity he enjoys today as one of the "kings" of zydeco, along with the late greats **Clifton Chenier** and **Rockin' Dopsie**. He and rival **Beau Jocque**, the urban zydeco czar, vie for top honors in an ongoing friendly "battle."

On stage, Chavis swaggers and dances as he pushes and pulls his single- or triple-row accordion. Wearing a Stetson with a silver deputy sheriff badge and an apron to protect his accordion from perspiration, he cuts a comical cowboy figure. He punctuates his idiosyncratic rhythms with down-home French and English lyrics either respectable or raunchy, depending on the audience. He and his band, the Magic Sounds, play up to four-hour sets with no intermission at clubs and dance halls. They also entertain for zydeco trail rides, horseback rides ending in a dance party. The band includes two of his sons.

Referring to the band's tours outside Louisiana, Chavis commented in liner notes for *Boozoo Chavis*, "Now that we're traveling, we're opening people's eyes. They're sayin' 'Where he come from that little man? That joker can *play*.'"

THE BEST

Live! At the Habibi Temple, Lake Charles, Louisiana 📖

r. 1993; i. 1994/Rounder 2130 CD, CS

A TOP 10 ZYDECO ALBUM

This CD accurately captures the live sound of Boozoo and the Magic Sounds as they pound and grind away at their own unique blend of zydeco, blues and waltzes. The band includes his two sons—Charles on rubboard and Rellis on drums—plus Carlton Thomas and Nathaniel Fontenot on guitars and the great bassman, Classie Ballou. They have been with Boozoo so long that they can follow his idiosyncratic styling to a "T". Boozoo's first hit, "Paper in My

Shoe," is here, as well as the great, driving blues, "Tell Me What's the Matter." The band cranks up on the rocking "Boozoo's Breakdown" and "Boozoo, That's Who." Close your eyes, and you'll be transported to Lake Charles for one hot zydeco show.

EXCELLENT

Boozoo, That's Who!

r. & i. 1993/Rounder 2126 CD, CS

Boozoo's first studio album for Rounder is a winner, even containing a wonderful cover version of Clifton Chenier's "You Used to Call Me." The polyrhythms produced by the grooving band propel Boozoo and his accordion to new heights. The sound quality obtained by the engineers at the New Orleans Recording Company is a step above that of any previous Boozoo album. Standout songs include the low-down blues, "I'm Going to the Country to Get Me a Mojo Hand," the rollicking "Boozoo's Payback" and the rocking autobiographical tale "Went to New York." Highly recommended.

Boozoo Chavis

r. 1990; i. 1991/Elektra/Nonesuch 61146 CD, CS

This CD finds Boozoo and Magic Sounds in fine form. The sound is not quite as full and sparkling as on the Rounder releases, but nevertheless many of Boozoo's signature tunes are here. Especially noteworthy are "Keep Your Dress Tail Down" and "Gilton."

Hey Do Right!

i. 1996/Antone's Discovery 74707 CD

Although Chavis was in his mid-60s on his latest CD, you'd never suspect it. The indefatigable man from Dog Hill just keeps on pumping out his individualistic zydeco tunes. He is the master of writing songs about the concerns of everyday life, as illustrated in "I Got a Camel," written about one of his race horses, and "Hey Do Right," about his daughter. The addition to the band of Terry Adams on electric piano for two cuts, "Goin' to the Zydeco" and "Zydeco Lady," gives the sound a little more push. One wishes the instrument had been used more, not that Chavis and band need much help to keep the groove rockin'. Just play "You're Gonna Look Like a Monkey" (Boozoo's theory on aging) or "The Spotted Cow Died" and try to keep your feet still.

Zydeco Trail Ride

r. late 1980s; i. 1989/Maison de Soul 1034 CD, CS, LP

This is the best of Boozoo's releases from Maison de Soul. It contains many Boozoo classics, like "Uncle Bud," "Deacon Jones," "Paper in My Shoe" and "Boozoo's Trail Ride Breakdown." Twenty-one songs, clocking in at over 60 minutes, make this rocking CD a great buy.

OTHER RECORDINGS

Boozoo Zydeco

i. 1987/Maison de Soul 1021 CS, LP

The Lake Charles Atomic Bomb (Original Goldband Recordings)

r. 1950s; i. 1990/Rounder 2097 CD, CS, LP

Louisiana Zydeco Music

i. 1986/Maison de Soul 1017 CS, LP

Paper in My Shoe

i. 1987/Ace (England) 214

Zydeco Homebrew

r. 1988; i. 1992/Maison de Soul 1028 CD, CS, LP

Zydeco Live

(with Nathan & the Zydeco Cha-Chas)/r. 1988; i. 1989/Rounder 2069 CD, CS, LP

C. J. CHENIER (Clayton Joseph Chenier)
Accordion, vocals

Arhoolie LP 1098

The son of zydeco king **Clifton Chenier**, C. J. Chenier learned accordion from the master. Today, he ably upholds the family name by taking his father's Red Hot Louisiana Band in creative new directions.

C. J. was born in 1957 to a house cleaner in Port Arthur, Tx. He saw his father, who was married to another woman and living in Lafayette, only intermittently during his childhood. At the time, he wasn't aware of his father's fame and thought zydeco was for old folks. He studied piano briefly as a young child and in his teens played saxophone in the school band, winning a music scholarship from Texas Southern University. He played in Top 40 bands and explored fusion jazz in his own garage band, Hot Ice, where he played sax, flute and keyboards and sang back-up vocals.

When Clifton suddenly invited the 20-year-old to sit in for his indisposed sax player in 1978, C. J. began a five-year trial by fire in zydeco and the French language, learning song lyrics phonetically from the band's drummer while touring coast to coast.

"It was hard at first. I didn't know the music, didn't understand it, didn't have the feel. But after about a year I caught on," Chenier said in liner notes for the 1995 album *Too Much Fun*. In 1983, an ailing Clifton taught his son the accordion–or rather, the son watched the father and practiced by himself–so C. J. could fill in for him when he was too sick to play.

After the elder Chenier's death in 1987, C. J. carried on with the Red Hot Louisiana Band, a seasoned ensemble blessed with the talents of such Clifton Chenier veterans as guitarist Harry Hypolite. C. J.'s accordion playing, smooth baritone voice and songwriting have developed a strength of their own. He usually writes songs in English, with a touch of French. His blues and R&B-tinged style differs from his father's, he has said, because he's a "Texas boy."

Chenier's versatility has worked against him at home, despite his star status at concerts and festivals. In Creole country, he is seldom heard on the radio or in dance halls, and some critics say he falls between the cracks stylistically. Despite the experimentation, he holds fast to his father's credo that a tune must have substance, as reflected in comments C. J. made in *Too Much Fun* liner notes:

"One thing we don't have is this new type of zydeco that's big in Louisiana now, where they just play one riff over and over and shout out some words and don't even ever change chords. What we're playing here are real songs." Another reason for the negative reaction in southwest Louisiana is his father's lingering shadow.

"At first they said about me, 'He's trying to be like his daddy.' And now they say, 'He'll never be like his daddy.' There's always something," Chenier told *Living Blues* in 1991.

Chenier stayed in his father's classic zydeco mode on his first album, *My Baby Don't Wear No Shoes*. But he spread his wings stylistically, to slightly less advantage, on later recordings. His recordings don't match his stellar live performances, which show a mature and greatly improved C. J. backed by one of the best bands in zydeco.

THE BEST

My Baby Don't Wear No Shoes 🪗

r. 1988; i. 1992/Arhoolie 1098 CD (Arhoolie 1098 CS & LP are entitled Let Me in Your Heart and do not include the song "Big Mama Blues.")

A TOP 10 ZYDECO ALBUM

Recorded within a year of Clifton Chenier's death, C. J.'s first album remains one of his two best. C. J. kept the same personnel as his father had in the band, adding only second guitarist Selwyn Cooper to round out the sound. Heavily blues-based, the songs were all written by Clifton or C.J. Highlights include re-recordings of Clifton's "I'm Coming Home" and "Banana Man," as well as C. J.'s own "Used and Abused" and "I'm All Shook Up." Chenier's considerable skills on the accordion are showcased on the low-down instrumental "Blue Flame Blues," put down with just rubboard and drums for backing.

EXCELLENT

Hot Rod

r. & i. 1990/Slash 26263 CD, CS

On a par with his first CD on Arhoolie, *My Baby Don't Wear No Shoes*, this follow-up release was also produced by Arhoolie's Chris Strachwitz, longtime friend and producer of Clifton Chenier. By this time, the great rubboard player Cleveland Chenier had died and was replaced by R. C. Carrier. Otherwise, the band on this album remained essentially the same as on C. J.'s first recording. Most of these tunes were penned by C. J., except for Clifton's hard-rocking instrumental, "Hot Rod," and the traditional "Jole Blon." Uptempo

rockers like "I Feel Alright" and "Old Fashioned Party" alternate with blues-drenched ballads such as "Your Time to Cry" and "It's a Shame." Another stand-out is C. J.'s tribute to his father, "You're Still the King to Me."

The Big Squeeze

i. 1996/Alligator 4844 CD, CS

C.J.'s latest Alligator release continues his quest to incorporate modern sounds while remaining true to his roots. He reaches back into time, putting the zydeco touch on Huey "Piano" Smith's "Don't You Just Know It," Elvis' "Teddy Bear" and an effective waltz treatment of Steve Alaimo's '60s hit, "Everyday I Have to Cry Some." Aided by his road band, he re-records a great moody rendition of his father's blues, "The Moon Is Rising"—zydeco blues at its best! Also in the blues vein is the driving shuffle, "I Can't Judge Nobody." C.J. and the band give a nod to the modern funk rhythms on "Mixed Up and Confused" and "Part Time Woman." "No Shoes Zydeco" is the only traditional cut on the CD, with just drums, triangle and rubboard for instrumentation.

Too Much Fun

i. 1995/Alligator 4830 CD, CS

This slickly produced CD cooks with traditional zydeco on "Louisiana Two Step" and simmers with the "Louisiana Down Home Blues." It features guests The Memphis Horns and blues guitarist Vasti Jackson. A step below his earlier recordings, this one is still enjoyable.

OTHER RECORDINGS

I Ain't No Playboy

i. 1992/Slash 26788 CD, CS

CLIFTON CHENIER

Vocals, accordion, harmonica

Arhoolie CD 313

As the undisputed "King of Zydeco" for four decades, Chenier reigned as its biggest star until his death in 1987. He virtually invented the style by blending rock and R&B with the old-time "la la," or Creole dance music. By adding guitar, drums, bass and horns to the traditional accordion and rubboard, he introduced the lineup characterizing zydeco bands today. In fact, the term "zydeco" is synonymous with Chenier, who popularized the old Creole song "Les Haricots Sont Pas Sales" (The Snap Beans Aren't Salty) as "Zydeco Sont Pas Sale." An endlessly inventive stylist, agile accordionist and gutsy vocalist, his talents have yet to find a match.

Born in 1925 to poor sharecroppers near Opelousas, Chenier grew up working in fields of cotton, rice, sugar and corn. His father played button accordion. At home, the boy heard old French songs as well as southern blues; an important early influence were the recordings of Creole accordionist **Amedee Ardoin**.

Clifton was one of the first black Creoles to play piano accordion, which has a wider range than the smaller Cajun-style button accordion, lending itself better to bluesy

sounds. His older brother Cleveland accompanied him on their mother's washboard–a talent he later developed into an art form, "scrubbing" bottle openers on the corrugated tin, vestlike rubboard designed by Clifton that has since become a fixture of zydeco and Cajun bands. In the late 1940s, the brothers drove oil refinery trucks for the Port Arthur, Tx., oil refineries, playing local dances evenings and working at their uncle Morris "Big" Chenier's club, where Morris sat in playing fiddle and guitar. Meanwhile, Clifton soaked up the music of bluesmen Lightnin' Hopkins and Muddy Waters, as well as R&B stars Ray Charles and Fats Domino.

Legendary talent scout J. R. Fulbright discovered Chenier one day in 1954, when he came across the brothers playing in the middle of a road, surrounded by a crowd, outside Lafayette. He recorded Chenier on his small Elko label. The next year, Specialty Records, a major R&B label based in Hollywood, signed Chenier, and recordings of "Ay-Tete-Fee" (Little Girl) and "Boppin' the Rock" hit nationwide. This success led to touring the R&B circuit as the "King of the South" with his band, the Zodico Ramblers, joining singer Etta James and others.

He hit a slump during the 1960s when recordings with Chess and Zynn labels proved disappointing and the rock 'n' roll craze all but wiped out ethnic Louisiana music. Then he was rediscovered in Houston by Arhoolie record producer Chris Strachwitz from Berkeley, Ca., who prized zydeco and Gulf Coast blues. Starting in 1964, Chenier returned to his zydeco roots. He recorded a string of albums and singles for Arhoolie while performing at concerts and clubs for largely white, blues-loving fans, as well as at Creole dance halls. He also recorded briefly for the

Crazy Cajun label in Pasadena, Tx., most notably his hit "Oh, Lucille," now a zydeco classic.

Chenier hit his stride in the 1970s with his splendid Red Hot Louisiana Band, whose strong lineup was a key factor in his success–especially Paul Senegal on guitar and John Hart on tenor sax, an instrument not heard much in zydeco until then. For the next two decades, Chenier ruled the Gulf Coast and toured nationwide and in Europe, where he was immensely popular. Wearing a jeweled crown, playing a rhinestone-studded accordion and flashing a gold-toothed smile, he performed a dazzling program of zydeco, southern blues, soul, R&B and country & western, adapting them to his own style. In his prime, he was featured in the 1973 film *Hot Pepper* by Les Blank.

The charismatic Chenier's powerful vocals mixed French patois, English and the "jure" (call-and-response) chanting of south Louisiana. He was reluctant, however, to sing French songs outside Louisiana and Texas, or to include them on recordings, believing the younger crowd would not take to them.

In the late 1970s, Chenier parted with Arhoolie and moved on to record for a variety of labels. Among the many honors coming to him late in life, Chenier won Grammys and a National Heritage Fellowship and played at the White House for President Ronald Reagan. After receiving his 1984 Grammy for the album *I'm Here!* he reflected on the importance of being true to oneself:

"I figured French music fit me and I stayed with it. Rock 'n' roll didn't get me that Grammy. Zydeco got me that Grammy. Maybe that's going to show some of the young ones that's where it's at, right here... Just got to do something with it, that's all."

By 1979, diabetes started to take its toll on Chenier, although he continued performing until his death. A hero to younger zydeco musicians and players in other styles, he inspired such second-generation artists as **Buckwheat Zydeco** and **Rockin' Dopsie**, as well as today's musicians. His son, **C. J. Chenier**, continues his legacy with the Red Hot Louisiana Band.

Chenier recorded a repertoire of mostly his own compositions for many labels, without rehearsals or retakes. At times on recordings, he was joined by artists like Katie Webster, Elvin Bishop, Steve Miller, Phillip Walker and Lonesome Sundown. Alone among zydeco artists, virtually everything he ever recorded is worth listening to.

Note: Chenier's early 1960s recordings for Louisiana's Jay Miller are reissued on Flyright 539, and his 1956-1957 recordings for Checker are available on Chess (Japan) PLP 6035.

THE BEST

Zydeco Dynamite: The Clifton Chenier Anthology

r. 1954-1984; i. 1993/Rhino 71194 CD, CS

A TOP 10 ZYDECO ALBUM

Attractively packaged with a 30-page booklet, this two-CD boxed set covers Clifton's entire career from his earliest recording on Elko Records in 1954 to his last on Caillier in 1984. The 40-song compilation touches all sides of Chenier's repertoire. Pure zydeco tunes such as the classic "Zydeco Sont Pas Sale" contrast with the blues of "I'm on the Wonder." Many of his most famous songs are here, including "I'm Coming Home," "I'm a Hog for You," "Bon Ton Roulet" and "Eh, 'Tite Fille." The informative booklet is loaded with great photos of the zydeco king.

EXCELLENT

Bogalusa Boogie

*r.1975; i. 1987/Arhoolie 347 CD, CS (contains Arhoolie
CS/LP 1076 & several tracks from CS/LP 1078 +
1 previously unissued cut)*

A TOP 10 ZYDECO ALBUM

This classic release features a session held in
Bogalusa, La. The red-hot band, including Hart,
Senegal and Clifton's brother, Cleveland, swings
like hell. You'll get up to dance while listening to
"One Step at a Time," "M'Appel Fou," "Ti Na Na"
and "Bogalusa Boogie." *Rolling Stone* considers
this popular recording Chenier's all-time best,
while the *Washington Post* called it "the best
zydeco album of all time."

Sings the Blues

*r. 1969, 1977; i. 1987, 1993/Arhoolie 351 CD (contains
Arhoolie CS/LP 1097 + 7 cuts from CS/LP 1078)*

This release proves that Clifton was a
consummate bluesman. On the first 12 tracks,
recorded in Houston in 1969, he was in
excellent voice and the blues mood was deep.
Particularly noteworthy songs include "Ain't No
Need of Crying," "Rosemary," "Gone a la
Maison" and "Blues After Hours." He recorded
the last seven selections in 1977 in New
Orleans. They feature what was probably
Clifton's best band: the great John Hart on
tenor sax, Cleveland Chenier on rubboard,
Paul Senegal on guitar, Joe Morris on bass,
Robert Peter (St. Julian) on drums and Stanley
"Buckwheat Zydeco" Dural on keyboards. Dural,
who has since become a top zydeco performer,
did many of the band's arrangements. Stand-out
songs are "Falksy Girl" and the incredibly
rocking "Highway Blues."

Zydeco Legend!

r. 1975, 1984; i. 1984/Maison de Soul 105 CD

Another great one, with most of the same
band as on *Bogalusa Boogie*. The first 10
selections are from his classic 1975 album,
Boogie n' Zydeco, on Maison de Soul; the last
eight are from *Country Boy Now*, recorded in
1984, three years before Clifton's death.
Hard-rocking fast tunes like "Johnny Can't
Dance," "Choo Choo Ch-Boogie" and "Hot
Tamale Baby" abound, while "Je Me Fu—Pas
Mal" and the beautiful blues waltz "You Used
to Call Me" swing sweet and mellow. The later
songs find Clifton squarely in the blues mood
with songs like "Driftin' Blues," "Love Me or
Leave Me" and "My Baby She's Gone to Stay."

Bayou Blues

r. 1955; i. 1970/Specialty 2139 CD, CS, LP

Talent scout J. R. Fulbright brought Chenier
to Los Angeles, where he recorded for the
legendary Specialty label in 1955. This
compilation of 12 old mono recordings from
that period shows a stomping style unique
for its time. Hard rockin' boogie and blues
like "All Night Long," "Zodico Stomp,"
"Clifton's Squeeze-box Boogie" and "I'm On
My Way" don't let up. This historic disc is
first-rate, if only because of the slice of
zydeco funk named "Opelousas Hop."

Live! At the Long Beach and San Francisco Blues Festivals

*r. 1982 (San Francisco), 1983 (Long Beach); i.
1985/Arhoolie 404 CD, CS (Arhoolie CS/LP 1093, Live at
the San Francisco Blues Festival, also available)*

Recorded late in Clifton's career, this rollicking
disc is the best of his five live recordings. The
19 songs and generous playing time of 74
minutes give an accurate representation of the
live Chenier experience and show the breadth
of his repertoire, from blues and boogie to old-
fashioned waltzes. Top tunes are "Rock Me,"
"You Gonna Miss Me," "Calinda" and "I'm
Coming Home."

Chapter 2 • Zydeco

Bon Ton Roulet

r. mid-1960s; i. 1990/Arhoolie 345 CD, CS (contains all of Arhoolie CS/LP 1031, half of CS/LP 1038, + several unissued tracks from 1964)

Dating from sessions in the mid-60s, this CD is filled with varied, wonderful performances and stands out because Chenier's uncle, Morris "Big" Chenier, joins in on fiddle on 11 tracks. One of them, "Black Gal," features Chenier's fine blues singing and became a huge hit. The classic rocking title cut, "Bon Ton Roulet," is a unique Chenier version of an older song popularized by Louis Jordan.

King of the Bayous

r. 1965, 1969, 1970; i. 1992/Arhoolie 339 CD, CS (contains Arhoolie CS/LP 1052 + 6 previously unissued tracks)

This CD contains worthwhile early material. Newly discovered songs such as "Coming Home Tomorrow" and old stand-bys like the poignant "I'm Coming Home" make for enjoyable listening. A good song selection, with a strong band.

Out West

r. 1971, 1973; i. 1974/Arhoolie 350 CD, CS (contains Arhoolie CS/LP 1072 + previously unissued tracks)

Recorded with guest rockers Elvin Bishop and Steve Miller, this 1974 release still sparkles. Bishop was then a young blues guitarist who had already made a name for himself with the Paul Butterfield Blues Band. Bishop's slide guitar and John Hart's powerful tenor lend a modern zydeco sound. Recorded in San Francisco on one of Chenier's regular trips to the West Coast to play for Louisiana expatriates and general pop/rock audiences, this disc contains excellent versions of "I'm on the Wonder" and "Just Like a Woman."

Live at St. Mark's

r. 1971; i. 1988/Arhoolie 313 CD, CS (contains Live at a French Dance/Arhoolie 1059 LP + 4 previously unissued tracks from the dance)

Clifton rocked hard for transplanted Louisiana Creoles at this dance at St. Mark's Church Hall in Richmond, Ca. Fortunately, Arhoolie captured the performance in its entirety, chatter and all. The disc bounces with the spirit and feeling of a "French dance," during which Chenier typically pounded hard for four to five hours without a break.

Frenchin' the Boogie

r. 1976; i. 1994/Verve 519724 CD

Featuring the sterling mid-1970s band of Hart, Dural, Senegal and Cleveland Chenier, this is another great rocker, with tunes such as "Caldonia," "Shake, Rattle & Roll," "Don't You Lie to Me" and "Le Blues de la Vache a Lait."

On Tour

r. 1978/EPM Musique FDC 5505 CD

This live concert of straight-ahead blues and boogie zydeco was recorded in Paris. Included are some songs not available elsewhere, such as "Travelin' Man," "Let's Talk it Over" and "Four in the Mornin'."

60 Minutes with the King of Zydeco

i. 1988/Arhoolie 301 CD, CS

A great 15-hit sampler culled from 10 previous Arhoolie recordings. There is nothing new here, but every cut is a winner. All styles are represented, from traditional zydeco to blues, in French and English. Highly recommended.

In New Orleans

r. 1978; i. 1979/GNP Crescendo 2119 CD, CS, LP

Another strong outing. Slow blues tunes like "Tous Les Jours" and "Cotton Picker Blues" alternate with driving boogies such as "J'Aime Pain de Mais" and "Boogie Louisiane."

I'm Here!

r. & i. 1982/Alligator 4729 CD, CS, LP

Although not his best, this album won a Grammy in 1983. By this time, the Red Hot Louisiana Band included Chenier's son, C.J. Chenier, on sax, Warren Caesar on trumpet and Danny Caron (who would later play with Charles Brown) on guitar. The dynamic young band helped revive Chenier's career after several years of illness and doctors' pronouncements that his career was over. "I'm Here!" is Chenier's response.

OTHER RECORDINGS

Bayou Soul

1966/Crazy Cajun 1002 CS, LP

Black Snake Blues

1966/Arhoolie 1038 CS, LP

Boogie in Black & White

(with Rod Bernard)/Jin 9014 CS, LP

Boogie n' Zydeco

r. 1975; i. 1979, 1990/Sonet (England) 801 CD; also Maison de Soul 1003 CS, LP

Cajun Swamp Music Live

(at Montreux)/r. 1975/Tomato 2696062 CD; 2696061 LP

Classic Clifton

Arhoolie 301 CD (contains Arhoolie 1082 CS, LP + 3 added tracks)

Clifton Chenier and Rockin' Dupsee

r. Chenier 1958-60; Dupsee 1970-74; i. 1991/Paula/Flyright 17 CD

Country Boy Now

(Grammy Award winner 1984)/Maison de Soul 1012 CS, LP

King of Zydeco

1985/Ace (England) 234 CD; Arhoolie 1086 CS, LP

King of Zydeco Live at Montreux

r. 1975; i. 1984/Arhoolie 355 CD, CS (contains Arhoolie 1086 CS, LP + 10 tracks)

Louisiana Blues and Zydeco

r. 1964, 1965, 1967/Arhoolie 329 CD, CS (contains Arhoolie 1024 CS, LP; half of Arhoolie 1038 CS, LP + 1 track from Arhoolie 1018 LP)

Red Hot Louisiana Band

i. 1978/Arhoolie 1078 CS, LP

We're Gonna Party

r. 1977; i. 1994/Collectables 5513 CD

Zodico Blues and Boogie

r. 1955; i.1993/Specialty 7039 CD (also available as Ace [England] 389 CD)

WILFRED CHEVIS
Accordion, vocals

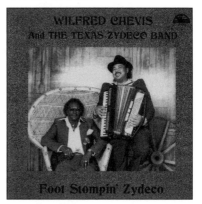

Maison de Soul LP 1013

A Houston-based musician, Wilfred Chevis plows the musical field of his mentor, **Clifton Chenier**. He was born in 1945 in Church Point, the same town as legendary Cajun accordionist **Iry Lejeune**. There he grew up hearing old-style Creole "la-la" music and learned how to play the accordion from his father. Inspired by Chenier, he was taught some tricks by the king of zydeco, who also sold him the accordion he plays today.

Chapter 2 • Zydeco

Chevis moved to Houston in 1969. He and his Texas Zydeco Band play clubs, church halls, and festivals from Houston to Lafayette. Chevis has also deejayed a zydeco show on KPFT-FM in Houston since the late 1980s. The band plays an urban style zydeco in the Chenier tradition.

THE BEST

Let's Go to P.T.'s

i. 1991/Maison de Soul 1040 CS, LP

Chevis and his eight-piece band cut some killer grooves on this, his second Maison de Soul album. It's a good album to party with, but Chevis' weak, off-key singing brings it down. Recorded at P.T.'s Cajun Club in Houston, the album has better sound than many Maison de Soul releases. With two tenor saxes riffing in the background, the band rocks solidly on "Don't Sell My Monkey" and Clifton Chenier's "Hey Teet Fille." D. L. Menard's "The Back Door" gets a spirited treatment, and the band creates a zydeco blues mood on Chenier's "Ti Na Na." Other highlights are the driving "Let's Go to P.T.'s" and the bouncy "If You Got Problems."

GOOD

Foot Stompin' Zydeco

i. 1985/Maison de Soul 1013 LP

Chevis' first album for Maison de Soul featured Phillip Steward as vocalist, a big improvement over Chevis. Unfortunately, the band here is not up to the standard of *Let's Go to P.T.'s*. The thin-sounding production doesn't help, either. Steward turns in creditable performances on the ballads "Keep on Sailin On" and "Why Did You Leave Me." "Geraldine" sounds suspiciously like Buster Brown's R&B hit "Fannie Mae," complete with the the same horn riffs. A purchase for zydeco fanatics only.

OTHER RECORDINGS

Makin' it Back to Louisiana

i. 1995/Collectables 5550 CD

CREOLE ZYDECO FARMERS
Group

The Creole Zydeco Farmers is an offshoot of **Fernest Arceneaux**'s band and features two of that group's veterans: singer/drummer Clarence "Jockey" Etienne and guitarist Chester Chevalier. Etienne's recording credits stretch back to Fats Domino records. The versatile blues guitarist Chevalier is Arceneaux's brother-in-law.

Based in Lafayette, the band plays unsophisticated zydeco in the style of **Clifton Chenier** and **Buckwheat Zydeco**, with a swamp pop tilt. Besides Louisiana, they have toured across the U.S. and performed in Europe. One band member is in fact a farmer—Murphy Richard raises pigs and grows soybeans.

THE BEST

Come to Party

i. 1996/Lanor 1059 CD

Well recorded at Lee Lavergne's funky country studio in Church Point, this is one of the Lanor label's best releases. The latest incarnation of the band features Murphy Richard and Morris Francis on accordion, Chester Chevalier and Joseph McKinley Rossyion on guitars, Clarence "Jockey" Etienne on drums and David Edmond on bass. Vocal chores are split between Richard, Francis and Edmond, while Richard also plays rubboard. Eight of the 11 cuts are originals—the best being "Thankful," a soul zydeco composition with a rolling rhumba beat, and "Don't You Think It's Time," a driving zydeco blues. Covers include an effective version of Wilson Pickett's "Don't

Let Green Grass Fool You," a heartfelt rendition of Johnny Ace's "Pledging My Love" and a typical zydeco treatment of Little Richard's "Keep A Knockin'."

EXCELLENT

Live in Louisiana

r. 1993; i. 1994/CMA (Germany) 10013 CD

Recorded live at the Friendly Lounge in Cecilia, this CD is solid, if unoriginal. It runs the gamut from blues to R&B to waltzes to old-time, rural zydeco. The songs are mostly cover versions of titles by Clifton Chenier, Boozoo Chavis, Tyrone Davis, Lonesome Sundown and others; there are only three originals on the album. Highlights are "We Gonna Boogie," the swamp pop standard "Irene" and "Turning Point." The band rocks solidly on all the tunes. The sound, while somewhat echoey, is acceptable, capturing the atmosphere of a big, old country dance hall. This German release may be difficult to obtain, but it is worth searching out.

OTHER RECORDINGS

Zydeco Train

Lanor 1050 CS

GENO DELAFOSE
Accordion, drums, rubboard, vocals

Rounder CD 2141

Delafose got his start at the age of eight, playing rubboard and drums with his father's band, **John Delafose** and the Eunice Playboys. He eventually learned accordion and is now one of only a few zydeco musicians to play both button and piano accordion. He is also one of a minority of zydeco sons to step out of their fathers' shadows and find success on their own.

John Delafose was a highly respected traditionalist, and his son in the big black Stetson has followed suit with old songs adapted from **Iry LeJeune** and **Canray Fontenot** and the Cajun repertoire, harking back to an era when Creole and Cajun music were closer in style than they are today. But the Eunice native is equally at home with modern R&B tunes.

He has been playing accordion since he was 13, learning both on his own and with the help of his dad. Bucking peer pressure as a teenager, he spoke French, attended French dances and sported a cowboy hat instead of cool high school clothes.

"I'm just a down-to-earth country boy, and I wouldn't want to change that for anything in the world," he told *Offbeat* in 1996.

Chapter 2 • Zydeco

After high school, Delafose found himself unable to attend college because of heavy band duties, so in 1989 he decided to make music his career. When John cut back on performing for health reasons in 1994, Geno took over the band; his father died that same year. Two years later, the six-piece band appeared at the New Orleans Jazz & Heritage Festival as "French Rockin' Boogie," the name of Delafose's debut album.

He maintains a hectic touring schedule across the U.S., has toured Europe and has opened shows for Robert Cray. Despite a growing national following, he remains unappreciated in his local region—one of many musicians dropped or overlooked by the fickle zydeco crowd of southwest Louisiana.

A still evolving artist, Delafose is a talented accordionist whose vocals, sung in both English and French, are improving. He cut his first solo album, *French Rockin' Boogie*, at the age of 22, after collaborating with his father on three previous albums for Rounder Records. His own CDs are better than the less realized ones he cut with his father.

THE BEST

That's What I'm Talkin' About!

i. 1996/Rounder 2141 CD

Multi-talented Delafose strikes gold on his second solo release for Rounder. He remains true to his Creole zydeco roots, while injecting his music with the driving rhythm and energy that current zydeco fans demand. His nods to the past are rollicking renditions of his father's "I Wanna Be Your Loving Man," "Bye Bye Mon Neg'" and Amedee Ardoin's "One Step des Cameaux." "Teardrops" is a nice original ballad on which Delafose contributes some Hammond B-3 organ as well as accordion playing. Also on this disc are

waltzes such as "La Valse de Pop" and swinging blues tunes like "Tell Me Why You're Always Late." Throughout, the band—Bobby Broussard on guitar, Stanislas Chambers on bass, Steve Nash on rubboard and cousin Jermaine Jack on drums—kicks ass. Delafose's vocals are improving, but still weak.

EXCELLENT

French Rockin' Boogie

r. & i. 1994/Rounder 2131 CD, CS

This solo debut is a solid effort, reflecting the fact that Delafose was a 15-year veteran of the zydeco scene when he recorded it. His touring band, the Eunice Playboys, also features here Shelton Broussard (of Zydeco Force) and Charles Prudhomme on guitars, Tony Delafose on bass, Jermaine Jack on drums and Steve Nash on rubboard. The saxophones of Joe Cabral and Derek Huston of the Iguanas are added on several numbers, notably "French Rockin' Boogie" and "C'est Pas la Peine Brailler," giving the band a full, driving sound. Although probably the weakest link here, Delafose's vocals have improved markedly since his collaborative recordings with his father. Other highlights of this rockin' CD are the frantic tunes "Do the Mill" and "Think it Over." The only cut where the pace slows is the "Wedding Day Waltz."

OTHER RECORDINGS

Blues Stay Away From Me

r. & i. 1993/Rounder 2121 CD, CS

Pere et Garcon Zydeco

r. 1991; i. 1992/Rounder 2116 CD, CS

JOHN DELAFOSE
Accordion, fiddle, vocals

Maison de Soul CD 1035

John Delafose and the Eunice Playboys exemplified the zydeco dynasty tradition. This dynamic family band included three of Delafose's sons, along with nephews and grandsons, at one time or another. He was a mainstay of the zydeco scene from the mid-1970s, when only a handful of musicians such as **Clifton Chenier**, **Rockin' Dopsie** and **Buckwheat Zydeco** carried the zydeco banner, to his death in 1994, when the field had become crowded with young performers.

The band held allegiance to its classic zydeco roots—reviving early Creole sounds, singing often in French (unlike the younger bands) and favoring two-steps and waltzes over blues and R&B. But they played with funk and fire enough to pack fans into dance halls in south Louisiana, east Texas and New Orleans for two decades. With his emotional vocals and percussive button-accordion style echoing Afro-Caribbean rhythms, Delafose expressed the true Creole style. He also drew on Cajun and country & western music. He occasionally played piano accordion on bluesy numbers as well as fiddle, rarely heard in zydeco music.

Actually, the fiddle was Delafose's first instrument. Born in Mamou in 1939 to sharecroppers, he made violins and guitars as a child out of windowscreen wire stretched over a board and cigar box. Then he switched to harmonica and, at 18, button accordion, and played harmonica for dances. After quitting performing to farm, then repair electric fans, Delafose returned to music in his 30s, playing harmonica and accordion with various bands. He formed his own band in the mid-1970s with Charles and "Slim" Prudhomme on guitar and bass, joined later by his teenaged sons, John "T.T." on rubboard and Tony Delafose on drums (now on bass). It became one of the most sought-after bands on the Lousiana/Texas Gulf Coast, at a time of Creole cultural revival.

In recent years, Delafose's son **Geno Delafose** traded lead vocals and accordion work with his father. Two other relatives —John's nephew, Jermaine Jack, and his cousin, Paul Delafose—also joined the band, sharing rubboard and drum duties. Geno, who started playing with the band at eight, became one of the best zydeco drummers around. He eventually learned accordion from his father. In 1994 when John cut back on touring for health reasons, Geno took over as bandleader.

An esteemed accordionist and singer, John Delafose was featured in the 1992 Hollywood film *Passion Fish* and several documentaries. A capable songwriter as well, he is best known for "Joe Pete Got Two Women" and "Ka-wann." He had a spontaneous composing style, explaining to *Offbeat* in 1994, "I don't write a song. I fool around with different notes during a dance, add on to it a little bit, and tomorrow night I finish it. When you're playing, you got people screaming at you, winking at you, waving at you, hollering at you, so it makes it exciting."

Chapter 2 • Zydeco

THE BEST

Heartaches and Hot Steps

r. & i. 1990/Maison de Soul 1035 CD, CS, LP

This enthusiastic recording finds Delafose in great form vocally, with strong accordion playing. Recorded in Crowley, the disc has a strong roster: Delafose sons Geno on drums and Tony on bass, nephew Jermaine Jack on rubboard, Charles Prudhomme on rhythm guitar and Gene Chambler on lead guitar. Chambler especially contributes to the enjoyment here; his sparkling runs propel the band to even more intense grooves than heard on other Delafose releases. Delafose's traditional, dance-oriented style is reflected in the many different rhythmic sounds, from waltzes and two-steps to slow blues and R&B. Highlights are the lead-off tune, "Ka-Wann," paying tribute to other zydeco stars, and the grinding "Hungry Man Blues."

GOOD

Pere et Garcon Zydeco

r. 1991; i. 1992/Rounder 2116 CD, CS

This father-son recording is as much Geno as John Delafose. From an early age, Geno was the propulsive drummer for the family band; but here he comes to the forefront with six cuts on accordion and vocals, while John switches to rubboard. Particularly rocking is Geno's version of "Watch That Dog." Another driving cut is John's cover of Clifton Chenier's "Morning Train." The pace slows with zydeco versions of "I Can't Stop Loving You" and "Friday Night Waltz." This well-recorded CD will definitely make you put on your dancing shoes.

Blues Stay Away From Me

r. & i. 1993/Rounder 2121 CD, CS

Once again, son Geno Delafose is featured on half the songs on this release. His vocals,

while maturing, still can't match his father's, but his cuts rock solidly with the driving support of the family band on "Slow Motion Zydeco" and "Let Me Take You in My Arms Tonight." Harking back to zydeco's common roots with Cajun music, John uses the fiddle on "Joe Simien Special" and "Co-Fe."

Joe Pete Got Two Women

r.1980, 1982; i. 1990/Arhoolie 335 CD, CS (compiled from Zydeco Man/Arhoolie 1083 CS, LP & Uncle Bud Zydeco/Arhoolie 1088 CS, LP)

This CD shows Delafose and his band in a formative state in the early 1980s. His regional hit "Joe Pete Got Two Women" is included, along with four powerful live tunes cut at the 1981 Festival de Musique Acadienne in Lafayette.

OTHER RECORDINGS

Zydeco Excitement

i. 1985/Maison de Soul 1015 CS, LP

Zydeco Live!

(with Willis Prudhomme)/i. 1989/Rounder 2070 CD, CS, LP

THOMAS "BIG HAT" FIELDS
Accordion, vocals

Newcomers to the zydeco scene, Fields and his Foot Stompin Zydeco Band play a cross between **Boozoo Chavis**-style rural zydeco and its modern, funked-up counterpart. Born in Rayne in 1947, Fields gained inspiration to play accordion while operating a zydeco club in Grand Coteau. Within a year he formed a band, starting with his wife, Geneva Fields, who taught herself bass. The five-piece ensemble has played local clubs and started touring since the 1994 release of its first recording.

THE BEST
Come to Louisiana

i. 1995/Lanor 1051 CD

As a newcomer, Fields has yet to develop a distinctive and varied playlist; the tunes on this debut album sound pretty much the same. However, Shelton Broussard's guitar helps give the music its propulsive beat and contributes greatly to Fields' overall sound. A couple of tunes rock along better than others: "The Mess Around" and "Ting a Ling." The disc is enjoyable enough, but Fields' best is still to come.

OTHER RECORDINGS
The Big Hat Man

i. 1994/Lanor 1045 CS

KEITH FRANK
Accordion, vocals

Maison de Soul CD 1055

Leading the pack of young *"nouveau zydeco"* musicians, Keith Frank is a top draw on the Acadiana zydeco circuit in south Louisiana and east Texas. He was born in 1972 in Soileau. Starting at the age of four he played a variety of instruments with his father, zydeco bandleader **Preston Frank**, in

the traditional-style Family Zydeco Band (also called the Soileau Playboys). Later, he fronted his own Soileau Zydeco Band as his father cut back on performing. The band includes his younger sister Jennifer on bass and brother Brad on drums.

Frank played his father's accordion off and on from the time he was six, hating zydeco music and his heavy band responsibilities until around eighth grade.

"That's when I started getting more into it. I realized it was a part of my life, and I couldn't stand being without it. I didn't know rap and stuff, but I always knew zydeco–I felt at home," Frank said in a 1995 *Offbeat* interview. Despite being laughed at by classmates, in the 10th grade he started his own zydeco band with a couple of friends. For a time he played guitar for accordionist **Jo Jo Reed**'s band before switching to accordion and creating a *nouveau zydeco* incarnation of the family band. The same band members play in two different groups with two different styles, with Preston Frank covering the traditional, French-lyric front.

Frank's idols are his father and **Boozoo Chavis**, whose highly rhythmic, simple style Frank found appealing to modern audiences. He was also heavily influenced by James Brown, Gene Chandler, Little Milton and Bob Marley. Merging these influences into a new style that spoke to his generation, Frank attracted a following. Later, as a college student at McNeese State University in Lake Charles, Frank stuck close to home, playing clubs, trail rides and festivals at an increasingly demanding pace.

His exciting, rap-suffused performances are studded with comical pop and TV music references and occasional digs at his arch-rival, urban zydeco star **Beau Jocque**. While Frank's critics call his style long on riffs and short on substance, lyrics and repertoire, the younger zydeco crowd loves his simple style with its heavy, danceable beat.

No one outdrew Frank's band in the zydeco dance halls and festivals of Acadiana in the mid-1990s. His main threat—from titan Beau Jocque—receded as Beau left the region more and more frequently to tour.

With two albums under his belt, Frank is also considered one of zydeco's emerging recording stars. Following two promotional releases on cassette, he hit big with his first album, *What's His Name?* It quickly turned into local label Maison de Soul's fastest-selling CD.

THE BEST

Movin' On Up!

r. & i. 1995/Maison de Soul 1055 CD, CS

Frank's latest is not necessarily the greatest, but it is still a solid effort in the R&B-influenced, nouveau zydeco, partyin' dance vein. In fact, two songs, "Rebel" and "Pieces to My Heart," are not zydeco at all, but reggae and R&B, respectively. The band —sister Jennifer Frank on bass, brother Brad Frank on drums, James "Chocolate" Ned on rubboard and George Attle on guitar —provides the funky backing that Frank's simple songs require. One tune, the medley "Watch My Step/Movin' On Up," contains an effective version of the theme song to the TV series "The Jeffersons." Other standout cuts are "Take It to the Highway" and "Bernadette C'est My 'Tit Creole." If you like your zydeco heavy on the beat and funky, you'll love to dance to *Movin' On Up*.

GOOD

What's His Name?

r. & i. 1994/Maison de Soul 1053 CD, CS

This release was Frank's first CD for Maison de Soul. Except for covers of a couple of Boozoo Chavis tunes and "Feel So Bad" (attributed to Little Milton but actually written by Chuck Willis), the rest of the songs are originals. Maison de Soul's rather flat-sounding production hampers the impact, but several tunes manage to overcome this drawback. Among these are "Everybody Get Up!" and "Get On Boy," zydeco funk grooves at their best. Don't expect meaningful lyrics—just dance.

OTHER RECORDINGS

Get On Boy

i. 1993/ZYH 1001 CS

On the Bandstand

i. 1993/Lanor 1035 CS

Only the Strong Survive

i. 1996/Maison de Soul 1062 CD, CS (unreviewed)

PRESTON FRANK
Accordion, vocals

Accordionist Preston Frank of Soileau puts down a stompin' traditional zydeco groove that isn't heard much these days. The group played in the area around Eunice, Opelousas, and Mamou for many years under the name the Preston Frank Family Band (also called the Soileau Playboys), in which Preston's son **Keith Frank** got his start at age four. The group recorded for Arhoolie and Lanor under the name Preston Frank's Swallow Band.

In recent years, the elder Frank (b. 1947, Oberlin) has performed less often, leaving his accordionist son to front the family's popular Soileau Zydeco Band. The *nouveau zydeco* group also includes Keith's sister, Jennifer, and brother, Brad.

Zydeco, Vol. 2 (Preston Frank and the Swallow Band/Ambrose Sam's Old Time Zydeco)

r. 1981; i. 1985/Arhoolie 1090 LP

For a slice of old-time zydeco, try this album. One of its unique features is the fiddle, rare in zydeco. Frank's uncle, Carlton Frank, fiddles with verve, especially on "Bals de Lake Charles." Not the strongest vocalist, Frank is assisted on three tunes by drummer Leo Thomas, who wrote two of the album's best tunes, "Why Do You Want to Make Me Cry" and "Shake What You Got," a song with the same basic riff as Clifton Chenier's "Hot Tamale Baby." The other side of this recording captures Ambrose Sam (uncle of the Sam Brothers) doing older, blues-influenced zydeco backed only by rubboard and drums, sounding like it did back in the formative years of the early 1950s. All in all, a good album exposing the roots of modern zydeco's tree.

MAJOR HANDY
Accordion, vocals, guitar

Born in 1947 in Lafayette, Major Handy was influenced primarily by **Clifton Chenier**.

Wolf Couchon

i. 1985/GNP Crescendo 2177 CS, LP

While certainly no Clifton Chenier, Major Handy turns in a few good cover versions of some zydeco standards on this release. Boozoo Chavis' classic "Paper in My Shoe" is given a rocking blues treatment, Chenier's minor key "I'm on a Wonder" floats in a moody manner and Tyrone Davis' oft-covered "Turning Point" rocks. But there isn't much else to get excited about. This recording lacks the spark that ignites a better-than-average zydeco disc.

JABO (Donald Glenn)
Accordion

Billing himself as "Jabo, the Texas Prince of Zydeco," Donald Glenn has made a splash in zydeco-happy Houston. In 1977, the Humble, Tx., native started experimenting with blending blues and zydeco after listening to **Clifton Chenier**, **Rockin' Dopsie** and **Buckwheat Zydeco**. By the late 1980s, Glenn saw a future in zydeco and approached Louisiana record producer Floyd Soileau about making an album; the result is *Texas Prince of Zydeco*. Unfortunately, Glenn returned to Houston without touring or otherwise following up this fine recording.

Texas Prince of Zydeco

i. 1990/ Maison de Soul 1032 CS, LP

As much blues as zydeco, this release is a solid debut. Along with his full band, Jabo rocks through zydeco-blues songs such as "Inflation Blues" and "Shame On You," in which his money-hungry woman has him standing in line waiting for food stamps. Also on this record is a track called "Zydeco Is Alright," a zydeco-ized version of the blues anthem, "The Blues Is Alright."

THE LAWTELL PLAYBOYS
Group

The original Lawtell Playboys represented the old-style, rural zydeco sound, although they used electric instruments and drums. They differed from urban zydeco bands in their inclusion of a violin and reliance on the one-row, button accordion; urban bands favor the more complex two- or three-row button accordion or piano-key accordion. They played little blues

Chapter 2 • Zydeco

and soul, featuring instead traditional Cajun tunes and zydeco versions of popular songs heard on the radio–an approach reflecting their family and friendship ties with the older-generation **Carriere Brothers**, who started the original Lawtell Playboys.

Eraste and Bebe Carriere played with Eraste's son, Calvin, on second violin and daughter, Beatrice, on guitar until the mid-1960s, when their old-style Creole "la-la" music fell out of favor. Calvin then joined accordionist/vocalist Delton Broussard (1927-1994), who had learned accordion from Eraste Carriere, and rubboard player J. C. Gallow in the new Lawtell Playboys. They played regularly at Slim's Y-Ki-Ki in Opelousas, a well-known family-style Creole club, where they held forth with zydecos, two-steps, waltzes and slow blues.

Broussard was the father of 11 children, four of whom regularly made up the rhythm section along with their cousin, Paul Newman, on drums. Broussard's staccato approach to melodies was due partly to the effect the small, "push-pull" accordion has on Cajun tunes, and partly to the influence of Eraste Carriere's playing and Broussard's more Afro-Caribbean cultural heritage from his birthplace in Arnaudville. While Broussard's sons increasingly took the band into more modern sounds–son Jeffery joined the band **Zydeco Force** in 1988–the Lawtell Playboys reflected a unique mix of Cajun, Afro-Caribbean and African-American music that echoed early Creole music. Another son, John, now leads the band.

THE BEST

Zodico: Louisiana Creole Music

(with the Ardoin family, Carriere Brothers, Inez Catalon & others)/r. 1976, i. 1979/Rounder 6009 CS, LP

Two cuts on side two feature the band in 1976. The recordings sound older than they are due to their rougher, early zydeco presentation. Delton Broussard does good vocal and accordion work. "Les Flammes d'Enfer" is just a great, old zydeco sound. The entire LP is worthwhile for anyone interested in the roots of zydeco music, and the 23-page booklet by Nick Spitzer enclosed with the album is highly informative.

EXCELLENT

La La: Louisiana Black French Music

(with the Carriere Brothers)/r. 1976; i. 1977/Maison de Soul 1004 CS, LP

Strong performances overcome a less-than-perfect sound quality. Delton Broussard's vocals are particularly good on "Eunice Two Step" and "Personne P'ole Danse Avec Moin," but the ensemble shines on "Baby Please Don't Go." The material on this LP–including excellent Carriere Brothers numbers on one side–represents a step in the progression from early Creole great Amedee Ardoin up through Clifton Chenier to the present-day zydeco.

OTHER RECORDINGS

A cassette tape of a live performance in the Augusta Heritage Center, Davis and Elkins College, W.Va., is available by calling 304 636-1903.

ROSIE LEDET
(Mary Rosezla Bellard Ledet)
Vocals, accordion

Maison de Soul CD 1056

"Zydeco Sweetheart" Rosie Ledet is a rising star with a promising future. She is a member of what *Offbeat* calls the *nouveau zydeco* "brat pack" who grew up during the 1980s era when zydeco was coming on strong. Having led her own band for just a few years, she is quickly drawing fans to her energizing performances and sweetly alluring voice.

Ledet stands out on two counts: She is one of very few female professional zydeco musicians, and she writes many of her own songs. But her tunes differ from her male counterparts' in the emphasis she places on lyrics and their content.

"Every one of their songs is either about a dog or a no-good woman… I meet the wives, and they don't seem no-good. Naw… that's not right. Give the girl a chance–and wait 'til I write mine," she said in a 1995 interview with *Offbeat*. Indeed, her songs show an expanded view of women. Other tunes are more traditionally R&B/zydeco, such as "Should've Been Mine" and "I'm Gonna Take Care of Your Dog." The boldness of her songs and her sensuous, dynamic stage persona are at odds with her shy off-stage personality.

Ledet's sturdy button-accordion playing is reminiscent of **Boozoo Chavis,** whom she admires. Other musical influences include Tina Turner, Koko Taylor, **Terrance Simien** and Carlos Santana. While her performances suffered early on from repetitious tempos and an unvaried repertoire, her latest live shows have improved.

Born in 1971 in Church Point, Ledet was raised in a French-speaking home by parents who used English with her so as to make school easier. She fell in love at 16 with zydeco and her husband, Morris Ledet, at the first zydeco dance she attended; Boozoo Chavis was performing, and she was hooked. She learned to play accordion by watching Morris, who had his own band, and then practicing on his accordion while he was away at work.

In 1994 at the age of 23, Rosie Ledet took over the accordion and bandleading spotlight. Now Morris happily plays bass in her band, along with his father Lanis Ledet on rubboard, nephew Corey Ledet on drums and Kent August on guitar. The band tours the zydeco circuit and is played often on zydeco radio shows in south Louisiana. In a sign of Ledet's growing stature, she was invited to "referee" the annual "battle" between Boozoo Chavis and **Beau Jocque** at Rock 'n' Bowl in New Orleans during the 1996 Jazz & Heritage Festival.

THE BEST

Sweet Brown Sugar

i. 1994/Maison de Soul 1052 CD, CS

She isn't Aretha Franklin, but Ledet possesses the best female voice in zydeco. Her plaintive vocals grow on the listener over time. On this debut disc, she also demonstrates her songwriting prowess, having penned all 15 tunes. Since many of her songs, such as "The Mardi Gras," "Shame On You" and "I Waited for

You," concentrate more on lyrics than do many contemporary zydeco songs, this disc is for listening as well as dancing. However, the grooves are certainly here to fuel the dancing fires; just listen to Ledet and the band funk it up on "Sweet Brown Sugar" and especially "Swing That Thing." She tries her hand at balladry on the soulful "Ever Love a Woman," the only downtempo song. A satisfyingly impressive first release.

EXCELLENT

Zesty Zydeco

i. 1995/Maison de Soul 1056 CD, CS

This follow-up release to *Sweet Brown Sugar* solidifies Ledet's promising future. Her songwriting skills continue to improve with songs like the risqué "Casino Nights" and "I'm Gonna Take Care of Your Dog." The Ledet family band once again provides the hard-driving backing, augmented by a sax and keyboard for a fuller sound. The tempos and rhythms on this CD are somewhat more varied than on her first, including the waltz "Dancing with the Devil" and a slow soul ballad, "Let the Sky Cry." Other outstanding tunes are "Fever Chill" and "C'est Tout Finis," where the band really cranks it up.

OTHER RECORDINGS

The Zydeco Sweetheart

Maison de Soul 1050 CS

L'IL BRIAN & THE ZYDECO TRAVELERS (Brian Terry)
Group

Rounder CD 2146

Just 21 when his album *Fresh* debuted in 1995, "L'il Brian" Terry is one of the young generation of performers broadening zydeco's audience. An accordionist, songwriter and singer, he got hooked on zydeco when he first heard **John Delafose**, a distant relative. Terry grew up in Crosby, Tx., where his parents exposed him to zydeco music. During a summerlong visit at the Delafose farm in Eunice, he learned button accordion at 13 from John's son, **Geno Delafose**, who once gave Terry an old-fashioned beating when he couldn't catch on to a song. He also taught himself piano accordion by watching **Buckwheat Zydeco** and listening to **Clifton Chenier** records.

When he was 14, Terry sent Rounder producer Scott Billington his first demo tape, at Buckwheat Zydeco's urging. Unsuccessful, he sent several more over the next seven years and acquired coaching from Lee Allen Zeno, Buckwheat's bass player, who produced the CD that finally satisfied Billington. Terry started his band with his two brothers while still in high school. The group was soon playing clubs and festivals in Texas, and in 1990 won an award for the youngest zydeco band at the annual Zydeco Festival in Plaisance. As a junior at Crosby High School, he won over a tougher audience: the lunchroom crowd. That experience taught him that if you mix zydeco with rap and hip-hop, the teens will follow.

THE BEST

Z-Funk

i. 1997/Rounder 2146 CD

This second Rounder release is miles ahead of L'il Brian's first, showing a continuing evolution and maturity in the band's music. They take influences from hip-hop, funk, blues and R&B and churn them all together into a caldron of fire and funk calculated to appeal to a young zydeco audience. Highlights are the funkiest tunes–covers of King Floyd's "Baby Let Me Kiss You," James Brown's "Back Up and Try It Again" and their own zydeco rap "Z-Funk." The deep grooves of the rhythm section are rock-solid, providing the perfect foundation for Brian's steadily improving accordion riffs. The band's strong harmony vocals, a rarity in zydeco, are particularly evident on the moody "Sunday Walk." On "You Got Me Crying," a straight zydeco blues, the band pays tribute to Clifton Chenier.

GOOD

Fresh

i. 1995/Rounder 2136 CD, CS

This debut release fits the mold of some of Buckwheat's recent recordings. Unfortunately, L'il Brian isn't the vocalist that Buckwheat is, which is the CD's greatest failing. However, the band is tight, and the sound quality of the album is excellent. The song styles run the gamut from waltzes to straight blues to soul and rap. It must be admitted that

Brian plays a mean accordion. The most effective cut on the CD is the zydeco-rap "FuNkABLUeSaDeCo." Cover versions of Clifton Chenier's "My Baby She's Gone" and Z. Z. Hill's "Givin' It Up for Your Love" should have been left alone; they pale in comparison to the originals. "Snap Bean" is a rocking instrumental that is another high point. This young zydeco artist does have some "fresh" ideas; they just need a little seasoning.

NATHAN & THE ZYDECO CHA-CHAS
Vocals, accordion

Rounder CD 2107

Nathan Williams is a gifted songwriter with a strong, distinctive voice. He is one of the few to play the piano accordion–a more versatile instrument than the button accordion favored by most contemporary artists. Stylistically, he follows in **Clifton Chenier**'s footsteps as a tradition-based innovator who has created his own repertoire of zydeco, blues, R&B and pop. Nathan & the Zydeco Cha-Chas are a dynamic young band with a bright future.

Williams (b. 1963) comes from St. Martinville, where early musical influences included his brothers Dennis and Allen, as well as his uncle Harry Hypolite, guitarist for many years with Chenier and for almost a decade with **C. J.**

Chenier. As a child, Williams used to watch Chenier by peeking through windows outside the local Casino Club, often getting run off. It was Chenier's blues that captured the youngster. He also listened to his uncle and friends singing old-style Creole "jure," unaccompanied call-and-response music.

In ninth grade, Williams left home to work with his older brother, Sidney, in Lafayette. Sidney bought Nathan his first accordion and virtually built his early career. Starting in 1985 he provided a place for him to play at his club, El Sid O's. There patrons were admitted for free until the young musician had honed his skills. But Williams' biggest mentor was Stanley "**Buckwheat**" Dural, who lived nearby and taught him how to play accordion.

Sid Williams had been the unofficial head of the tight-knit Williams family since their father died when Nathan was seven. His tireless entrepreneurial efforts to pull the family of eight children out of poverty have resulted in economic successes like his convenience store and club, as well as that of Nathan in music and another brother, Dennis Paul, in art. A talented painter, Dennis Paul also plays guitar in the band.

Furthermore, Sid provided a record label, El Sid O's, for Nathan to cut 45s early on. His first single, "Everybody Calls Me Crazy," became a best-seller in south Louisiana and appealed to Rounder Records producer Scott Billington when he heard it in 1987. After a recommendation from Buckwheat, the result was *Zydeco Live!*, which Williams recorded with Boozoo Chavis live at Richard's Club in Lawtell.

Williams was 25 when he recorded his own first album, *Steady Rock*, in 1988. The release produced his first regional hit, the title track penned by R&B songwriter Paul Kelley. Another Rounder release, *Your Mama Don't Know*, also caught on and propelled Williams to touring dates outside the bayou state. Largely due to this quick succession of Rounder releases, Williams' musical career took off with lightning speed.

One of zydeco's best songwriters, Williams writes with wit and a good ear for dialect, drawing on his family and everyday life around Sid's One Stop convenience store. In his trademark cowboy hat and sunglasses, he leads one of zydeco's best and most popular bands.

THE BEST

Steady Rock

r. 1988; i. 1989/Rounder 2092 CD, CS, LP
A TOP 10 ZYDECO ALBUM

Williams burst upon the scene with this spectacular debut when he was 25. Heavily influenced by Clifton Chenier and Stanley "Buckwheat" Dural, Williams is nevertheless his own man—a creative songwriter who penned eight of the 12 songs on this CD. The title cut, the reggae-tinged "Steady Rock," became so popular that even the Lafayette high school marching band began playing it. There are no duds here, just fresh material and good hard-rocking music, from the blues of "Why Can't I Get Over You?" to the steamrolling vamp of "Zydeco Joe" to the French cover of the Fats Domino R&B classic, "You Got Me Walkin' the Floor." The zydeco groove cuts deep with "Big Fat Mama" and "I Don't Know Why I'm So Crazy About You."

EXCELLENT

Your Mama Don't Know

r. 1990; i. 1991/Rounder 2107 CD, CS

Just an iota below "Steady Rock" in excitement, Williams' follow-up CD still bubbles with soul-stirring blues and R&B-influenced zydeco.

From the bouncy opener, "Outside People," to the steaming last cut, "El Sid O's Zydeco Boogaloo," this release hardly lets up. Once again, Williams' songwriting skills are featured on eight of the 12 tracks, making this disc anything but a rehash of zydeco standards. Other standout songs are the slow blues, "Slow Horses and Fast Women," and the hypnotic "You Got Me Baby Now You Don't."

GOOD

Follow Me Chicken

r. & i. 1993/Rounder 2122 CD, CS

Williams continues expanding zydeco's harmonic boundaries and honing his songwriting skills on his third Rounder release. The funk influence is felt on the title cut, which Williams based on an old country saying ("Follow me chicken, I'm full of corn."), while the blues surfaces on the Z. Z. Hill composition "I Need Someone to Love Me." The Stevie Wonder song "Elle Est Jolie" (Isn't She Lovely) is given the zydeco treatment, and Williams and the band smoke on "Zydeco Road" and "Tout Partout Mon Passe." Another wonderful effort from one of zydeco's most energetic and original stylists.

Creole Crossroads

(featuring Michael Doucet)/i. 1995/Rounder 2137 CD, CS

Along with guest Cajun fiddler Michael Doucet of Beausoleil fame, Nathan and the Zydeco Cha Chas take a step backward into zydeco tradition to remind today's younger crowd where the music comes from. The spirit of Clifton Chenier is here, since four of the songs on this disk are associated with him. Williams' vocals continue to improve with each release, especially on the blues "Black Snake Blues/I Can't Go Home No More." *Creole Crossroads* is worthwhile;

however, it is a cut below Williams' previous recordings and doesn't do justice to these two fine musicians.

OTHER RECORDINGS

Zydeco Live!

(with Boozoo Chavis)/r. 1988; i. 1989/Rounder 2069 CD, CS

WILLIS PRUDHOMME
Accordion, vocals

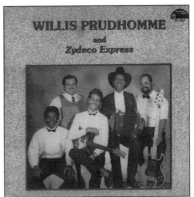

Maison de Soul LP 1033

An exponent of the **Boozoo Chavis** school of rural zydeco, relative newcomer Willis Prudhomme plays a bouncy button accordion and sings in both French and English. Like Chavis, his repertoire includes plenty of barnyard tunes like "Chicken Head Zydeco," "Making Love in the Chicken Koop" and "Backyard Dog" (complete with dog barks).

Prudhomme and his band, Zydeco Express, are popular in the zydeco clubs, church halls and festivals in Louisiana and east Texas with their mix of zydeco, R&B and–unusual for a modern zydeco band–Cajun music. Like the old-style Creole performers, Prudhomme plays the occasional Cajun waltz. In fact, his inspiration comes from Cajun accordionists like **Iry LeJeune** and **Nathan Abshire**, his idol.

Born in 1931 or 1932 in Kinder, Prudhomme grew up working in the rice fields and is a rice farmer today. At the age of 45, he taught himself harmonica, which he practiced while riding his tractor and plowing. Soon after, he switched to accordion and played with the Leo Thomas band for seven or eight years before forming his own band. In 1988, he recorded his first album, for Rounder, followed since by three others. Prudhomme writes many of his own songs.

THE BEST

Chicken Koop

i. after 1991/Goldband 7820 CD

Prudhomme and his band chug their way through a dozen traditional tunes on his most recent CD. The sparse liner notes don't identify the musicians, but the guitar player must be Cornelius Guidry, so distinctive is his style. All the songs are uptempo except "Roseland Waltz" and were written by Prudhomme, Guidry and W. P. Guidry. They are solid examples of old-time rural zydeco, updated by the influences of younger bands such as **Zydeco Force** and **Beau Jocque**.

GOOD

Zydeco Live! Vol. 2

r. 1988; i. 1989/Rounder 2070 CD, CS

This CD recorded live at Richard's Club in Lawtell showcases Prudhomme and the band as part of a series of in-person recordings by Rounder Records. The music rocks throughout, slowing down only for the waltz "Those Tears in Your Eyes Are Not for Me." The disc accurately captures the flavor of a zydeco dance. As a plus, the first half contains a rollicking performance by John Delafose and the Eunice Playboys.

OTHER RECORDINGS

Crawfish Got Soul

i. 1991/Maison de Soul 1039 CS, LP

Willis Prudhomme and Zydeco Express

i. 1990/Maison de Soul 1033 CS, LP

QUEEN IDA (Ida Guillory)
Accordion, vocals

GNP Crescendo CD 2181

Queen Ida was the first woman to lead a zydeco band. Originally from Lake Charles, the vivacious Ida Guillory has pumped out her pleasing brand of modern zydeco for the Creole community of San Francisco for many years. As a result of two decades of international tours and nine albums, this Grammy winner long ago caught on beyond the West Coast.

Born Ida Lewis in 1930, Guillory comes from a musical farming family whose mother and two uncles played accordion and whose father played harmonica. She used to practice on the accordion her mother brought home for the family. After World War II, the family moved to the San Francisco Bay Area, where Guillory married and raised three children. After a 20-year break from accordion-playing, she picked it up again in her 40s, practicing during off-duty moments as a school bus driver. Eventually, she and her older brother, Wilbert Lewis, started playing at local parties. Meanwhile, her younger brother, Al Lewis (later **Al Rapone**), was working as a professional guitarist, and she began sitting in with his band in the mid-1970s.

Guillory's break came at a Mardi Gras zydeco party which she played with Al Lewis and his Barbary Coast Bon Ton Band. In a story on the event, Peter Levine of the *San Francisco Chronicle* dubbed her "Queen Ida," and her career took hold. She played functions backed by brother Al's band, which eventually became Queen Ida and Her Zydeco Band. Tom Mazzolini, a Bay Area promoter and founder of the San Francisco Blues Festival, lined her up for the festival and other appearances in the area. Next came engagements at music festivals around the country.

Guillory plays the triple-row button accordion and sings in a six-member band that increasingly features her son, Myrick "Freeze" Guillory, a singer/songwriter who plays accordion and rubboard. Brother Wilbert Lewis played percussion in her band until her latest recording. While the rest of the group's usual line-up includes drums, bass, guitar and violin, horns are added on her latest CD.

She has turned out nine albums for GNP Crescendo Records, one every few years since 1976. Most of them benefited from production and songwriting by Rapone, who served as lead guitarist/vocalist/arranger with the band for seven years before moving to New Orleans recently. He produced her 1982 Grammy-winning album, *Queen Ida & the Bon Ton Zydeco Band on Tour*, and composed one of her most popular tunes, "Frisco Zydeco." Three other albums have won Grammy nominations. She also appeared in the Francis Ford Coppola film *Rumble Fish*.

While Guillory's traditional female credentials are impeccable–she has even authored a cookbook, *Cookin' with Queen Ida*–she had to buck a culture that regarded accordion-playing as unladylike. She remains one of a tiny minority of female zydeco artists. She explains why in liner notes for *In San Francisco*:

"[W]omen in Louisiana were expected to raise their children, tend chickens, go to church and bake bread. And the lyrics to the Cajun songs were about unfaithful women. I'm changing that. The only thing women did not do was play zydeco. Well, I'm changing that, too!"

THE BEST

Caught in the Act

i. 1988/GNP Crescendo 2181 CD, CS, LP

Caught in the act at the Great American Music Hall in San Francisco, this live CD well represents a Queen Ida show and showcases her many zydeco styles. The sound quality is very good, and the queen's singing is as good as it gets for her. The best songs are the blues-based ones–the traditional "Hey Negress," the slow "Sad, Lonesome and Blue" and especially the hard-driving shuffle "Raywood Texas." She gives Rockin' Sydney's megahit, "My Tu Tu," an effectively funky treatment, but one still wonders why this song hit so big. Guillory's Cajun influences show through on "Willie on the Washboard," "Cotton-Eyed Joe," featuring some nice fiddling by Peter Allen, and on the Cajun anthem "Jolie Blon." Another highlight is the rollicking "Half a Boy, Half a Man."

Chapter 2 • Zydeco

GOOD

In San Francisco

i. 1991/GNP Crescendo 2158 CD, CS, LP

Nobody can fault Queen Ida and Her Zydeco Band for a lack of diversity. This, her best studio effort, has it all, from waltzes to blues shuffles to covers of rock and R&B tunes. The finest cut is "Every Now and Then," a hard-rocking English version of Clifton Chenier's "Tu le Ton Son Ton." Credence Clearwater Revival's "Bad Moon Rising" moves along nicely, but Fats Domino won't have to lose any sleep over the queen cutting him on "My Girl Josephine." "Zydeco Taco" shows a Latin influence. Hank Williams' "Jambalaya" has been done better by other zydeco artists, but this version is O.K. and sports some nice fiddle work. The Cajun side is represented by adequate renditions of "Fais Deaux Deaux" and D. L. Menard's "Back Door."

Mardi Gras

i. 1994/GNP Crescendo 2227 CD, CS

Queen Ida's latest release is certainly her biggest production, utilizing saxes, trumpet and even trombone. Whether this makes for a better CD is open to debate. However, there are a few good selections here, most notably a swinging "Home on the Bayou"; a nice ballad with sweet backing by the horns, "Where Are You Now"; and a rocking version of Delbert McClinton's "Object of My Affection." "Mr. Fine" is a nice midtempo blues with a solid sax solo by Bernard Anderson. Queen Ida even tries her hand at reggae with Johnny Nash's "I Can See Clearly Now," but she shouldn't have—her version pales in comparison with the original. Not a bad release, but for Queen Ida devotees only.

OTHER RECORDINGS

Cookin' with Queen Ida

i. 1989/GNP Crescendo/Sonet 1021 CD, CS, LP

In New Orleans

i. 1980/GNP Crescendo 2131 CS, LP

On a Saturday Night

i. 1984/GNP Crescendo 2172 CS, LP

On Tour

i. 1986/GNP Crescendo 2147 CD, CS, LP

Zydeco

i. 1976/GNP Crescendo 2101 CS, LP

Zydeco a la Mode

i. 1977/GNP Crescendo 2112 CS, LP

AL RAPONE (Al Lewis)
Accordion, vocals, guitar

Al Rapone is best known for his work with his sister, **Queen Ida**. He helped shape her career and produced her 1982 Grammy-winning album *Queen Ida & the Bon Ton Zydeco Band on Tour*. But his own musical career has held steady through moves to the West Coast and back to Louisiana. With his band, the Zydeco Express, he has played the West Coast and Europe for many years.

Rapone was born in 1936 in Lake Charles, where he was surrounded by musicians and heard various relatives perform at *fais do-dos*. His mother and two uncles played accordion, and his father played harmonica. At 13, Rapone learned accordion. By 15, he was playing the squeezebox at dances in California, where his family had moved. But he found more work as a blues guitarist in San Francisco, backing such artists as Big Mama Thornton, Jimmy Reed and Clarence Gatemouth Brown. After studying writing, arranging and producing in college, Rapone formed a trio, which his sister soon joined.

Rapone stayed with the Bon Ton Zydeco Band seven years, serving as composer, guitarist, vocalist and accordionist. He worked at creating a unique zydeco sound with a distinctive guitar backing to the accordion and a C&W beat. Then he struck out on his own, finding his greatest fans in Germany. After touring with fiddler Allen Fontenot, he moved to New Orleans recently.

Rapone's stylistic range encompasses zydeco, Cajun, country and New Orleans blues and R&B. His best known composition is "Frisco Zydeco."

THE BEST

Zydeco to Go

i. 1990/Blind Pig 73790 CD, CS, LP

Rapone's latest CD is an enjoyable, Cajun-tinged recording. He is joined by musical luminaries such as Allen Fontenot on fiddle and vocals, former B. B. King guitarist Leonard Gill on bass and guitar, Mark Naftalin on Hammond B-3 organ and Rapone's cousin Roy Chantier singing soulful vocals on some cuts. Instrumentation includes fiddles, banjo and synthesizer–not usually heard in zydeco. Production and sound are first-rate, something that unfortunately can't be said for Rapone's other releases. Highlights of this danceable disc include the lovely Louisiana ballad "Our Hearts Will Dance in Love Again" and the blues-influenced "Yvette U.B. Dancin'"–both featuring Chantier's wonderful voice. The rollicking Cajun-styled "Chere Duloone" features Fontenot's fiddling.

GOOD

C'est La Vie

r. & i. 1984/L&R (Germany) 4012 CD

This German release is worth searching out if you like zydeco on the blues side. Four of the 10 songs are blues-based, including "Married Man Blues," "Alice Mae," "Walkin' Papers Blues" and "Je Vas Revenir." Two complaints, however: (1) Who told Patty "LaRue" Harrison she could sing blues, as she attempts on "Married Man Blues," failing miserably? (2) Why does Rapone take credit for writing "Je Vas Revenir," a thinly disguised cover of Clifton Chenier's "I'm Coming Home"? Still, there is some enjoyable music here. The rhumbalike "Without You" swings like hell, as does "Alice Mae." Rapone's Cajun side comes out on "Benladette" and "Chere Duloone." He gets low down and dirty on "Walkin' Papers Blues," featuring some great blues accordion.

OTHER RECORDINGS

Cajun Creole Music

r. 1982; i. 1994/CMA (Germany) 8023 CD

Let's Have a Zydeco Party

i. 1985/JSP (England) 1092 LP

JO JO REED
Accordion, vocals

Jo Jo Reed is trying to break from the pack of young zydeco performers spreading the *nouveau zydeco* gospel. At the time of his 1995 debut CD, *Funky Zydeco*, he was 25 and had been playing zydeco for 10 years. He tours the southwest Louisiana-east Texas circuit, elsewhere in the South, and the West Coast.

Funky Zydeco

i. 1995/Maison de Soul 1057 CD, CS

On Reed's first CD, his music spans contemporary funky zydeco, blues and old-time zydeco. Most of the 12 tunes are self-penned. Somebody should tell him that Jimmy Reed did "Baby What You Want Me to Do"; Jo Jo isn't a blues singer. The best performances here, such as "Somebody Tell Them," "Gettin' Funky" and "Going to See My Baby," are all in the modern, funk-zydeco mode, although he also does a credible version of the swamp pop ballad "Irene." The only instrumental, "JD Special," rocks solidly, and the novelty tune "Pullin' for the Saints" is amusing. More good things can be expected in future from this young zydeco artist.

ROCKIN' DOPSIE (Alton Rubin Sr.)
Vocals, accordion

Maison de Soul CD 104

Rockin' Dopsie never did become a master of the accordion, which he played upside down, or left-handed. Nor was his voice top-notch. But as he used to say, "If you want the real zydeco, you come to me."

Fans did come to him, in droves. He was one of zydeco's most popular artists, earning international acclaim following a string of fine albums, tours and a zydeco turn on Paul Simon's *Graceland* album. After **Clifton Chenier's** death, the "King of Zydeco" title fell to Dopsie when he was crowned in 1988 by the mayor of Lafayette, although others laid claim to the title. His death in 1993 renewed rivalry for the crown that continues today.

Born Alton Rubin in 1932, he was the oldest of four children. He frequently missed school to help his parents work in the fields in Carencro, just outside Lafayette. He was through with school by 13. His sharecropper father, who played a simple, Cajun-style accordion, educated him musically by taking his son with him when he played at house dances. To learn how to play the $2 accordion his father bought him, the 14-year-old youngster spent three intensive weeks practicing under a tree in the fields. Later, he hung out in clubs to hear blues greats like B. B. King, Ray Charles, Muddy Waters and Lightnin' Hopkins.

Dopsie started his musical career in 1955 playing the accordion in local clubs with a distant relative, Chester Zeno, on rubboard. He soon picked up his stage name from imitating a 1950s Chicago dancer named Doopsie. After he married, he worked construction by day to support his family and played gigs at night for 13 years—a tough lifestyle reflected in his raw, relentless musical style. Somehow, he knew how to make music people couldn't help dancing to, and his local popularity grew. Clifton Chenier struck up a friendship with him and convinced him to play zydeco and blues, rather than the more popular rock 'n' roll. At first, young people laughed at him, calling the music "chanka-chank," but he heeded Chenier's advice to stick with his roots.

Possibly the longest running act in zydeco, Dopsie led his band continuously from the

1950s until the mid-1990s. His earliest recording, in 1959, sank into obscurity, but a decade later he found success recording blues singles for two committed Louisiana zydeco producers, Floyd Soileau and Jay Miller. In 1973, Sam Charters from Sweden's Sonet label signed him. The resulting six albums led to wider recognition–especially in Europe–and years of tours with his R&B-oriented band, the Zydeco Twisters.

"What I liked about his band was that it sounded so raw. Clifton Chenier was more polished. Dopsie had a sound that was incredibly alive. And he plays sharps and flats on his accordion so it gives a real wail," Charters wrote in liner notes for *Zy-De-Co-In*.

Dopsie's band bristled with top talents like tenor saxman John Hart, who joined Dopsie in 1978 at Charters' suggestion after retiring from Clifton Chenier's band. Since the early 1980s, the band has also included two of Dopsie's sons, Alton on drums and David on rubboard.

During the 1980s, Dopsie recorded with Bob Dylan and Cyndi Lauper, won two Grammy nominations and made commercials for Burger King. His *Graceland* break came in 1985, when Paul Simon went to Lafayette to hear Dopsie play, then asked him to record with him on the album that introduced zydeco to millions of music-lovers. Dopsie topped his career in 1991 with an Atlantic Records contract.

Dopsie didn't play in a great variety of styles on his push-button accordion, although his early albums are more bluesy than his later, more contemporary-sounding ones. He stuck to what he knew: belting out earthy, down-home zydeco. In comments to *Offbeat* in 1992, he called zydeco a "high-steppin' party. A foot-stompin' party all night long." The party goes on with his son, David Rubin–**Rockin' Dopsie Jr.**–leading the band.

THE BEST
Louisiana Music 📖

i. 1991/Atlantic 82307 CD, CS

A TOP 10 ZYDECO ALBUM

This CD, the last before he died, captures the sound and feel of a live Rockin' Dopsie show. The only thing better would be a recording of one of his legendary, smoldering performances at the Maple Leaf Bar in New Orleans. The band used on this date was Dopsie's working ensemble of the time, including his sons, Alton Jr. and David; saxman John Hart; Alonzo Johnson on bass and Selwyn Cooper on guitar. The songs include many from his live repertoire. Slow and midtempo blues such as "Since I Lost My Baby" and "That's Alright" alternate with hard drivers like "Keep a Knockin" and "Hot Tamale Baby." Traditional zydeco two-steps are here also, including "Jesephin C'est Pas Ma Femme" and "Zydeco Two Step."

EXCELLENT
Good Rockin'

i. 1984/GNP Crescendo 2167 CS, LP

This 1984 Grammy-nominated record is one of the few to document the actual sound of Dopsie and his band. Most of his last, greatest, band is here: sons Alton Jr. and David, John Hart on sax and the great Paul Senegal playing guitar. Not the best of singers, Dopsie enlisted second guitarist Russell Gordon and friend Joshua Jackson Sr. to handle the vocals on five of the 10 tunes, including two of the bluesiest on the album, "Driving Wheel" and the stellar "I'm a Country Boy." The band cooks like crazy on "Zydeco 'Round the World" and "Whole Lot of Loving," sung in French. "Good Rockin' " describes the album perfectly.

Chapter 2 • Zydeco

Saturday Night Zydeco

r.1987; i. 1988/Maison de Soul 104 CD (a reissue of a previously released LP of the same title [Maison de Soul 1025], with some added tracks)

A Grammy nominee, this release could have been better with more polished production. Still, the rockin' zydeco groove is there, propelled by the likes of Paul Senegal on guitar, John Hart on sax and Alonzo Johnson on bass. "Dopsie's Boogie" and "I Can't Lose With the Stuff I Use" are great tunes.

Crowned Price of Zydeco

i. 1987/Maison de Soul 1020 CS, LP

The same flat production sound that hinders *Saturday Night Zydeco* is heard here as well, but this LP is still well worth acquiring for the good song selection and driving band. Standout songs include the low-down zydeco blues, "Why You Do the Things You Do" and the high-energy "Crazy 'Bout That Married Woman."

OTHER RECORDINGS

Big Bad Zydeco

i. 1988/GNP Crescendo 2154 CS, LP

French Style

i. 1982/Sonet (England) 872 LP

Hold On!

i. 1979/GNP Crescendo 2156 CS, LP

Rockin' Dopsie and the Twisters

r. 1976-77; i. 1977/Rounder 6012 CS, LP

Rockin' Dupsee

r. 1970-1974/Flyright (England) 592 LP

Zy-De-Co-In'

i. 1989/Gazell 3003 CD (contains his first two Sonet [England] LPs, Doin' the Zydeco/1976/Sonet 718 & Zy De Blue/1977/Sonet 761)

ROCKIN' DOPSIE JR. (David Rubin)
Vocals, rubboard

As "Rockin' Dopsie Jr.," David Rubin carries the banner for his late father, **Rockin' Dopsie** (Alton Rubin Sr.). He pumps out a blend of zydeco, R&B and Cajun music with his father's band, the Zydeco Twisters. One of the best in the business, the group includes two of Rubin's brothers—Anthony on accordion/vocals and Alton Jr. on drums—as well as the fabulous duo of Paul Senegal on guitar and Alonzo Johnson on bass, plus keyboards, guitar and sax. A singer and rubboard player with a flamboyant stage presence featuring whirling-dervish acrobatics and splits, Rubin is the James Brown of zydeco.

After Rockin' Dopsie's death in 1993, Rubin (who is from Carencro) continued the band's scheduled tours and performed its regular gig at the Maple Leaf Bar in New Orleans. He is updating the band by venturing into funk and rock occasionally, and he has added a keyboard player.

"I kept the same style of music, but I took it into the era of what's going on today," he commented in the 1996 *New Orleans Jazz & Heritage Festival Program*.

Rubin's star is rising. He won the "Best of the Beat" award for best zydeco band/performer in 1996 from *Offbeat*, Louisiana's authoritative music magazine. He intended his debut album to be a tribute to his father.

Feet Don't Fail Me Now

i. 1995/AIM (Australia) 5001 CD

Besides Rockin' Dopsie Jr., this debut disc also features his three brothers, Anthony and Dwayne on accordions and Alton Jr. on drums. Also present are guitarist Paul Senegal and bassist Alonzo Johnson from Dopsie's last and best band. (Unfortunately, the sax of John

Hart, who also played with Dopsie, is missing.) The elder Dopsie's repertoire is well represented, notably with a driving version of "Don't You Lie to Me," "Let Me Be Your Chauffeur," "Jambalaya" and "Mountain Jack Blues." New Orleans bandleader Wardell Quezerque produced this well-recorded CD. It may be hard to get because of its Australian origin, but it is worth finding for its good-time zydeco party atmosphere.

ROCKIN' SIDNEY (Sidney Semien)
Vocals, accordion, harmonica, guitar

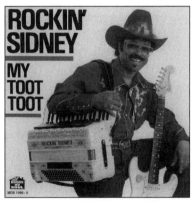

Maison de Soul CD 1009

Rockin' Sidney's claim to fame is his catchy 1985 novelty tune "My Toot Toot," zydeco's first international smash hit. The song's triple-entendre line "Don't mess with my toot toot!" refers to the French word "tout" (all), as in the Cajun French expression "ma cher tout tout," a term of endearment something like "my dearest everything." Fans read into it innuendos of sex and cocaine, as well. But Sidney is not just a one-hit wonder; the highly versatile pop zydeco artist has been a mainstay of the south Louisiana music scene since the 1950s.

Sidney Semien was born in 1938 in Lebeau, near Ville Platte. He started playing guitar and harmonica professionally as a teenager,

emulating Louisiana R&B artists such as Cookie & the Cupcakes and Slim Harpo. He recorded a string of appealing tunes in the late 1950s-early 1960s on Floyd Soileau's local Fame and Jin labels, and had his first regional hit in 1962 with the bluesy "No Good Woman." A second hit was "You Ain't Nothing But Fine," covered later by the Fabulous Thunderbirds. Europe discovered him when the English Flyright label reissued a 1974 collection of Fame and Jin singles, *They Call Me Rockin'.*

With another Louisiana label, Goldband, Sidney recorded more than 50 R&B and soul songs less successfully from 1965 to the late 1970s before learning the accordion and switching to zydeco. In Sidney's hands, the style became a happy-go-lucky combination of zydeco, R&B, soul, blues and country music. In 1982, he put out his first all-zydeco album, *Give Me a Good Time Woman.* With that recording, the versatile musician returned to his roots, for both his grandfathers had played zydeco music and inspired him to become a musician. Subsequently, he released several cassette albums on his own ZBC label.

When Sidney recorded "My Toot Toot" for Floyd Soileau's Maison de Soul label, he and Soileau considered it one of the weaker tunes on the 1984 album *My Zydeco Shoes Got the Zydeco Blues.* But the single from the album became a jukebox hit, forcing local radio stations who at first spurned it as too down-home to broadcast it. Quickly spreading in underground style, the million-plus seller put out by a small local label eventually won a Grammy, rode the charts in the U.S. and England and spawned a dozen popular covers. In Mexico and Central America, a cover called "Mi Cu Cu" reportedly sold more than a million records.

My Zydeco Shoes was put together in what has become Sidney's characteristic way–single-handedly, in his own Lake Charles studio. He sang and played all the instruments (harmonica, accordion, rhythm and lead guitar, bass) except his omnipresent drum machine. This solo approach has not fulfilled the promise of his early recordings or produced a hit to match "My Toot Toot," but Sidney stays active. One of zydeco's most prolific recording artists, he produces and records his own albums and produces other artists for his Bally Hoo label. He continues to perform throughout the Gulf Coast, tours abroad and devotes time to his radio stations, KAOK-AM and KEAZ-FM. Recently, he developed a six-acre entertainment complex called "Festival City" in Lake Charles.

THE BEST

Boogie Blues 'n' Zydeco

i. 1983/Maison de Soul 1008 CS, LP

It's too bad the quality of Rockin' Sidney's many recordings doesn't match their quantity. What sets this 1983 album apart is the hot band backing Sidney, who is far from a great vocalist and only an average accordion player. Swamp boogie queen Katie Webster contributes her pounding piano, along with Thomas Shreve on guitar, drummer Warren Storm, saxman Willie Tee and bass player Mark Miller. The selections are about evenly divided between boogie, blues and zydeco. "Slim's Y-Kee Kee" is a low-down blues with the same theme as the blues standard "Tin Pan Alley." Zydeco tunes "Cochon de Lait" and "Every Nickel, Every Dime" rock along nicely, while the band boogies on "Creole Rock and Roll" and "Boogie for Me."

GOOD

Creola the Talk of the Town

i. 1987/ZBC 102 CS, LP

A pop-zydeco album with almost no blues-based songs, this recording at least uses a real band. On several other recordings, Sidney plays and overdubs all the instruments and uses a drum machine. More accordion is heard here than usual, on tunes that are bouncy, light and pleasant enough, with good band backing. Highlights are "Rock-a-body," "Sunny Side Up" and "Crippled Crab a Crutch."

Squeeze That Thang!

ZBC 103 CS, LP

This is the best of Sidney's self-produced albums on which he plays all the instruments while using a drum machine. There is a good version of Bob & Earl's "Harlem Shuffle" and a rockin' cut called "Kicking, Asking and Taking Names." One of Sidney's best ballads, "May I Have the Pleasure," features good vocals and accordion work, and he gets funky on "Put Your Clothes Down." This is a reasonably enjoyable album, although the drum machine wears on you after awhile.

Mais Yeah Chere!

i. 1992/Maison de Soul 2046 CD, CS

This is the best of Sidney's CDs, but be warned: this is Sidney rockin' all by himself in his own studio, playing all instruments accompanied by the cursed drum machine. There are some decent tunes, such as the title cut, the rap "Funky Attitude," "Color Me Zydeco" and "Sex it Up Baby." The highlights, however, are two Mardi Gras tunes, "Mardi Gras Zydeco" and especially "Mardi Gras Second Line," a funky little ditty that gets airplay at Carnival time.

Zydeco is Fun

i. 1996/Maison de Soul 1061 CD, CS

Sidney's latest CD contains mostly tunes from previous albums with performances of Rockin' Sidney, the one-man band. Fans will probably want this disc instead of the LPs because of its superior sound quality. There are a few good cuts, nobably "I'm Your Man," a medium-tempo blues rocker; "May I Have the Pleasure," a sweet ballad; and "Harlem Shuffle," the R&B chestnut. However, the rest are forgettable.

OTHER RECORDINGS

Give Me a Good Time Woman

i. 1982/Maison de Soul 1007 CS, LP

A Holiday Celebration

i. c. 1987/ZBC 100 LP

Hot Steppin'

i. 1986/ZBC 101 LP

Joy to the South

i. 1982/Bally Hoo 2001 LP

Live with the Blues

i. 1988/JSP (England) 213 CD

My Toot Toot/My Zydeco Shoes

r. 1982-1984, 1990; i. 1991/Maison de Soul 1009 CD, CS

My Toot Toot

i. 1986/Ace (England) 160 CD, LP (contains all but 1 track of Maison de Soul 1009 LP + 3 tracks from the Jin label, 1959-1964)

My Toot Toot

i. 1986/Epic PET 40153 CS (unreviewed)

They Call Me Rockin'

i. 1974/Flyright (England) 515 LP (reissue of 1960s recordings for Jin and Fame labels)

THE SAM BROTHERS
Group

Maison de Soul LP 1029

The Sam Brothers (also known as the Sam Brothers Five) first delighted audiences in 1979 as a teen-age group from Opelousas by way of Houston. The group brings their **Clifton Chenier**-inspired sound to clubs and church halls on the zydeco circuit in Louisiana and Texas.

They got their first musical inspiration from their father, Herbert Sam, who started playing accordion at house dances around Opelousas and later performed with his own five-piece band in Houston, where he moved his family in 1951. While their father was away working as a roofer by day, the boys borrowed the band's instruments and learned to play in the family garage. One by one, Herbert incorporated the boys into his band to replace troublesome band members, and they eventually became the Sam Brothers.

Arhoolie Records producer Chris Strachwitz heard them in 1979 at the New Orleans Jazz & Heritage Festival and arranged a California tour as well as recorded a live album of the group. That year, they returned to Louisiana and started playing zydeco clubs and touring outside the state. The "brotherhood" includes

Chapter 2 • Zydeco

(from oldest to youngest) Carl on lead guitar; Rodney on drums and washboard; Leon, bandleader and vocalist who plays keyboards and accordion; Glen on bass and Calvin on washboard and drums.

THE BEST

Zydeco Brotherhood

i. 1989/Maison de Soul 1029 CS, LP

Standing in the large shadow of zydeco king Clifton Chenier, the Sam Brothers were all in their 20s when this rockin' LP was cut at Greybeard Studios in Lafayette. Three Chenier compositions, "Tu le Ton Son Ton," "Josephine C'est Pas Ma Femme" and the touching "I'm Coming Home" are included. One can waltz to the strains of "Joe Pete Took My Woman" and groove to the soul sounds of "Be Honest With Me," a song also recorded by the influential R&B singer Tyrone Davis. "Louise" and "Shoe Box" are great, driving zydeco blues tunes composed by the Sam Brothers. Boozoo Chavis' signature song "Paper in My Shoe" is given a speeded-up treatment with only accordion, rubboard and drums for accompaniment. It's hard to believe that such young musicians could put out such a good album of hard-rockin' zydeco blues.

GOOD

Cruisin' On

i. 1981/Blues Unlimited 5014 LP

This early album is strong musically, but marred by immature vocals—not surprising, since the brothers were in their teens at the time. "Early One Morning," "Baby Where Did You Go Last Nite" and "Baby Please" are straight zydeco blues. The brothers' dad, "Good Rockin'" Herbert Sam, makes a guest appearance on "My Baby Don't Wear No

Shoes," backed by only accordion, rubboard and drums. Four of the cuts on the album are effective instrumentals, the best of which is the funky "Jam (Jam with Sam)." Not a bad release by a young, developing zydeco blues band.

OTHER RECORDINGS

Leon Sam & the Sam Brothers

i. 1996/Master Track

The Sam Brothers 5

r. 1979/Arhoolie 1081 CS, LP

TERRANCE SIMIEN
Vocals, accordion

Black Top CD 1096

Terrance Simien is an incendiary performer with a soulful voice reminiscent of Aaron Neville. He does his part for multiculturalism by adding other styles to zydeco, annoying purists but pleasing crowds from California to Khartoum. Soul, funk, reggae and gospel all find a home in his repertoire, in line with his philosophy that "there's room for all styles of music. There's room for all kinds of people."

Simien was born in 1965 in Mallet, near Lafayette. He first heard zydeco at church dances. Like most of his modern zydeco peers, he thought it was unhip. But by the time he learned to play the accordion and began writing songs with his brother Greg, the growing popularity of zydeco offered opportunity. At 16 he formed a band and began playing church dances and local zydeco clubs on week-ends while working during the week with his father, a bricklayer.

An appearance at the 1984 New Orleans World's Fair shot Simien out of the rural zydeco orbit. The breaks came fast after that, starting with meeting zydeco fan Paul Simon through Louisiana composer and sax player Dickie Landry, and cutting a single with Simon of the Clifton Chenier song "You Used to Call Me." Landry became Simien's manager and producer–a relationship since severed; Simien and his wife, Cynthia Simien, now run their own business. Landry also lined up an appearance for Simien in the Hollywood film *The Big Easy*, in which he co-wrote and performed a song with Dennis Quaid, the film's star.

With his band, the Mallet Playboys, Simien has maintained a tireless touring schedule, even headlining a U.S. State Department "Arts America" tour of North Africa in 1988. Audiences respond wildly to his athletic, sensuous performances and rubboard player Earl Sally's on-stage antics (*Billboard* rated Terrance Simien and the Mallet Playboys one of the top 10 performance acts of 1987). But what sets him apart from other modern zydeco artists is his voice, a soaring falsetto well-suited to the 1970s soul-style ballads featured on both his albums.

THE BEST

There's Room for Us All

r. 1992,1993; i. 1993/Black Top 1096 CD, CS

With this second recording, Simien continues to incorporate other music styles into his own brand of modern zydeco. Guest appearances

by New Orleans funkmasters the Meters on two songs, the King Floyd classic "Groove Me" and Charles Wright's "Love Land," solidify Simien's forays into the funk and soul arena. The reggae influence is especially apparent on "Come Back Home" and "Will I Ever Learn," with guest performances by former Neville Brothers' band members Willie Green on drums and Daryl Johnson on bass/piano/background vocals. Only four tunes, "Uncle Bud," "Dog Hill," "Zydeco Boogaloo" and "A Ma Maison," mine the more traditional zydeco sounds. This CD features Simien's voice while burying his accordion further down in the mix. Overall, the release is tight, good-sounding and well produced. But fans of traditional zydeco should be warned: there isn't much of it here.

GOOD

Zydeco on the Bayou

i. 1990/Restless 72368 CD, CS

Simien's first release gave an indication of where his music was heading after years of one-nighters. The traditional zydeco grooves such as those on the title track and "Zydeco Zambada" are there, but reggae rears its head on Peter Tosh's "Stop That Train." Simien ventures into the ballad area on two lovely songs, "I'll Do It All Over Again" and "I'll Say So Long." One of the highlights of the CD is the chilling gospel tribute to Clifton Chenier, "Will the Circle Be Unbroken." Those who like pop music mixed with their zydeco will go for this album.

JUDE TAYLOR
Accordion, vocals

A disciple of the zydeco blues of **Clifton Chenier** and **Buckwheat Zydeco**, Taylor is a fine singer and musician. Like many zydeco artists, his performances are family affairs that include his sons, "Curly" and Errol, in a group called Jude Taylor and His Burning Flames. An accomplished songwriter, he wrote half the tunes on his *Best of Zydeco* album.

Born in 1949 in the French-speaking Creole hamlet of Grand Coteau, he has stayed in the area most of his life. He sang first with his church and school choirs and later with blues bands as a young adult, until his brother-in-law gave him an accordion and he turned to zydeco.

Best of Zydeco

i. 1994/Mardi Gras 5011 CD, CS

Taylor makes an impressive debut on this CD. Recorded with his sons "Curly" on drums and Errol on rubboard, the great Paul Senegal on guitar and Rockin' Dopsie veteran Alonzo Johnson on bass, Jude rocks the house. He establishes a zydeco blues feeling throughout, especially on the slow songs, "Revenge Lover" and "Cold Hearted Woman." The band cooks relentlessly on the two Clifton Chenier tunes, "My Baby, She's Gone" and "Bogalusa Boogie." Taylor covers Clarence Carter's "Strokin'" and B. B. King's "The Thrill is Gone" to good effect, while representing more traditional zydeco sounds with "La La Zydeco" and "Everybody Zydeco." Let's hope this solid disc will be followed by many more.

T-LOU (Louis Joseph Eaglin)
Accordion, vocals

T-Lou and his Zydeco Band are based in Los Angeles, where they have played their pop zydeco everywhere from weddings to Warner Bros. Studios. Born to sharecroppers in Grand Coteau and raised in Kinder, T-Lou taught himself guitar at 15 and then played bass in a teenage R&B band. After high school graduation, he moved to Houston, where he worked in a furniture factory for three years.

His next move was to Los Angeles, where he worked as an inspector with a large company, married and raised a family.

Inspired by hearing **Clifton Chenier** at a dance, T-Lou taught himself accordion and formed a band that played church halls for a time before breaking up. By 1985, he had formed a new Los Angeles Zydeco Band and released his first LP. He was playing with yet another group as T-Lou and His Zydeco Band at the time of their 1993 CD, *Super Hot*.

THE BEST

Super Hot

i. 1993/Maison de Soul 1047 CD

This aptly named CD is slickly recorded and augmented by a full band including two saxes and background singers. T-Lou wrote nine of the 11 tunes, the remainder being nicely done covers of the classic R&B ballads "Shake a Hand" and "Since I Met You Baby."

There is no funk zydeco here–just the good old blues-influenced style for which T-Lou's idol, Clifton Chenier, was known. Noteworthy rockers are the steaming instrumental "Hop Jump-Skip" and the two-chord vamp "Emily" featuring the hot guitar of Paul Davis. Another highlight is "They Call Me T-Lou," with slashing guitar and sax solos. Recommended for any party, this well-recorded CD showcases T-Lou's talents as vocalist and accordion player.

OTHER RECORDINGS

T-Lou and His Los Angeles Zydeco Band

i. 1985/Maison de Soul 1014 LP

JOE WALKER
Vocals, accordion, guitar, rubboard

Joe Walker's zydeco walks on the soulful side. In fact, it could be called '60s soul with accordion and rubboard. Two other things distinguish him from the zydeco pack: his rich, expressive voice and the fact that he writes all his own songs. A veteran session musician with an up-and-down career, he was only recently rediscovered.

Walker was born in Lafayette in 1944. As a youngster, he took to the guitar and blues and played with **Rockin' Dopsie**'s band in his teens. In the1960s, he had his own band and joined **Rockin' Sidney** for some singles for Goldband Records. After moving to Lake Charles (his home base today) in 1967, he formed another band that opened for soul and blues stars such as Tyrone Davies and Barbara Lynn. However, the group was washed out by the advent of disco music and end of the oil boom, leaving Walker on his own to play keyboard with a drum machine in lounges and, for eight years, gospel music.

In 1984, the blues revival brought Walker back into the recording studio. A seasoned musician, he had been a sideman for many other performers' recording sessions for three decades. When Cajun producer Lee Lavergne rediscovered Walker, he recorded the following three albums in short order at his funky Sound Center studio in Church Point for release by Zane Records in England.

THE BEST

Soulful Side of Zydeco

r. & i. 1991/Zane (England) 1003 CD

This aptly named CD contains several lovely soul-blues ballads, most notably Walker's classic country soul tune "When I Get to Know You Better," "Business in the Street" and the moving "Love and Hate." Walker's plaintive vocals and sophisticated piano accordion playing create his characteristic soulful zydeco mood. The bouncy "Zydeco All

Night" carries a melody similar to Wilson Pickett's "Don't Let Green Grass Fool You." Eight of the 15 tunes on this CD are by Walker; the rest are by zydeco man Roy Carrier.

GOOD

In the Dog House

r. & i. 1993/Zane (England) 1006 CD

Besides the soul zydeco songs for which Walker is known, this release also contains waltzes such as "Tante Sarah," straight blues like "Watch That Black Cat" and more modern groove-oriented songs such as "I Screwed Up." The soul blues highlights are "Bullet Through My Heart" and "Seen It for Myself," a story of cheatin' love. A good, strong effort by a modern zydeco singer, songwriter and musician.

OTHER RECORDINGS

Zydeco Fever

r. & i. 1992/Zane (England) 1004 CD

THE ZYDECO BLAZERS
Group

The Zydeco Blazers

i. 1995/Jewel 5040 CD

When they talk about the impoverished state of lyrics in modern zydeco, this CD could serve as a prime example. The songs are mostly grooves with the titles sung over and over. The music is good enough, but unless you need some background dance music for a party, this disc will wear thin on repeated listening. A few of the tunes, notably "Let Me Pass Through Your Window," have some catchy melodies, but a few sweet notes and some semi-intense grooves do not make for a good zydeco album.

ZYDECO FORCE

Group

Maison de Soul CD 1045

This young band from Opelousas is one of the most vital groups on the zydeco scene today. Formed in 1988, "Z-Force" started out with an old-time style reflecting their roots in the **Lawtell Playboys**; vocalist/accordionist Jeffery Broussard, one of the driving forces in the band, is the son of Delton Broussard, the late leader of the Playboys. For a time they followed **Clifton Chenier**'s bluesy zydeco path, but lately they have veered toward **Beau Jocque**-like zydeco funk with a heavy bass and drum foundation and sublimation of lyrics to instrumentalism.

Bandleader Robby "Mann" Robinson writes and arranges the group's songs along with playing bass, accordion, piano and singing. A former R&B musician, he formed the band with several young Broussard clan members when he noticed the demand for zydeco rising in the late 1980s. The group's original roster included Hebert Broussard on *frottoir* (rubboard), Shelton Broussard on lead guitar and vocals and Raymond Thomas on drums.

Zydeco Force's solid, dance-hall-boogie sound has kept folks in Louisiana and east Texas dancing, even inspiring a lambada-like dance craze when the band came out with the tune "The Zydeco Push" in 1994. With several creditable recordings behind them already, the group is an up-and-coming force in the zydeco world.

THE BEST

It's La La Time 🪗

r. & i. 1995/Maison de Soul 1054 CD, CS

A TOP 10 ZYDECO ALBUM

The band's latest release is their most varied and best produced to date, showing a wide range of influences. Of the 14 cuts, all but four are written by bandleader Robby "Mann" Robinson. The best of these originals , including "I Don't Know," "Back to the Beginning," "Paul's Playhouse" and "Kush-Mal," all feature the funky, double-clutching rhythm so popular in zydeco now. Party time for sure! Of the cover tunes, the most impressive are the funked-up version of John Delafose's "Broken Hearted" and a touching rendition of Clifton Chenier's "You Used to Call Me," dedicated to the late Delton Broussard, accordionist Jeff Broussard's father. Another highlight is the final track, a funk-zydeco version of the blues classic "Hoochie Coochie Man."

EXCELLENT

Shaggy Dog Two-Step

r. & i. 1992/Maison de Soul 1045 CD, CS

If you're a serious fan of hard-rocking modern zydeco, you'll want this first CD release by Zydeco Force. One doesn't listen to this band for meaningful lyrics, but for the bubbling, complex rhythms created by the interaction of the instruments. Listen to the aptly named "Double Clutching," "Shake That Thang" and the title cut to appreciate the band's rhythmic grooves. There are also the obligatory nods to tradition with reprises of Clifton Chenier's "I'm a Farmer" and "Oh My Lucille." Another standout track is "Forget About Me," a clone of Zydeco Force's biggest hit, "I'm on My Way."

GOOD

The Zydeco Push

r. & i. 1994/Maison de Soul 1048 CD, CS

Their second CD is a slight let-down, but still contains some good, funky tunes. The hypnotic "Where'd You Get That Thing?" is a tour de force of zydeco-funk. Other good examples in the same vein are "Big Dog, Lil' Dog" and the "Zydeco Push." The title cut was written by bandleader Robinson to express the movements he saw in a lambada-like dance performed by a couple in Ville Platte, and the tune helped turn the dance into a "zydeco push" craze among Creoles in rural Louisiana. The band also covers the Clifton Chenier minor key blues masterpiece "I'm on a Wonder."

OTHER RECORDINGS

The Sun's Going Down

r. & i. 1991/Maison de Soul 1038 CS, LP

Zydeco Force

r. & i. 1990/Maison de Soul 1031 CS, LP

THE ZYDECO HURRICANES
Group

Guitarist Selwyn Cooper has toured with many prominent zydeco artists, including **Clifton Chenier**, **Buckwheat Zydeco**, **Rockin' Dopsie**, **C. J. Chenier**, **Lynn August** and **Fernest Arceneaux**. He recently formed the Zydeco Hurricanes, using two talented veterans–drummer Nathaniel Jolivette, who

has recorded with Buckwheat; and bassist Alonzo Johnson Jr., formerly with Clifton Chenier and Rockin' Dopsie–as well as newcomers Adam Robinson on washboard and John Wilson on accordion and vocals.

Louisiana Zydeco!

r. & i. 1994/Mardi Gras 5012 CD

This is a solid, but not essential, recording by the New Orleans Mardi Gras label. Most of the songs are cover versions of zydeco and blues classics such as "I'm Coming Home," "Night Time is the Right Time," "Hot Tamale Baby" and "Big Mamou."

Chapter 3 • Collections

CHAPTER 3: COLLECTIONS

CAJUN

The following collections are recommended. The best are listed first, in alphabetical order.

THE BEST

Allons Cajun Rock 'n' Roll

i. 1992/Ace (England) 367 CD

Aldus Roger, Lawrence Walker, Nathan Abshire, Blackie Forestier, Vin Bruce, Rufus Thibodeaux, Happy Fats, Louis Cormier, Doc Guidry, Jimmy C. Newman, Jimmy Breaux, Michael Doucet, Cajun Born.

Ace Records, a major player in Louisiana music for 40+ years, always packages a fine product –in this case, two dozen songs from La Louisianne Records in Lafayette by 13 different performers. The focus is on 1950s favorites Aldus Roger and Lawrence Walker.

Cajun & Creole Masters

r. 1987; i. 1996/Music of the World 138 CD

Canray Fontenot, Alphonse "Bois Sec" Ardoin, Sady Courville, Dennis McGee, Michael Doucet, Billy Ware.

A live 1987 recording made at a gathering in New York arranged by Michael Doucet and the World Music Institute. Doucet and Beausoleil mate Billy Ware back the masters in a wonderful session.

Cajun Dance Favorites

i. 1993/Swallow 6104 CD, CS

Jambalaya, Cajun Gold, D. L. Menard, Joe Bonsall, Walter Mouton, Belton Richard, Dewey Balfa, Nathan Abshire, Sheryl Cormier, Le Band Passepartout.

A mix of contemporary Cajun dance bands with some older artists plus D. L. Menard, a major artist of today whose musical career goes back to the early 1960s.

Cajun Dance Hall

i. 1996/Rounder/EasyDisc 7011 CD

Bruce Daigrepont, Jo-El Sonnier, Steve Riley, Jimmy C. Newman, Beausoleil, David Doucet, Eddie LeJeune, Mamou, D. L. Menard, Michael Doucet, Cajun Brew.

The artists, but not the songs, on this disc overlap with Rounder's earlier *Cajun Dance Hall Special*. Each of the 10 songs is a gem, and the CD's low price makes it all the more attractive.

Cajun Dance Hall Special

i. 1992/Rounder 11570 CD, CS

Beausoleil, Bruce Daigrepont, David Doucet, Michael Doucet, Eddie LeJeune, D. L. Menard, Jimmy C. Newman, Zachary Richard, Steve Riley, Jo-El Sonnier.

A super 24-song overview of the best contemporary Cajun performers in the huge Rounder lineup–a refreshing change from the typical compilation featuring older sounds.

Cajun Honky Tonk: The Khoury Recordings–The Early 1950s

i. 1995/Arhoolie 427 CD

Nathan Abshire, Lawrence Walker, The Texas Melody Boys, Harry Choates, Floyd LeBlanc, The Musical Four Plus One, Vincent and Cagley, Elise Deshotel with Dewey Balfa, Shuk Richard & Marie Falcon.

George Khoury captured some big names in the 1950s with his Khoury Records in Lake Charles–Nathan Abshire, Lawrence Walker and Harry Choates–as well as interesting performances by less well known artists. Includes Dewey Balfa's first recordings with Elise Deshotel.

Cajun Hot Sauce

i. 1995/Ace (England)/Arhoolie 591 CD

Beausoleil, Savoy-Doucet Cajun Band, California Cajun Orchestra, Dewey Balfa, D. L. Menard, Canray Fontenot/Beausoleil, Octa Clark & Hector Duhon, Chuck Guillory, Harry Choates, Wallace "Cheese" Read, Hackberry Ramblers, Breaux Brothers, Wade Fruge, Michael Doucet, Joseph Falcon.

A good cross section of leading lights covering a wide time span from Joe Falcon in the 1920s to today's California Cajun Orchestra.

Cajun Saturday Night

i. 1988/Swallow 102 CD

Dewey Balfa & Friends, Austin Pitre, Aldus Roger, Jim Olivier, Belton Richard, Paul Daigle & Cajun Gold, Nathan Abshire, Michael Doucet/Beausoleil, Jambalaya, Balfa Brothers, Cedric Benoit, Camey Doucet Et Musique, Adam Hebert, Lawrence Walker, Warren Cormier, Sundown Playboys, The Cajun Tradition, Sheryl Cormier.

A wonderfully diverse collection from the vast vaults of Floyd Soileau's Swallow Records in Ville Platte. The generous 23 choice songs guarantee a good time Saturday night–or any night.

Cajun Spice: Dance Music from South Louisiana

i. 1989/Rounder 11550 CD, CS

The Balfa Brothers, Beausoleil, Octa Clark & the Dixie Ramblers, Bruce Daigrepont, Michael Doucet, Eddie LeJeune, D. L. Menard, Jo-El Sonnier.

These 21 exceptionally fine recordings represent a wide range of material from eight of Rounder's Cajun stars.

15 Louisiana Cajun Classics

i. 1996/Arhoolie 103 CD

Beausoleil, Nathan Abshire, Wade Fruge, Dewey Balfa, Marc Savoy & D. L. Menard, Wallace "Cheese" Read, California Cajun Orchestra, Harry Choates, Hackberry Ramblers, Savoy-Doucet Cajun Band, Canray Fontenot, Austin Pitre, Magnolia Sisters, Dewey Balfa with Nathan Abshire, Michael Doucet, Joe Falcon.

An outstanding collection from the huge Arhoolie vault, featuring superb players and a near-perfect song selection. As a bonus, it's part of the new American Masters Budget Series. Arhoolie's Chris Strachwitz was recording and releasing Cajun music from Louisiana long before most folks (including those living there) saw its value. Consequently, he has the songs and knows how to pick the best.

Folksongs of the Louisiana Acadians

i. 1994/Arhoolie 359 CD, CS (contains all of Arhoolie LP 5009, most of Arhoolie LP 5015 + several previously unreleased tracks)

Chuck Guillory, Wallace "Cheese" Read, Mrs. Odeus Guillory, Mrs. Rodney Fruge, Isom J. Fontenot, Savy Augustine, Bee Deshotels, Shelby Vidrine, Austin Pitre, Milton Molitor.

Most of Dr. Harry Oster's field recordings from the late 1950s (formerly available only on rare Folklyric, Arhoolie and Prestige LPs), together with some unissued material. These vibrant down-home recordings of ballads, ceremonial songs and dance music can transport you back to the '50s dance halls and home *fais do-dos*. An informative booklet is included.

Great Cajun Accordionists: Cajun Country French Classics, Vol. 3

i. 1987/La Louisianne 145 LP

Nathan Abshire, Aldus Roger, Blackie Forestier, Ambrose Thibodeaux.

An album featuring the accordion masters who have recorded for La Louisianne–an interesting concept that works.

J'ai Ete au Bal (I Went to the Dance), Vol. 1 & 2

i. 1990/(soundtrack on 2 CDs of the film by Les Blank, Chris Strachwitz & Maureen Gosling + 7 additional tracks)

Vol. 1

Arhoolie 331 CD, CS

Walter Mouton, Queen Ida, Lionel LeLeux, Michael Doucet, Canray Fontenot, Dennis McGee, Amede Ardoin, Bois Sec Ardoin, Nathan Abshire, Marc Savoy, Marc & Ann Savoy, Joe Falcon & Cleoma Breaux, Odile Falcon, Solange Falcon, Luderin Darbone & The Hackberry Ramblers, Leo Soileau, Chuck Guillory with Preston Manuel, Harry Choates, Iry LeJeune.

Vol. 2

Arhoolie 332 CD, CS

Joseph Jones, Jimmy Peters, Sidney Babineaux, Clifton Chenier, D. L. Menard & The Louisiana Aces, D. L. Menard & The California Cajuns, Belton Richard, Johnny Allen, Dewey Balfa, Balfa Brothers Band, Rodney Balfa, Michael Doucet & Beausoleil, Paul Daigle, Paul Daigle & Cajun Gold, John Delafose, Boozoo Chavis, Rockin' Sidney, Wayne Toups & Zydecajun.

An essential blockbuster survey of Cajun music, this soundtrack includes 49 songs by 36 artists, from recording pioneers Joe Falcon and Cleoma Breaux Falcon to Cajun and zydeco artists of today such as Wayne Toups & Zydecajun. Compare the Falcon and Toups versions of "Allons a Lafayette."

Louisiana Cajun Music, Vol. 3: The String Bands of the 1930s

i. 1971/Old Timey 110 LP

Miller's Merrymakers, J. B. Fuselier, Leo Soileau, Hackberry Ramblers, Cleoma Falcon, Rayne-Bo Ramblers.

The strongest LP in the excellent series put out by Arhoolie's Chris Strachwitz under his Old Timey label. The choice of artists, song quality and performances set this compilation above others covering this period.

La Musique Chez Mulate's

i. 1986/Swallow 6071 CD, CS, LP

File, Beausoleil, Dewey Balfa, D. L. Menard, Hector Duhon & Octa Clark.

A stellar collection of musicians from the stable of famed Mulate's Cajun Restaurant in Breaux Bridge. Includes distinguished performances by some of the best talents in Cajun music.

21 Cajun Classics

i. 1990/Swallow 6079 CD

Dewey Balfa, D. L. Menard, Zachary Richard, Jesse Lege, Joe Bonsall, Nathan Abshire/Dewey Balfa & the Balfa Brothers, Cajun Tradition, Jo-El Sonnier, Jambalaya, Cajun Gold, Belton Richard, Ivy Dugas, Bruce Daigrepont, Fred Charlie & Acadiana Cajuns, Johnnie Allan, Michael Doucet/Beausoleil, Balfa Brothers, Harry Fontenot, Jim Olivier, Nathan Abshire.

A wide range of artists covering an equally broad time period, from Swallow Records in Ville Platte, the major force in Cajun compilations.

OTHER RECORDINGS

Acadian Two-Step, Vol. 2

i. 1988/Flyright (England) 610 LP

Alligator Stomp, Vol. 4: Cajun Christmas

r. 1973-1992; i. 1992/Rhino 71058 CD

Allons au Fais Do-Do

Swallow 6009 CS, LP

American French Music from the Bayous of Louisiana, Vol. 2

i. 1995/Goldband 7777 CD, CS, LP

The Best of Cajun Country

i. 1989/ERA/K-tel 339 CD, CS

The Best of the Cajun Hits

Swallow 6001 CS, LP

The Best of the Cajun Hits, Vol. 2

Swallow 6003 CS, LP

The Best of the Cajun Hits, Vol. 3

i. 1978/Swallow 6033 CS, LP

The Best of the Cajun Hits, Vol. 4

i. 1982/Swallow 6045 CS, LP

Bon Temps Rouler

i. 1981/Swallow 103 CD; 6040 CS, LP

Cajun, Vol. 1: Abbeville Breakdown

i. 1990/Columbia 46220 CD

Cajun Classics

i. 1993/Ace (England) 431 CD

Cajun Country French Classics

La Louisianne 130 LP

Cajun Fais Do-Do

r. 1966; i. 1995/Arhoolie 416 CD

Cajun Music: The Early 50s

i. 1975/Arhoolie 5008 CS, LP

A Cajun Music Anthology, Vol. 1: Le Gran Mamou—The Historic Victor Bluebird Sessions 1928-1941

i. 1990/Country Music Foundation 013 CD, CS

A Cajun Music Anthology, Vol. 2: Raise Your Window—The Historic Victor Bluebird Sessions 1928-1941

i. 1993/Country Music Foundation 017 CD, CS

A Cajun Music Anthology, Vol. 3: Gran Prairie—The Historic Victor Bluebird Sessions 1935-1940

i. 1993/Country Music Foundation 018 CD, CS

Cajun Social Music

i. 1990/Smithsonian/Folkways 40006 CD, CS, LP

Crowley Two-Step

i. 1985/Flyright (England) 604 LP

Festival de Musique Acadienne '81 Live

i. 1982/Swallow 6046 CS, LP

Floyd's Cajun Fais Do-Do

i. 1990/Ace (England) 304 CD

14 Cajun Classics

i. 1989/Swallow 6079 CS, LP

14 Cajun Hits

i. 1987/Swallow 6066 CS, LP

J'etais au Bal

Swallow 6020 CS, LP

Louisiana Cajun French Music from the Southwest Prairies, Vol. 1 & 2

r. 1965-66; i. 1989/Rounder 6001 & 6002 CD, CS, LP

Louisiana Cajun Music, Vol. 1: First Recordings—The 1920s

i. 1970/Arhoolie/Old Timey 108 (19028) LP

Louisiana Cajun Music, Vol. 2: The Early 1930s

Old Timey 109 LP

Louisiana Cajun Music, Vol. 4: From the 30s to the 50s

i. 1972/Old Timey 111 LP

Louisiana Cajun Music, Vol. 5: The Early Years—1928-1938

i. 1973/Old Timey 114 LP

Louisiana Cajun Music, Vol. 1: First Recordings

Arhoolie/Old Timey 213 CS (contains Old Timey LPs 108 & 109)

Louisiana Cajun Special No. 1

i. 1985/Ace (England)/Swallow 141 LP

More Cajun Classics

i. 1994/Ace (England) 519 CD

Pioneers of Cajun Accordion 1929-1935 (Louisiana Cajun Music, Vol. 9)

i. 1989/Old Timey 128 CS, LP

Les Sacalaits Sont Pas Sale

i. 1991/Swallow 6095 CD, CS

Swallow Records Louisiana Cajun Special, Vol. 2

i. 1992/Ace (England) 368 CD

Swampland Jewels

i. 1991/Goldband 7763 CD

ZYDECO

The following collections are recommended. The best are listed first, in alphabetical order.

THE BEST

101 Proof Zydeco

i. 1990/Maison de Soul 1030 CD, CS, LP

Lynn August, Zydeco Force, Terrance Simien, Sam Brothers 5, Clifton Chenier, Nathan & the Zydeco Cha Chas, Major Handy, Boozoo Chavis, Rockin' Sidney, Zachary Richard, Jo Jo Reed, John Delafose, Zydeco Brothers.

A fine representation of different zydeco stylists, mostly from Maison de Soul releases. This CD has 18 tracks, including Major Handy's zydeco funk version of Slim Harpo's classic "Tee Na Ni Na Nu."

Rockin' Zydeco Party!

i. 1994/Maison de Soul 1049 CD, CS

Boozoo Chavis, Zydeco Force, Rockin' Sidney, Beau Jocque, Keith Frank, Cory Arceneaux, John Delafose, T-Lou, Clifton Chenier, Rockin' Dopsie, Preston Frank, Roy Carrier, Ann Goodly, Lynn August, Wilfred Chevis, Rosie Ledet.

A good mixture of many different styles, old and new, blues to waltzes to funky. Selections from Maison de Soul, Lanor and Zydeco Hound Records.

Stomp Down Zydeco

i. 1992/Rounder 11566 CD, CS

Buckwheat Zydeco, Zydeco Force, John Delafose, Lynn August, Nathan & the Zydeco Cha Chas, Boozoo Chavis, Pee Wee & the Zydeco Boll Weevils.

An excellent introductory compilation of late 1980s to early 1990s recordings. All but one are previously unissued cuts, many recorded live at El Sid O's and Richard's zydeco clubs in Louisiana. Buckwheat's "Let the Good Times Roll" and Nathan's "You're My Mule" alone are worth the price.

A Tribute to John Delafose

i. 1995/Deep South 1001 CD

Willis Prudhomme, Terrance Simien, Leo Thomas, C. J. Chenier, Jo Jo Reed, L. C. Fontenot, Buckwheat Zydeco, Jude Taylor, Geno Delafose, Tony Delafose.

A hard-rockin', good-sounding tribute by friends and family of the late John Delafose, featuring many all-star zydeco musicians from southwest Louisiana, including members of the Magic Sounds, Boozoo Chavis' band. Get it if you can find it.

Zydeco Champs

i. 1992/Arhoolie 328 CD, CS

Clifton Chenier, C. J. Chenier, John Delafose, Amedee Ardoin, Lawrence Ardoin, Canray Fontenot, Bois Sec Ardoin, Clarence Garlow, Ambrose Sam, Sam Brothers 5, Herbert "Good Rockin'" Sam, Preston Frank, Leo Thomas.

An intriguing mixture of old-time and blues-based zydeco, mostly previously released on the Arhoolie label. Spans 60 years of recorded zydeco, from Amedee Ardoin in the 1920s to C. J. Chenier in the 1980s. Includes the first zydeco record from 1949, Clarence Garlow's "Bon Ton Roula." A must have.

Zydeco Festival

i. 1988/Maison de Soul 101 CD; 1024 CS, LP

Buckwheat Zydeco, Carriere Brothers, Terrance Simien, Rockin' Dopsie, Chuck Martin, Morris Francis, Clifton Chenier, John Delafose, Rockin' Sidney, Boozoo Chavis, Wilfred Chevis, Michael Doucet & Beausoleil, Zydeco Brothers.

A generous, 20-track, hour-long CD of zydeco excitement from Maison de Soul and other labels. Some of zydeco's biggest stars bring you a release full of toe-tappin' music. Nothing here not previously released, but a good introduction to the music.

Zydeco Party

i. 1992/K-tel 60591 CD, CS

Clifton Chenier, Boozoo Chavis, John Delafose, Roy Carrier, Lynn August, Terrance Simien, Rockin' Sidney, Buckwheat Zydeco, Nathan & the Zydeco Cha Chas, Rockin' Dopsie, Joe Walker, C. J. Chenier.

An inexpensive sampler of some of the best zydeco artists culled from several different labels. A good mixture of different styles, recommended especially for the new zydeco fan.

Zydeco Shootout at El Sid O's

i. 1991/Rounder 2108 CD, CS

Lynn August, Zydeco Force, Pee Wee & the Zydeco Boll Weevils, Warren Ceasar & Creole Zydeco Snap, Morris Ledet & the Zydeco Playboys, Jude Taylor & the Burning Flames.

A fine live CD recorded at Sid Williams' zydeco nightspot in Lafayette. Six hot bands battle, and the result is high-energy dance music.

Zydeco, Vol. 1—The Early Years: 1961-62

i. 1989/Arhoolie 307 CD, CS (contains Arhoolie LP 1009) (Zydeco, Vol. 2/Arhoolie LP 1090 also available [unreviewed])

McZiel & Gernger, Sidney Babineaux, Albert Chevalier, George Alberts, Peter King, Willie Green, Herbert Sam, Clifton Chenier, Clarence Garlow.

A fascinating look at the origins of modern zydeco. Most of these cuts were recorded at taverns and house dances in Houston and southwest Louisiana in 1961 and 1962 and are primitive by today's standards. Bonus tracks are Clifton Chenier's first two recordings from 1954 and Clarence Garlow's 1949 "Bon Ton Roulet," the first zydeco recording.

Zydeco's Greatest Hits

i. 1996/Rounder/EasyDisc 7025 CD

Buckwheat Zydeco, Nathan & the Zydeco Cha Chas, Geno Delafose, Beau Jocque, Rockin' Sidney, Clifton Chenier, Boozoo Chavis, John Delafose.

A budget-priced sampler of 10 popular zydeco tunes such as "Hot Tamale Baby," "My Toot Toot" and "Uncle Bud." Mostly from Rounder Records, with nothing new. However, it rocks hard beginning to end.

OTHER RECORDINGS

Let's Go Zydeco

i. 1994/Ace (England)/Arhoolie 543 CD

Louisiana Dance Party!

i. 1991/Gazell 3004 CD

Rockin' Accordion

i. 1989/Flyright (England) 622 LP

Texas Zydeco Greats

Collectables 5286 CD (unreviewed)

Zodico: Louisiana Creole Music

r. 1976; i. 1979/Rounder 6009 CS, LP

Zydeco Birth

i. 1987 Folk-Star/Charly (England) 103 LP

Zydeco Blues

i. 1978/Flyright (England) 539 LP (Flyright 36 CD also available)

Zydeco Blues, Vol. 2

i. 1984/Flyright (England) 600 LP

Zydeco Blues 'n' Boogie

i. 1991/Rykodisc 10198 CD, CS

Zydeco Dance Party

i. 1993/GNP Crescendo 2220 CD, CS

CAJUN/ZYDECO

THE BEST

Alligator Stomp: Cajun & Zydeco Classics

i. 1990/Rhino 70946 CD, CS

Rockin' Sidney, Queen Ida & Her Zydeco Band, Rocking Dopsie & the Cajun Twisters, D. L. Menard & the Louisiana Aces, Clifton Chenier, Cleveland Crochet, Bruce Daigrepont, Johnnie Allan, Jo-El Sonnier, Rusty & Doug, Boozoo Chavis, Beausoleil.

The first in a wonderful Rhino series, this disc captures classics by a good cross section of artists. Mostly mid-period recordings featuring strong performances.

Alligator Stomp, Vol. 2

i. 1991/Rhino 70740 CD, CS

Terrance Simien & the Mallet Playboys, Lesa Cormier & the Sundown Playboys, Nathan Abshire, The Balfa Brothers, Queen Ida & Her Zydeco Band, Iry LeJune, Clifton Chenier, Fats Domino & Doug Kershaw, Jo-El Sonnier, Rusty & Doug, Boozoo Chavis, Beausoleil, Buckwheat Zydeco, D. L. Menard, Rockin' Dopsie, Belton Richard, John Delafose.

This second Rhino offering mixes old and mid-period Cajun and zydeco with excellent performances by some of the best artists.

Bayou Dance Party

i. 1996/Rounder/EasyDisc 7014 CD

Steve Riley & the Mamou Playboys, Nathan & the Zydeco Cha-Chas, Geno Delafose, Bruce Daigrepont, David Doucet, Beausoleil, John Delafose, Beau Jocque, Buckwheat Zydeco, L'il Brian & the Zydeco Travelers.

It's short, with only 10 songs, but each one is a gem from Rounder's powerhouse of Cajun and zydeco artists. The low price makes it even more attractive.

Cajun Music and Zydeco

i. 1992/Rounder 11572 CD, CS

Dennis McGee, Bois-Sec Ardoin & Canray Fontenot, Aldus Roger, Clifton Chenier, Felix Richard, Boozoo Chavis, Zachary Richard, John Delafose & the Eunice Playboys, The Savoy-Doucet Cajun Band, Preston Frank, Dewey Balfa, Zydeco Force, Beausoleil, Buckwheat Zydeco, Bruce Daigrepont, Nathan & the Zydeco Cha-Chas, Steve Riley & the Mamou Playboys.

For its scope, thoughtful mix of artists and consistently superb performances, this is the best Cajun/zydeco compilation available.

The Real Louisiana

i. 1996/Rounder/EasyDisc 9002 CD

Dennis McGee, Bois-sec Ardoin & Canray Fontenot, Zachary Richard, John Delafose, Dewey Balfa, David Doucet, Zydeco Force, Beausoleil, Buckwheat Zydeco, Beau Jocque, Bruce Daigrepont, Nathan & the Zydeco Cha Chas, L'il Brian, Steve Riley.

If you haven't fallen in love with Cajun and zydeco music by now, this release should do the trick. From early to recent Cajun greats and contemporary zydeco near its best, this is one of the strongest compilations out there, and it's on Rounder's new, more affordable EasyDisc label.

OTHER RECORDINGS

Alligator Stomp, Vol. 3

i. 1992/Rhino 70312 CD, CS

Alligator Stomp, Vol. 5: Cajun & Zydeco—The Next Generation

i. 1995/Rhino 71846 CD, CS

Louisiana Dance Party!

i. 1991/Gazell 3004 CD

More Cajun Music and Zydeco

i. 1995/Rounder 11573 CD, CS

The Very Best of Cajun

i. 1996/Dino Entertainment 127 CD

Appendix

MUSIC SOURCES

If you can't find a Cajun or zydeco recording in your local record store, try the following specialized stores or contact a record company directly.

RECORD COMPANIES

The following companies issue the vast majority of Cajun and zydeco recordings. They will send a catalog or sell directly to individuals. Some also operate retail stores.

Ace Records Ltd.

46-50 Steele Rd.
London NW 10 7AS
England
Phone: +44 (0) 181 453-1311
Fax: +44 (0) 181 961-8725
Web site: http://www.acerecords.co.uk

Alligator Records

Box 60234
Chicago, IL 60660
Phone: 800 344-5609 or 312 973-7736
Fax: 312 274-3391
Web site:
http://www.visualradio.com/vrtour2/al/al1.html

Arhoolie Records

10341 San Pablo Ave.
El Cerrito, CA 94530
Phone: 888 274-6654 or 510 525-7471
Fax: 510 525-1204
E-mail: mail@arhoolie.com
Web site: http://www.arhoolie.com/

Record producer Chris Strachwitz, who has played a significant role in bringing Cajun and zydeco musicians to wider recognition, started Arhoolie in 1960. Its labels include **Arhoolie**, **Folklyric** and **Old Timey**, among others. All Arhoolie releases (including remaining LPs) are also in stock at its **Down Home Music Store**, at the same address. For phone orders, call 510 525-2129.

Black Top Records

P.O. Box 56691
New Orleans, LA 70156
Phone: 504 895-7239
Fax: 504 891-1510

Flat Town Music Co./Floyd's Record Shop

P.O. Drawer 10
434 East Main St.
Ville Platte, LA 70586
Phone (Flat Town Music Co.): 318 363-2177
Phone (Floyd's Record Shop): 800 738-8668
or 318 363-4893
Fax (Flat Town Music Co.): 318 363-2094
Fax (Floyd's Record Shop): 318 363-5622

One of Cajun/zydeco's longtime guardian angels, Floyd Soileau, produces Cajun and zydeco recordings under the **Swallow** and **Maison de Soul** labels, respectively.

Interstate Music Ltd.

*(Flyright & **Krazy Kat** labels)*
20 Endwell Rd.
Bexhill-on-Sea
East Sussex TN40 1EA
England

GNP Crescendo Record Co., Inc.

8400 Sunset Boulevard
Hollywood, CA 90069
Phone: 800 654-7029 or 213 656-2614
Fax: 213 656-0693

Goldband Recording Corp.

P.O. Box 1485
313 Church St.
Lake Charles, LA 70602
Phone: 800 259-3263 or 318 439-8839
Fax: 318 491-0994
Web site: http://cust.iamerica.net/goldband

Now a mail order record company, Goldband has been in business for more than 50 years under the leadership of record producer Eddie Shuler.

Jadfel Record Co. (Jadfel Publishing)

204 Kevin Dr.
Lafayette, LA 70507
Phone: 318 232-2368

Jewel/Paula/Ronn Records

P.O. Box 1125
Shreveport, LA 71163-1125
Phone: 800 446-2865 or 318 227-2228
Fax: 318 227-0304
The Paula label has zydeco recordings.

La Louisianne Records

P.O. Box 52131 (711 Stevenson St.)
Lafayette, LA 70505-2131
Phone: 318 234-5577
E-mail: laloumus@iamerica.net
Web site: http://cust.iamerica.net/laloumus

Lanor Records/Sound Center

P.O. Box 233
329 N. Main St.
Church Point, LA 70525
Phone: 318 684-2176

Record producer Lee Lavergne started the Lanor label in 1960.

Mardi Gras Records

3331 St. Charles Ave.
New Orleans, LA 70115
Phone: 800 895-0441
Fax: 504 891-4214

Master Trak Enterprises/Modern Music Center

P.O. Box 856
413 N. Parkerson
Crowley, LA 70526
Phone: 318 783-1601
Fax: 318 788-0776

Master-Trak Audio-Video Studios and record company and Modern Music Center are run by Mark and Bill Miller, sons of record producer J.

D. Miller, who died in 1996. Jay Miller's earlier labels include, among others, **Feature**, **Fais Do-Do**, **Kajun**, **Cajun Classics** and **Blues Unlimited**. (Many recordings released on Flyright in England.)

Rhino Records

P.O. Box 60008
Tampa, FL 33660-0008
Phone: 800 432-0020
Web site:
http://cybertimes.com/rhino/welcome.html

Rounder Records

One Camp St.
Cambridge, MA 02140
Phone: 617 354-0700
Fax: 617 491-1970

Rounder Mail Order

Phone (info.): 617 661-6308
Phone (orders): 800 443-4727
Fax: 617 868-8769
E-mail (info): info@rounder.com
E-mail (orders): order@rounder.com
Web site: http://www.rounder.com

Record producer Scott Billington at Rounder Records is a major player in Cajun/zydeco music.

SPECIALIZED RETAIL/MAIL ORDER STORES

Ace Video & Music

(mail order)
P.O. Box 1934
285 Caillavet St.
Biloxi, MS 39533-1934
Phone: 601 374-0777

The Magic Bus

527 Conti St.
New Orleans, LA 70130
Phone: 504 522-0530

Record Ron's

(retail store—used vinyl & new CDs)
1129 Decatur St. & 239 Chartres St.
New Orleans, LA 70130
Phone: 800 234-6889
or 504 522-9444 or 504 522-2239
Fax: 504 522-7305 or 504 527-0934
E-mail: al stuff@aol.com

Roots & Rhythm, Inc.

(mail order)
P.O. Box 2216
San Leandro, CA 94577
Phone: 888 ROOTS 66 or 510 614-5353
Fax: 510 614-8833
E-mail: roots@hooked.net
Web site:
http://www.bluesworld.com/roots.html

Savoy Music Center

(music store owned by musician/accordion
maker Marc Savoy)
Hwy. 190
Eunice, LA
Phone: 318 457-9563

OTHER LOUISIANA RECORD STORES

Lousiana Music Factory

210 Decatur St.
New Orleans, LA 70130
Phone: 504 586-1094
Fax: 504 586-8818

Tower Records

408 N. Peters
New Orleans, LA 70130
Phone: 800 ASK TOWER or 504 529-4411

*Many large on-line record stores carry Cajun and zydeco music. The one with the most information, including short bios on artists, is **CD now**: http://cdnow.com*

INTERNET RESOURCES

We highly recommend these sites on the World Wide Web. New Cajun/zydeco web sites are arriving all the time–just start exploring and you'll find them.

All Music Guide

http://allmusic.com

A massive on-line database of albums, artists' bios, reviews, ratings, song lists, release dates, discographies and prices. Updated regularly and open to public participation, this service is a companion to the book *All Music Guide*, ed. by Michael Erlewine, with Chris Woodstra & Vladimir Bogdanov (Miller Freeman Books).

The Cajun & Creole Pages

http://http.tamu.edu:8000/~skb8721/

Compiled by Shane K. Bernard from Lafayette and Herman Fuselier from Opelousas, Cajun and Creole journalists respectively. An interesting introduction to the culture and music of south Louisiana.

Cajun/Zydeco Music & Dance

http://www.bme.jhu.edu/~jrice/cz.html

Contains music and dance information for cities across the U.S. and numerous links to other useful web sites; also has instructions on how to dance Cajun and zydeco.

Cajun Zydeco Web Resources, Virtually Live from San Francisco

http://www.slip.net/~arubinst/

A nicely annotated, selected list of Cajun and zydeco information on the Web, plus detailed listings for the Cajun/zydeco scene in the San Francisco Bay Area.

Gary Hayman's ZydE-Magic Cajun/Zydeco Web Page (home of the ZydE-zine)

http://www.nmaa.org/member/ghayman

A great first stop, with regional, national and international schedules as well as articles, dance lessons and reviews of recent shows.

The Music Page of New Orleans, Louisiana–A Virtual Library

http://www.satchmo.com/nolavl/nomusic.html

A treasure trove of music news and artists' information including discographies, reviews and tour schedules.

The New Orleans & Cajun Country Newsletter

http://www.noconnect.com/forms/cajunews.htm

Informative regional information, music, festivals, reviews, recipes and more.

Offbeat

http://www.offbeat.com

Offbeat is the magazine of New Orleans and Louisiana music and entertainment. The web site is a great home base for Cajun/zydeco fans.

WWOZ

http://www.wwoz.org

WWOZ 90.7 FM Radio in New Orleans is a good place to hear Cajun and zydeco music. The web site has lots of music info.

BOOKS

The following books offer a wealth of interesting material about Louisiana music.

Allan, Johnnie

Memories: A Pictorial History of South Louisiana Music 1910s-1990s. Lafayette, La.: Johnnie Allan/JADFEL Publishing, 1995.

Ancelet, Barry Jean

Cajun Music: Its Origins and Development. Lafayette: Center for Louisiana Studies, University of Southwestern Louisiana, 1989.

Ancelet, Barry Jean

with photographs by Elemore Morgan Jr. *The Makers of Cajun Music.* Austin: University of Texas Press, 1984.

Ancelet, Barry Jean, Jay Edwards, and Glen Pitre

Cajun Country. Jackson: University Press of Mississippi, 1991.

Broven, John

South to Louisiana: The Music of the Cajun Bayous. Gretna, La.: Pelican, 1983.

Daigle, Pierre V.

Tears, Love and Laughter: The Story of the Cajuns and Their Music. Ville Platte, La.: Swallow Publications, 1987.

Fry, Macon and Julie Posner

Cajun Country Guide. Gretna, La.: Pelican, 1992.

Gould, Philip

(photographs), with an introduction by Barry Jean Ancelet. *Cajun Music and Zydeco.* Baton Rouge: Louisiana State University Press, 1992.

Lichtenstein, Grace and Laura Dankner

Musical Gumbo: The Music of New Orleans. New York: W. W. Norton, 1993.

Savoy, Ann Allen

Cajun Music: A Reflection of a People. Eunice, La.: Bluebird Press, 1984.

MAGAZINES & NEWSPAPERS

The following are good sources of current information about the Cajun and zydeco scene.

Living Blues

Room 206
Sam Hall
University, MS 38677

The magazine carries a column on zydeco.

New Orleans Times-Picayune

3800 Howard Ave.
New Orleans, LA 70130
Phone: 504 821-1455

See the newspaper's Friday entertainment section.

Offbeat

333 St. Charles Ave., Suite 614
New Orleans, LA 70130-3117
Phone: 504 522-5533
Fax: 504 522-1159
Web site: http://www.offbeat.com

Billed as "New Orleans & Louisiana's Music & Entertainment Magazine," *Offbeat* is THE main print source for Cajun and zydeco music.

The Times of Acadiana

201 Jefferson St.
Lafayette, LA 70501
Phone: 318 237-3560
Fax: 318 233-7484
Web site: http://www.timesofacadiana.com

This weekly newspaper is distributed throughout Cajun country. It also publishes *Allons!* magazine six times a year.

There are many Cajun and zydeco newsletters in major cities around the country. A good way to find one near you is to check your local music store or the Internet (see "Internet Resources" appendix).

VIDEOS

The following listings are gathered from many sources. We have not reviewed the videos.

Belizaire the Cajun

A feature film with soundtrack by Michael Doucet of Beausoleil. Produced, written, directed by Glen Pitre. 113 min. Cote Blanche, 1986.

Best of the Fest

Performances at the New Orleans Jazz & Heritage Festival; narrated by Quint Davis. 50 min. Ken Erlich Productions, 1989.

Big Easy, The

A Hollywood film with music by well-known Cajun and zydeco musicians. Directed by Jim McBride. 100 min. HBO Video, 1987.

Buckwheat Zydeco: Taking it Home

Filmed live at a concert in London. Directed by Bob Portway. 55 min. Island, 1990.

Cajun Country: Don't Drop the Potato

"A taste of Cajun music and culture." Episode from the television series American Patchwork. 60 min. Pacific Arts Video Publishing, 1990.

Cajun Visits/Les Blues de Balfa

Two productions on one 60-min. tape:

- **Cajun Visits**

  Six masters of traditional Cajun music sing, play and talk—Canray Fontenot, Robert Jardell, Dennis McGee, Wallace "Cheese" Read, Leopold Francois and Dewey Balfa.

- **Les Blues de Balfa**

  With the Balfa Brothers, Dewey Balfa, Rockin' Dopsie, Nathan Abshire and others.

Both produced and directed by Yasha Aginsky. In Cajun French with English subtitles. Flower Films, 1983.

Clifton Chenier

Produced and directed by Carl Colby. 58 min. Phoenix Films & Video, 1978.

Clifton Chenier, The King of Zydeco

Includes live performances at 1982 San Francisco Blues Festival and 1977 Jazz Fest, plus interviews with Chenier. Produced by Chris Strachwitz. 55 min. Arhoolie, 1987.

Dance for a Chicken: (Cajun Mardi Gras)

Rural Louisiana Carnival scenes with a Cajun music soundtrack. 57 min.

Dedans le Sud de la Louisiane

Documentary in Cajun French with English subtitles. Directed by French filmmaker Jean-Pierre Brunot. 43 min. Cote Blanche, 1983. Sequel c. 1993.

Dewey Balfa: The Tribute Concert

Documents a musical gathering of Balfa's friends at the Liberty Theatre in Eunice a month before he died in 1992. Directed by Glenn Orkin. 58 min. Motion, Inc., 1994.

Dry Wood

Documentary featuring the older, rural style of Cajun music. With Alphonse "Bois Sec" (Dry Wood) Ardoin and family, plus Canray Fontenot. A 1974 film directed by Les Blank. 37 min. Flower Films, 1979.

Hot Pepper

A 1972 documentary on Clifton Chenier's music and its sources, with lots of music. Directed by Les Blank. 54 min. Flower Films, 1973.

J'ai Ete au Bal (I Went to the Dance): The Cajun and Zydeco Music of Louisiana

Documentary with Michael Doucet, Clifton Chenier, Queen Ida, Walter Mouton, Rockin' Sidney, the Balfa Brothers, Marc and Ann Savoy, D. L. Menard, Nathan Abshire, Beausoleil, John Delafose, Wayne Toups, "Bois Sec" Ardoin, Chuck Guillory, the Hackberry Ramblers, Dennis McGee, Boozoo Chavis, Odile Falcon, Canray Fontenot, Paul Daigle & Cajun Gold and others. Historical sequences about Joe Falcon, Amedee Ardoin, Iry LeJeune, Harry Choates and others. Narrated by Barry Jean Ancelet and Michael Doucet. Produced by Chris Strachwitz, directed by Les Blank, edited by Maureen Gosling. 84 min. Brazos Films, 1989.

Kingdom of Zydeco, The

An entertaining look at the zydeco king controversy, with a 1993 Beau Jocque/Boozoo Chavis "battle" in Lake Charles; also Nathan Williams and John Delafose. Directed by Bob Mugge. 71 min. BMG Video, 1994.

Laissez les Bons Temps Rouler, Vol. 1 (1990-1994)

Live bands from the Cajun Music Television Series. 40 min.

Let the Good Times Roll

Ninety minutes of music from the New Orleans Jazz & Heritage Festival, 1992.

Marc and Ann

A visit to Cajun country with musicians Marc and Ann Savoy. By Les Blank, Maureen Gosling and Chris Simon. 27 min.

Passion Fish

A Hollywood film directed by John Sayles, with scenes in rural zydeco dance halls. 135 min. 1992.

Spend it All

With Balfa Brothers, Marc Savoy, Nathan Abshire and others. A 1971 film directed by Les Blank, Skip Gerson. 41 min. Flower Films, 1979.

Zarico: The Creole Sound of Louisiana

Documentary in French with English subtitles.

Zydeco: Creole Music and Culture in Rural Louisiana

With Amedee Ardoin, Alphonse "Bois Sec" Ardoin and others. A 1983 film by Nicholas R. Spitzer and Steven Duplanier. 57 min. Flower Films, 1984.

Zydeco Gumbo

Live performances at the 1987 Zydeco Festival in Plaisance, three months before Clifton Chenier's death. With Chenier, Boozoo Chavis, John Delafose, Terrance Simien and Willis Prudhomme. By Dan Hildebrandt. 28 min. Rhapsody Films, 1990.

Zydeco Nite 'n' Day

With Boozoo Chavis, Rockin' Dopsie, Buckwheat Zydeco, Terrance Simien, John Delafose, Nathan Williams and the Zydeco Cha Chas, Clifton Chenier, Alphonse "Bois Sec" Ardoin, Canray Fontenot and others. Produced by Karen Anderson and Robert Dowling. 70 min. Island Visual Arts, 1991.

INSTRUCTIONAL–DANCE

Advanced Cajun Dancing

Jitterbug moves as well as a group dance for three people called the troika. Also contains a documentary on the Cajun culture.

Allons Danser! (Let's Dance!)

Dance instruction by Randy Speyrer; music by Dewey Balfa, Michael Doucet, Beausoleil and others. 30 min. Bruce Conque, Inc., 1987.

I Love to Cajun Dance

Dance instruction by Betty Cecit; music by Nous Autres. 30 min. Cote Blanche, 1988.

Introduction to Cajun Dancing

Shows the basics of the waltz, two-step and Cajun jitterbug. Also contains a documentary on the Cajun culture.

Learn to Zydeco Dance Tonight

38 min. Cote Blanche.

INSTRUCTIONAL–INSTRUMENTAL

How to Play Cajun Accordion

Instruction by master accordionist Marc Savoy. 60 min.

Learn to Play Cajun Fiddle

Easy intermediate lessons by Michael Doucet of Beausoleil. 90 min.

Note: If you have trouble finding these videos in your local video store, try ordering from Floyd's Record Shop or Arhoolie Records. Both are listed under "Music Sources" in this Appendix. Or contact Louisiana Catalog in Cut Off, La.: Phone: 800 375-4100; fax: 504 632-4129.

FESTIVALS

LOUISIANA

Where better to hear Cajun and zydeco music than in Louisiana? For general information on the state's many festivals, call 800 633-6970 or 800 334-8626. The following are the most important events:

Festivals Acadiens, Lafayette

Cajun, zydeco and traditional French bands, plus indigenous crafts and food. Third week of September. Info.: 800 346-1958 or 318 232-3737, or web site at:
http://fil.net-connect.net.

Festival International de Louisiane, Lafayette

Participants from all over the French-speaking world; emphasis on indigenous music and food. Usually third week of April. Info.: 318 232-8086.

New Orleans Jazz & Heritage Festival (JazzFest)

The world's greatest non-classical music festival, featuring all Louisiana musical styles including Cajun and zydeco. Last week of April and first week of May.

Info.: 504 522-4786 or web site at http.//www.nojazzfest.com.

Southwest Louisiana Zydeco Festival, Plaisance

Zydeco performers, regional cuisine and African-American arts and crafts. August: Saturday before Labor Day. Info.: 800 884-7329 or 318 942-2392 or web site at http://www.zydeco.org.

OUTSIDE LOUISIANA

Cajun and zydeco music abounds at festivals across the U.S. Just consult your local newspaper or the Internet, which offers detailed regional information. The following are just a selected few of the bigger events:

Bay Area Cajun/Zydeco Festival, Marin, Ca.

Big Easy Bash and Cajun & Blue Grass Festival, Escoheag, R.I.

Chicago Blues Festival

Jambalaya Jam, Philadelphia, Pa.

Long Beach/San Diego Blues Festival

Newport Folk Festival, Newport, R.I.

San Francisco Blues Festival

Southern California Cajun & Zydeco Fest, Long Beach, Ca.

LOUISIANA MUSIC CLUBS

The best way to hear Cajun and zydeco music is live in a club. There may be one near you–check your local newspaper or record store. Cajun/zydeco web sites on the Internet also carry club listings for major cities throughout the U.S. If you are in Louisiana, by all means visit the clubs, whose listings can be found in newspapers and *Offbeat* magazine, as well as on the Internet. The following is a selective list.

NEW ORLEANS (area code 504)

Cajun Cabin (Cajun)

501 Bourbon St.
529-4256

House of Blues (zydeco, Cajun)

225 Decatur St.
529-2583; Concert line: 529-1421

Maple Leaf Bar (Cajun, zydeco)

8316 Oak St.
866-9359

The Mardi Gras Cabaret & Restaurant (zydeco)

829 Convention Center Blvd.
522-6020

Michaul's (Cajun, zydeco)

840 St. Charles Ave.
522-5517

Mid-City Bowling Lanes (zydeco, Cajun)

(Home of the Rock 'n Bowl)
4133 S. Carrollton Ave.
482-3133

Mulate's (Cajun)

201 Julia St.
522-1492

Tipitina's (Cajun, zydeco)

501 Napoleon Ave.
895-8477

SOUTHWEST LOUISIANA (area code 318)

BREAUX BRIDGE

Harry's Lounge (Cajun)

519 Parkway Dr.
332-6852

La Poussiere Club (Cajun)

1215 Grand Point Rd.
332-1721

Mulate's Cajun Restaurant
(the original Mulate's) (Cajun)

325 Mills Ave.
800 634-9880 or 332-4648

ERATH

Smiley's Bayou Club (Cajun)

Rt. 14

EUNICE

Gilton's Club (zydeco)

U.S. 190 & Rt. 95
457-1241

Liberty Theatre (Cajun)–Saturday night radio broadcasts

2nd St. & Park Ave.

Savoy Music Center (Cajun)–Saturday morning jam sessions

Hwy. 190
457-9563

LAFAYETTE

Cajun Pier (Cajun & zydeco)

1601 W. Pinhook Rd.
233-8640

El Sid O's (zydeco)

1523 N. St. Antoine St.
237-1959 or 235-0647

Hamilton's Place (zydeco, Cajun)

1808 Verot School Rd.
984-5583

Prejean's Restaurant (Cajun)

I-49 Service Rd.
896-3247

Randol's Restaurant & Cajun Dancehall (Cajun)

2320 Kaliste Saloom Rd.
800 YO-CAJUN or 981-7080

LAWTELL

Roy's Offshore Lounge (zydeco)

Parish Road 643
543-7359

Richard's Club (zydeco)

Hwy. 190
543-6596 or 543-8233

LEWISBURG

Borque's (Cajun)

948-9904

Guidry's Friendly Lounge (Cajun)

942-9988

LOREAUVILLE

Clifton Chenier's Zydeco Club (zydeco)

Croche Lane
269-9390

MAMOU

Fred's Lounge (Cajun)—Saturday morning jam sessions

420 Sixth St.
468-5411 or 468-2300

Papa Paul's Club (zydeco)

Poinciana (Rt. 1160) & 2nd St.
468-5538

OPELOUSAS

Slim's Y-Ki-Ki Lounge (zydeco)

Hwy. 182 (Main Street)
942-9980

PARKS

Double D Cotton Club (zydeco)

St. Louis Rd.
394-9616

VILLE PLATTE

Snook's Bar and Cajun Dance Hall (Cajun)

Rt. 190 W.
363-0451

QUOTE SOURCES

CHAPTER I: CAJUN

Nathan Abshire: "A musician's life…" Barry Jean Ancelet, *The Makers of Cajun Music* (Austin: University of Texas Press, 1984), p. 103.

Amedee Ardoin: "Then Amadie would really get hot…" Canray Fontenot, by Michael Doucet, in John Broven, *South to Louisiana: The Music of the Cajun Bayous* (Gretna, La.: Pelican, 1983), p. 103; "Everybody went crazy…" Dennis McGee in Ann Allen Savoy, *Cajun Music: A Reflection of a People* (Eunice, La.: Bluebird Press, 1984), p. 67.

Dewey Balfa: "Don't be ashamed…" obituary by Jon Pareles, *The New York Times*, June 18, 1992, Section D, p. 22.

Basin Brothers, The: "We went to Canada…" Michael Tisserand, liner notes for *Dans la Louisiane*, 1996 (Rounder 6065).

Beausoleil: "you can take…" Michael Doucet, in Grace Lichtenstein and Laura Dankner, *Musical Gumbo: The Music of New Orleans* (New York: W. W. Norton & Co., 1993), p. 213.

Shirley Bergeron: "Son, beat on it…" Savoy, *Cajun Music*, p. 222.

Vin Bruce: "Well, he can see me…" Broven, *South*, p. 70.

Cajun Gold: "I knew that…" Pierre V. Daigle, *Tears, Love and Laughter* (Ville Platte, La., 1987), p. 100.

Carriere Brothers: "I was a young fella…" Nicholas Spitzer, liner notes for *La La: Louisiana Black French Music*, 1977 (Maison de Soul 1004).

Octa Clark: "I always thought…" Doucet, liner notes for *Old Time Cajun Music*, 1982 (Arhoolie 5026).

Michael Doucet: "Before I could go…" Spitzer, liner notes for *The Mad Reel*, 1981 (Arhoolie 397).

John DuBois: "Maurice Chevalier of the Bayous," Bouziane Damoudi, *Liberation Magazine* (France), in liner notes for *Rendez-Vous Louisianais*, c. 1995 (Chaud Dog Jean).

Joseph Falcon: "If all of the United States…" Johnnie Allan, in Broven, *South*, p. 17.

Canray Fontenot: "I just play…" Savoy, *Cajun Music*, p. 331.

Wade Fruge: "yokery yoke-ery," Savoy, *Cajun Music*, p. 44.

Doug Kershaw: "With rhythm and blues…" Broven, *South*, p. 160.

Eddie LeJeune: "It makes me feel like…" Barry Jean Ancelet, liner notes for *It's in the Blood*, 1991 (Rounder 6043).

Iry LeJeune: "When you hear…" Crawford Vincent, in Savoy, liner notes for *Cajun's Greatest–The Definitive Collection* (Ace 428).

Dennis McGee: "I play *French*!" Will Spires, liner notes for *The Complete Early Recordings of Dennis McGee 1929-1930*, 1994 (Shanachie/Yazoo 2012).

D. L. Menard: "Most of us was raised poor…" Jim and Carlotta Anderson, "The Good Times Are Rolling in Cajun Country," *Smithsonian*, February 1988, p. 115.

Belton Richard: "Country music was…" Savoy, *Cajun Music*, p. 290.

Zachary Richard: "Louisiana singer-songwriter…" Scott Aiges, "The Bayou's in His Blood," *New Orleans Times-Picayune*, Jan. 29, 1993, p. L6; "discovering that who I really was…" Keith Spera and Michael Tisserand, "Zachary Richard," *Offbeat*, May 1993, p. 55.

Steve Riley and the Mamou Playboys: "People long to…" Tisserand, "Cajun Crusader," *Offbeat*, April 1992, p. 21.

Marc Savoy: "People listen to this cheap…" Herman Fuselier, "Marc, Ann March to Different Beat," Opelousas, La. *Daily World*,

May 11, 1995; "Some Cajuns…" Michael Walsh, "Hot Off the Bayou," *Time*, May 8, 1995; "An imitation…" Simon Broughton et al, eds., in *World Music: The Rough Guide* (London: Rough Guides, Ltd., 1994), p. 617.

Savoy-Doucet Cajun Band: "I've always thought…" Marc Savoy, liner notes for *Home Music with Spirits*, 1992 (Arhoolie 389).

Leo Soileau: "I was too busy…" *Ville Platte Gazette*, 1974, in Savoy, *Cajun Music*, p. 129.

Jo-El Sonnier: "I think ethnic music…" Douglas B. Green, liner notes for *Cajun Life*, 1988 (Rounder 3049).

Wayne Toups: "a Cajun, R&B, Southern rock sound," interview with David Babb, Dec. 5, 1995; "the Cajun counterpart…" Todd Mouton, "Dirty Rice," *Offbeat*, August 1995, p. 30.

CHAPTER 2: ZYDECO

Chris Ardoin: *"nouveau zydeco"*–expression used by Michael Tisserand in "Nouveau Zydeco," *Offbeat*, April 1995, p. 32.

Beau Jocque: "Actually, it was an answer…" Arsenio Orteza, "Beau Jocque," *Offbeat*, September 1996, p. 49.

Buckwheat Zydeco: "The music my father played…" Brooke Wentz, "Reclaiming His Roots," *Downbeat*, August 1990, p. 29; "played straight…" Grace Lichtenstein and Laura Dankner, *Musical Gumbo: The Music of New Orleans* (New York: W. W. Norton, 1993), p. 231.

Boozoo Chavis: "old-style, natural zydeco," Jim Macnie, liner notes for *Boozoo, That's Who!*, 1993 (Rounder 2126); "Now that we're traveling…" Ben Sandmel, liner notes for Boozoo Chavis, 1991 (Elektra/Nonesuch 61146).

C. J. Chenier: "It was hard…" Sandmel, liner notes for *Too Much Fun*, 1995 (Alligator 4830); "One thing we don't have…" ibid.; "At first…" Sunny Slim Baker, "C. J. Chenier," *Living Blues*, July/Aug. 1991, p. 33.

Clifton Chenier: "I figured…" Barry Jean Ancelet, "Clifton Chenier," *Living Blues*, November/December 1994, p. 52.

Geno Delafose: "I'm just a…" Orteza, "Back Talk with Geno Delafose," *Offbeat*, October 1996, p. 92.

John Delafose: "I don't write a song…" Michael Tisserand, "John Delafose," *Offbeat*, October 1994, p. 50.

Keith Frank: *"nouveau zydeco"*–expression used by Michael Tisserand, "Nouveau Zydeco," *Offbeat*, April 1995, p. 32; "That's when…" Tisserand, "Nouveau Zydeco," *Offbeat*, April 1995, p. 35.

Rosie Ledet: "Every one of their songs…" ibid., p. 41.

Queen Ida: "[W]omen in Louisiana…" liner notes for *In San Francisco*, 1991 (GNP Crescendo 2158).

Rockin' Dopsie: "If you want the real zydeco…" Sam Charters, liner notes for *Zy-De-Co-In*, 1989 (Gazell 3003); "What I liked…" Edward Silverman, "Rockin' Dopsie," *Living Blues*, July/August 1991, p. 13; "high-steppin' party," Rick Coleman, "Dopsie Rules," *Offbeat*, February 1992, pp. 14-18.

Rockin' Dopsie Jr.: "I kept the same…" Don Hoffman, "Rockin' Dopsie Jr.," *New Orleans Jazz & Heritage Festival Program '96*, p. 32.

Terrance Simien: "there's room for all styles…" Keith Spera, "Terrance Simien," *Offbeat*, September 1993, p. 27.

BIBLIOGRAPHY

Quotations appearing in this book and background information came from the following sources.

BOOKS

Allan, Johnnie. *Memories: A Pictorial History of South Louisiana Music, 1910s-1990s*. Lafayette, La.: Johnnie Allan/Jadfel Publishing, 1995.

Ancelet, Barry Jean. *Cajun Music: Its Origins and Development*. Lafayette: Center for Louisiana Studies, University of Southwestern Louisiana, 1989.

Ancelet, Barry Jean (photographs by Elemore Morgan Jr.) *The Makers of Cajun Music*. Austin: University of Texas Press, 1984.

Ancelet, Barry Jean, Jay Edwards, and Glen Pitre. *Cajun Country*. Jackson: University Press of Mississippi, 1991.

Broven, John. *South to Louisiana: The Music of the Cajun Bayous*. Gretna, La.: Pelican, 1983.

Daigle, Pierre V. *Tears, Love and Laughter: The Story of the Cajuns and Their Music*. Ville Platte, La.: Swallow, 1987.

Fry, Macon, and Julie Posner. *Cajun Country Guide*. Gretna, La.: Pelican, 1992.

Gould, Philip (photographs), with an introduction by Barry Jean Ancelet. *Cajun Music and Zydeco*. Baton Rouge: Louisiana State University Press, 1992.

Lichtenstein, Grace, and Laura Dankner. *Musical Gumbo: The Music of New Orleans*. New York: W. W. Norton, 1993.

Savoy, Ann Allen. *Cajun Music: A Reflection of a People*. Eunice, La.: Bluebird Press, 1984.

MAGAZINES & NEWSPAPERS

In addition to the following publications, we found background information in *Atlantic, Gambit* and *Newsweek*. By far the most helpful source was *Offbeat*, 333 St. Charles Ave., Suite 614, New Orleans, LA 70130-3117.

Aiges, Scott. "The Bayou's in His Blood," *New Orleans Times-Picayune*, Jan. 29, 1993, p. L6.

Ancelet, Barry Jean. "Clifton Chenier," *Living Blues*, November/December 1994, pp. 51-52.

Anderson, Jim and Carlotta. "The Good Times Are Rolling in Cajun Country," *Smithsonian*, February 1988, pp. 112-124.

Baker, Sunny Slim. "C. J. Chenier," *Living Blues*, November/December 1994, pp. 31-33.

Coleman, Rick. "Dopsie Rules," *Offbeat*, February 1992, pp. 14-18.

Fuselier, Herman. "Marc, Ann March to Different Beat," Opelousas (La.) *Daily World*, May 11, 1995 (on-line).

Hoffman, Don. "Rockin' Dopsie Jr.," *New Orleans Jazz & Heritage Festival Program '96*, p. 32.

Mouton, Todd. "Dirty Rice," *Offbeat*, August 1995, pp. 21-22, 30.

Orteza, Arsenio. "Back Talk with Geno Delafose," *Offbeat*, October 1996, pp. 91-93.

_____. "Beau Jocque," *Offbeat*, September 1996, pp. 46-49, 52.

Pareles, Jon. Dewey Balfa obituary, *The New York Times*, June 18, 1992, Section D, p. 22.

Silverman, Edward. "Rockin' Dopsie," *Living Blues*, July/August 1991, pp. 10-15.

Spera, Keith. "Terrance Simien," *Offbeat*, September 1993, pp. 24-29.

Spera, Keith, and Michael Tisserand, "Zachary Richard," *Offbeat*, May 1993, pp. 53-58.

Tisserand, Michael. "Cajun Crusader," *Offbeat*, April 1992, p. 20-22.

_____. "John Delafose," *Offbeat*, October 1994, p. 50.

_____. "Nouveau Zydeco," *Offbeat*, April 1995, pp. 32-37, 39-41.

Walsh, Michael. "Hot Off the Bayou," *Time*, May 8,1995, pp. 94-98.

Wentz, Brooke. "Reclaiming His Roots," *Downbeat*, August 1990, p. 29.

ALBUM LINER NOTES

Album liner notes proved indispensable to our biographical research, although they cover a wide spectrum in terms of accuracy. We relied most heavily on these authoritative writers:

- Barry Jean Ancelet, University of Southwestern Louisiana
- Scott Billington, Rounder Records
- John Broven, author
- Sam Charters, author/producer
- Michael Doucet, musician
- Jeff Hannusch, author
- Ben Sandmel, writer/musician/producer
- Ann Savoy, author/musician
- Nicholas Spitzer, folklorist/writer
- Chris Strachwitz, Arhoolie Records
- Michael Tisserand, author/*Offbeat* writer

Barry Jean Ancelet. *It's in the Blood*, 1991 (Rounder 6043).

Charters, Sam. *Zy-De-Co-In*, 1989 (Gazell 3003).

Doucet, Michael. *The First Black Zydeco Recording Artist*, 1981 (Old Timey 124).

_____. *Old Time Cajun Music*, 1982 (Arhoolie 5026).

Green, Douglas B. *Cajun Life*, 1988 (Rounder 3049).

Humphrey, Mark. *Cajun Dance Party Fais Do-Do*, 1994 (Columbia CK46784).

In San Francisco, 1991 (GNP Crescendo 2158).

Macnie, Jim. *Boozoo, That's Who!*, 1993 (Rounder 2126).

Rendez-Vous Louisianais, c. 1995 (Chaud Dog Jean).

Sandmel, Ben. *Boozoo Chavis*, 1991 (Elektra/Nonesuch 61146).

_____. *Too Much Fun*, 1995 (Alligator 4830).

Savoy, Ann. *Cajun's Greatest–The Definitive Collection* (Ace 428).

Savoy, Marc. *Home Music with Spirits*, 1992 (Arhoolie 389).

Spires, Will. *The Complete Early Recordings of Dennis McGee 1929-1930*, 1994 (Shanachie/Yazoo 2012).

Spitzer, Nicholas. *La La: Louisiana Black French Music*, 1977 (Maison de Soul 1004).

_____. *The Mad Reel*, 1981 (Arhoolie 397).

_____. *Zodico*, 1976 (Rounder 6009).

Strachwitz, Chris. *J'ai Ete au Bal*, 1990 (Arhoolie 331 & 332).

Tisserand, Michael. *Dans la Louisiane*, 1996 (Rounder 6065).

CATALOGS & GUIDES

Our discographical information was taken primarily from our own recordings and cross-checked with the Schwann and record company catalogs. We also consulted other CD guides, the following of which have the biggest Cajun/zydeco sections:

Broughton, Simon, et al, eds. *World Music: The Rough Guide*. London: Rough Guides Ltd., 1994.

Erlewine, Michael, with Chris Woodstra and Vladimir Bogdanov, eds. *All Music Guide*. San Francisco: Miller Freeman Books, 1994.

Scott, Frank, et al. *The Down Home Guide to the Blues*. Pennington, N.J.: A Cappella Books, 1991.

INTERNET SOURCES

We found useful biographical and discographical material in the following sites on the World Wide Web:

All Music Guide. http://allmusic.com

The Cajun & Creole Pages.
http://http.tamu.edu:8000/~skb8721/

CD now. http://www.cdnow.com

The Music Page of New Orleans, Louisiana–A Virtual Library.
http://www.satchmo.com/nolavl/nomusic.html

OTHER SOURCES

Babb, David. Interview with Wayne Toups, Dec. 5, 1995.

PHOTO CREDITS

Front cover: Photo of C.J. Chenier by David Babb

Back cover: Photo of Michael Doucet by Robley Dupleix, courtesy Rhino Records

CHAPTER I ALBUM COVERS

Nathan Abshire: Photo by Chris Strachwitz, courtesy Arhoolie Records

Alphonse "Bois Sec" Ardoin: Photo by Michael P. Smith, courtesy Arhoolie Records

Amedee Ardoin: Cover by Ann A. Savoy, courtesy Arhoolie Records

Balfa Brothers: Photo by Jesse Breaux, design by Susan Marsh, courtesy Rounder Records

Dewey Balfa: Courtesy Flat Town Music Co.

Balfa Toujours: Photo by Rick Olivier, design by Jean-Pierre LeGuillou, courtesy Rounder Records

Beausoleil: Photo by Chris Strachwitz, courtesy Arhoolie Records

Joe Bonsall: Courtesy Flat Town Music Co.

Vin Bruce: Courtesy Flat Town Music Co.

Cajun Gold: Courtesy Flat Town Music Co.

California Cajun Orchestra: Photo by Heather Hafleigh, courtesy Arhoolie Records

Hadley J. Castille: Photo by Philip Gould, courtesy Flat Town Music Co.

Harry Choates: (Photo courtesy the Choates family) Courtesy Arhoolie Records

Octa Clark: Photo by Nicholas R. Spitzer, design by Marsh Graphics/Elisa Tanaka, courtesy Rounder Records

Sheryl Cormier: Photo by Joe Besse, courtesy Flat Town Music Co.

Bruce Daigrepont: Photo by Philip Gould, design by Nancy Given, courtesy Rounder Records

Michael Doucet: Photo by Phillipe Gould, courtesy Arhoolie Records

Cleoma Breaux Falcon: (Photo courtesy Lu Lu Falcon Langlinais) Courtesy Jadfel Publishing

Joseph Falcon: Photo by Chris Strachwitz, courtesy Arhoolie Records

Canray Fontenot: Photo by Chris Strachwitz, courtesy Arhoolie Records

Wade Fruge: Photo by Chris Strachwitz, courtesy Arhoolie Records

Chuck Guillory: Photo by Philip Gould, courtesy Arhoolie Records

Kristi Guillory: Photo by Lemoine Studio, courtesy Flat Town Music Co.

Hackberry Ramblers: (Photo courtesy Luderin Darbone) Courtesy Arhoolie Records

Jambalaya Cajun Band: Photo by Ronald Guidry, courtesy Flat Town Music Co.

Robert Jardell: Courtesy Flat Town Music Co.

Eddie LeJeune: Photo by Rick Olivier, design by Joanna Bodenweber, courtesy Rounder Records

Magnolia Sisters: Photo by Kim Andrus, courtesy Arhoolie Records

Mamou: Photo by Philip Gould, design by Nancy Given, courtesy Rounder Records

D. L. Menard: Photo by Rick Olivier, design by Scott Billington, courtesy Rounder Records

Jimmy C. Newman: Courtesy Flat Town Music Co.

Jim Olivier: Photo by Carol Rachou Sr., courtesy Flat Town Music Co.

Austin Pitre: Courtesy Flat Town Music Co.

Belton Richard: Photo by Lemoine Studio, courtesy Flat Town Music Co.

Zachary Richard: Photo by Daniel Poulin, courtesy Zachary Richard/Arzed Records

Steve Riley & the Mamou Playboys: Photo by Philip Gould, design by Scott Billington and Nancy Given, courtesy Rounder Records

Marc Savoy: Photo by Chris Strachwitz, courtesy Arhoolie Records

Savoy-Doucet Cajun Band: Photo by Ken Light, courtesy Arhoolie Records

Leo Soileau: (Photo from collection of Leo Soileau) Courtesy Arhoolie Records

Jo-El Sonnier: Photo by Rick Olivier, design by Scott Billington, courtesy Rounder Records

Wayne Toups & Zydecajun: Photo by Lake Star Photographics, courtesy Flat Town Music Co.

CHAPTER 2 ALBUM COVERS

Chris Ardoin: Photo by Rita Manuel, courtesy Flat Town Music Co.

Lynn August: Photo by Rick "Rico" Olivier, courtesy Black Top Records

Beau Jocque: Photo by Jean Hangarter, design by Scott Billington, courtesy Rounder Records

Buckwheat Zydeco: Photo by Stanley Rowin, design by Scott Billington, courtesy Rounder Records

Boozoo Chavis: Courtesy Flat Town Music Co.

C. J. Chenier: Photo by Mark Sarfati, courtesy Arhoolie Records

Clifton Chenier: Photo by Chris Strachwitz, courtesy Arhoolie Records

Wilfred Chevis: Courtesy Flat Town Music Co.

Geno Delafose: Photo by Philip Gould, design by Scott Billington, courtesy Rounder Records

John Delafose: Courtesy Flat Town Music Co.

Keith Frank: Photo by Lemoine Studio, courtesy Flat Town Music Co.

Rosie Ledet: Courtesy Flat Town Music Co.

L'il Brian & the Zydeco Travelers: Photo by Philip Gould, design by Scott Billington, courtesy Rounder Records

Nathan & the Zydeco Cha-Chas: Photo by Rick Olivier, design by Scott Billington, courtesy Rounder Records

Willis Prudhomme: Courtesy Flat Town Music Co.

Queen Ida: Photo by Lyn Guy, courtesy GNP Crescendo Records

Rockin' Dopsie: Photo by Allen Breaux Studio, courtesy Flat Town Music Co.

Rockin' Sidney: Courtesy Flat Town Music Co.

Sam Brothers: Courtesy Flat Town Music Co.

Terrance Simien: Photo by Brian Ashley White, courtesy Black Top Records

Zydeco Force: Courtesy Flat Town Music Co.

ARTIST INDEX

W

Z